Food and Agriculture Security

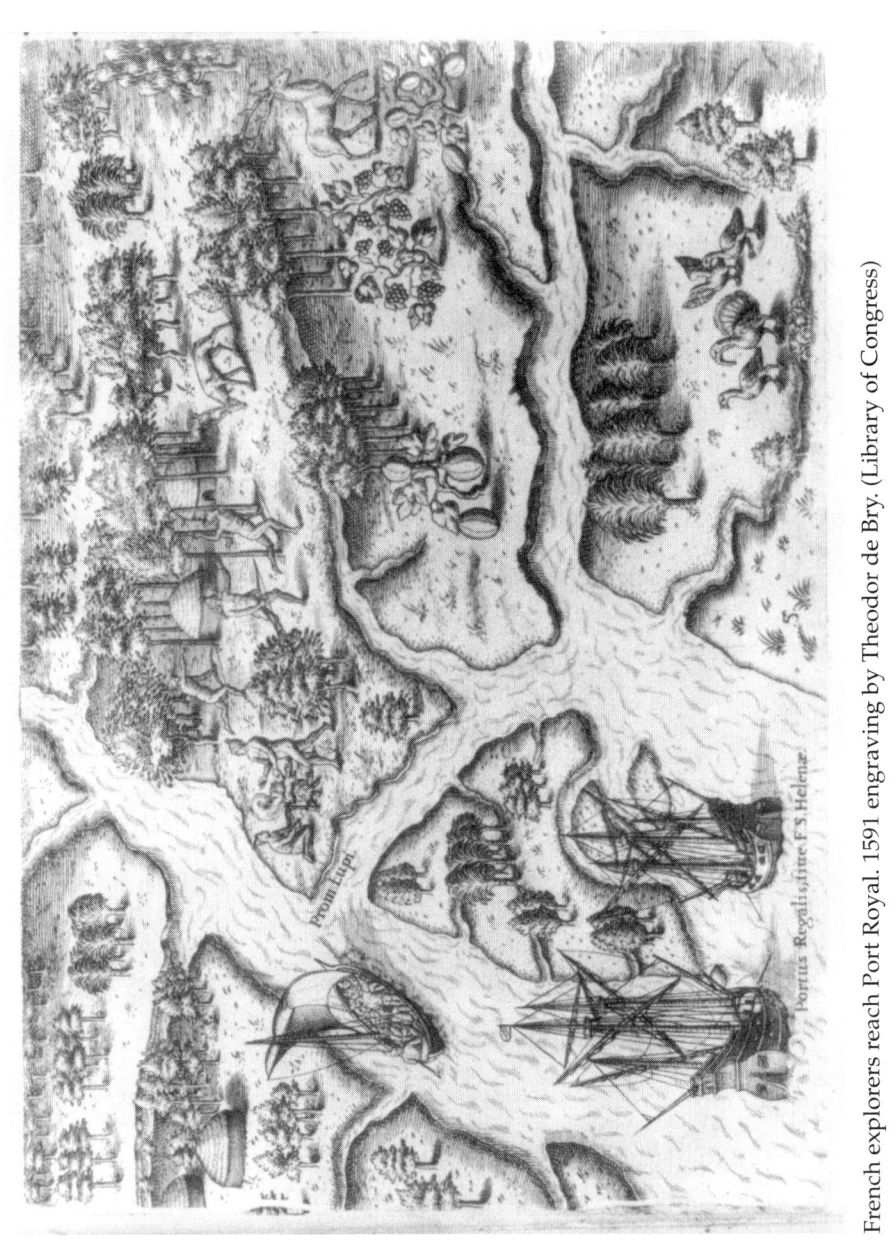

French explorers reach Port Royal. 1591 engraving by Theodor de Bry. (Library of Congress)

Food and Agriculture Security

An Historical, Multidisciplinary Approach

JUSTIN KASTNER, EDITOR

PRAEGER SECURITY INTERNATIONAL

AN IMPRINT OF ABC-CLIO, LLC
Santa Barbara, California • Denver, Colorado • Oxford, England

Copyright 2011 by ABC-CLIO, LLC

All rights reserved. No part of this publication may be reproduced, stored in a retrieval system, or transmitted, in any form or by any means, electronic, mechanical, photocopying, recording, or otherwise, except for the inclusion of brief quotations in a review, without prior permission in writing from the publisher.

Library of Congress Cataloging-in-Publication Data

Food and agriculture security : an historical, multidisciplinary approach / Justin Kastner, editor.
    p. cm.
  Includes bibliographical references and index.
  ISBN 978-0-313-38322-9 (hard copy : alk. paper) — ISBN 978-0-313-38323-6 (ebook)
  1. Food supply—Government policy—United States. 2. Food security—United States. 3. Agriculture and state—United States. I. Kastner, Justin.
  HD9006.F58 2011
  338.1'973—dc22   2010032070

ISBN: 978-0-313-38322-9
EISBN: 978-0-313-38323-6

15 14 13 12 11   1 2 3 4 5

This book is also available on the World Wide Web as an eBook.
Visit www.abc-clio.com for details.

Praeger
An Imprint of ABC-CLIO, LLC

ABC-CLIO, LLC
130 Cremona Drive, P.O. Box 1911
Santa Barbara, California 93116-1911

This book is printed on acid-free paper ∞

Manufactured in the United States of America

I dedicate this book to my wife Susie, with whom I have shared innumerable adventures and joys, and to our children, Ian and Sally.

May this book inspire each and every reader to find real joy in learning.

Contents

Foreword ix
Jason Ackleson

1 Introduction 1
   Justin Kastner

2 Food and Agriculture Security: An Historical Illustration
   of Contemporary Challenges 5
   Justin Kastner

3 Food and Agriculture Security Along the Farm-to-Table
   Continuum 33
   Kathryn Krusemark

4 Historical and Contemporary Cases Illustrating the
   Vulnerability of Specific Commodities and Sectors 61
   Kathryn Krusemark and Cobus Block

5 Import Security: U.S. and Global Approaches 83
   Edward Nyambok

6 Managing Human and Animal-Health Threats: Additional
   Lessons from the 19th-century Trading World 105
   Justin Kastner

7 Looking Forward 129
   Cobus Block, Jason Ackleson, and Justin Kastner

Appendix: Available Resources Related to Food and Agriculture Security 147
Kathryn Krusemark and Justin Kastner

Index 153

About the Editor and Contributors 161

Foreword

Jason Ackleson

One of the most important walks of my life took place on a mild evening in London during the autumn of 1998. I had recently met a bright young Fulbright Scholar from Kansas who, like me, was pursuing a graduate degree in the United Kingdom. We agreed one evening to take advantage of the abnormally warm weather to chat about issues that we studied—for me, border security, and for him, food safety and security.

In many ways, on that evening, the *Frontier* program for the historical studies of border security, food security, and trade policy was born. Over the next 12 years, and at campuses 1,000 miles apart, Justin Kastner and I developed this unique research and training initiative that unites not only scholars across these disciplines but also students across campuses and from around the world.

As the only program of its kind in the United States, *Frontier* employs a unique multidisciplinary approach. We believe that border, food security, and trade issues cannot be examined adequately within rigid disciplinary silos. Rather, we believe in the utility of a broad approach that unites and blends the best thinking from scholars and practitioners across these disciplines. Such an approach, in our view, sheds fresh light on both old and new problems.

This book represents the best of what *Frontier* seeks to achieve: informed, policy-relevant, and historically rooted analysis of food and agriculture security. In the chapters that follow, readers will find insightful case studies, theoretical perspectives, and evaluation of some of the major evolving issues in food and agriculture today. From food safety policy in China to best practices in risk management to tumultuous agricultural trade disputes, this volume highlights some of the key issues facing consumers, regulators, traders, and producers across the world.

A key signature of Kastner's approach is his dedication to mentoring students. He deliberately and consistently fosters their critical writing, research, and thinking skills. His instruction always includes a carefully considered historical angle so that students can appreciate the deeper dimensions of today's policy issues. The results of this focus are available in these pages: both undergraduate and graduate students contributed valuable research-based chapters to this important effort. It is gratifying to see them included here and to know they represent the next generation of thought-leaders who will grapple with and help solve these problems.

Securing the world's food and agriculture sector is not a new challenge, but it is one that has grown increasingly important and complex in today's international security environment. By adding new knowledge and perspectives to our understanding of these issues, this volume provides unique, timely, and salient insights for policymakers and citizens concerned about one of the primary and most fundamental social and economic concerns of our time: food and agriculture security.

CHAPTER 1

Introduction

Justin Kastner

A comprehensive understanding of food and agriculture security is best wrought through multidisciplinary analysis. Indeed, multiple academic disciplines provide lenses through which the multiple dimensions of food and agriculture security may be comprehensively examined. Food and agriculture security—a stated priority research area of the U.S. Department of Homeland Security—concerns the safety, security, and ongoing operation of the agricultural and food system in a global society that values both trade and security. Any attempt to understand the food system must involve multidisciplinary, multidimensional study.[1] This book offers a bona fide multidisciplinary as well as historical approach to help students appreciate such a complex and multifaceted subject. Authored by scholars within the *Frontier* program for the historical studies of border security, food security, and trade policy, the book reviews some of the most salient and trade-related food and agriculture security concerns of the 19th century, describes the modern-day policy and industry contexts in which food and agriculture security issues arise, provides historical and contemporary illustrations of the vulnerability in the food and agriculture sector, identifies modern-day domestic (United States) as well as international (e.g., China) challenges, and highlights the role that public-private partnerships and cross-border cooperation must play in ensuring food and agriculture security in a globalized world.

This book opens (chapter 2) by giving due attention to somewhat-neglected perspectives and lessons from an important episode in the history of food and agriculture security, when U.S. and other food and agricultural regulatory officials were forced to come to grips with animal disease-related problems that occurred in the 19th-century, transatlantic trading world. Illuminated by a treasure trove of primary source material that includes diplomatic as well as regulatory correspondence, the historical case offers important perspectives for today's policymakers at U.S. and international regulatory agencies, the World Trade Organization, and other venues where food and agriculture security issues and policies are discussed. During the 19th century, the United States and Great Britain were engaged in a significant trade in agricultural products, including livestock and meat. America's agricultural exports were praised for providing Britain with good-quality, affordable food; however, when animal disease concerns surfaced among U.S. livestock exported to Britain, Britain's importation policies required review. While other risks would become topics in the dispute, Britain and America soon wrangled about how to manage contagious bovine pleuro-pneumonia, a biosecurity concern for cattle populations. Students of food and agriculture security will learn that U.S.-British sanitary trade relations were characterized by much more than merely straightforward considerations of public health, agricultural biosecurity, and microbiological science. As transatlantic correspondence and other primary-source materials illustrate, the trade questions were interwoven with noteworthy factors of influence, most notably economic considerations and regulatory cooperation involving the two countries. An in-depth review of the case yields several valuable lessons for decision makers in today's era of globalization. These lessons relate to the benefits of innovation and foreign direct investment in food and agricultural technology, the necessity of food and agriculture regulators backing up safety and security claims with robust risk management practices, the often-forgotten value of bilateral regulatory coordination, and the reminder, for biological and physical scientists (and their critics), that food and agriculture security decision making is often undertaken under the dim light of new and still-unfolding science.

The book then (in chapter 3) turns to the farm-to-table continuum in which today's food and agriculture security issues arise. After clarifying issues of terminology related to "food safety, "food defense," "food protection," and "food security," the author—a former Homeland Security Career Development Fellow in the *Frontier* program—discusses noteworthy threats and risk-management approaches including the Hazard Analysis Critical Control Point (HACCP) system, birthed by the Pillsbury Company and U.S. agencies in the 1960s. A review of the U.S. policy objectives of critical infrastructure protection and food and agriculture security appears, followed by an overview of the way the U.S. government envisions public and private actors working together to achieve food and agriculture security. New approaches to food systems security and defense, including analytical tools such as CARVER plus Shock, are also explained. Chapter 4 illustrates the vulnerability of the food and agriculture sector to intentional as well as accidental contamination and disruption. Several

U.S. case studies from the 20th and 21st centuries illustrate the common vulnerability of diverse commodity sectors. One of the authors of chapter 4 is a *Frontier*-affiliated research student presently studying abroad in China, and one of the cases illustrates the vulnerability of a particular commodity—milk—in the Chinese agricultural and food system.

Returning to issues of international trade policy, chapter 5 provides perspectives on import security and its relationship to food and agriculture security as well as public health. New laws (e.g., the 2002 Public Health Security and Bioterrorism Preparedness and Response Act in the United States) have markedly changed the import security policy environment. The author of chapter 5—a *Frontier* research assistant studying import security-related issues—highlights approaches to ensuring the safety and security of imported food products. Both sanitary (food safety and animal health) as well as phytosanitary (plant health) import security considerations (as well as regulatory approaches) are discussed in the chapter.

Chapter 6 provides additional historical illustrations (again drawn from the 19th century) of the challenges faced in the food and agriculture security realm and, like chapter 2, offers lessons worthy of contemplation. Chapter 7, entitled "Looking Forward," offers an analysis of food and agriculture security challenges (including food safety) in China and an overview of two noteworthy and innovative models of international cooperation. The chapter concludes with a prescription for students of food and agriculture security: to enthusiastically embrace the spirit of cross-border cooperation. The book concludes with an appendix, entitled "Available Resources Related to Food and Agriculture Security," that provides students of food and agriculture security with noteworthy public- and private-sector resources (many of which are available online) for future consultation.

The principal aim of this book is not to merely provide more informational sources but rather to whet its readers' appetites for an approach to learning that will help them develop valuable, lifelong skills. This is where the multidisciplinary and historical approach embodied in this book is example-setting and, the editor hopes, inspiring. Thought-leading institutions have affirmed the value of interdisciplinary research, in part because integrating multiple academic disciplines can help paint truer pictures of today's complex problems.[2] To be sure, this is indeed the case in the complex and interconnected domains of food and agriculture security, border security, food safety and security, and international trade. However, and perhaps more important, multidisciplinary approaches can actually help students develop critical thinking skills that, regardless of the issue or policy domain in which they will one day operate, will serve them well. As students blend academic disciplines and cross disciplinary frontiers, they not only examine issues through multiple perspectives but also necessarily translate discipline-specific language and interpret discipline-specific assumptions; these tasks of translation and interpretation are challenging and inevitably require the honing of critical thinking skills.

As readers hone their critical thinking skills, they enhance their abilities to navigate tomorrow's challenges—whatever they may be. If recent history is any indication, these challenges will involve a number of complex issues related to agricultural biosecurity, public health, food safety, and international trade. From the close of the 20th to the beginning of the 21st centuries, stakeholders in food and agriculture have grappled with disagreements and problems regarding a wide range of topics—including, but not limited to, agricultural biotechnology, beef produced with growth-promoting hormones, bovine spongiform encephalopathy (BSE), foot and mouth disease (FMD), and Novel Influenza A. The food and agriculture sector is a dynamic decision-making environment, especially in a globalized world. If there ever was a need for multidisciplinary, historically minded thought leaders, the time is now.

NOTES

1. David F. Smith and Jim Phillips, "Chapter 1: Food Policy and Regulation: A Multiplicity of Actors and Experts," in *Food, Science, Policy and Regulation in the Twentieth Century*, ed. David F. Smith and Jim Phillips (New York: Routledge, 2000), p. 2.

2. Committee on Facilitating Interdisciplinary Research et al., *Facilitating Interdisciplinary Research* (Washington, D.C.: The National Academies Press, 2004).

BIBLIOGRAPHY

Committee on Facilitating Interdisciplinary Research, Committee on Science Engineering and Public Policy, National Academy of Sciences, National Academy of Engineering, and Institute of Medicine of the National Academies. *Facilitating Interdisciplinary Research*. Washington, D.C.: The National Academies Press, 2004.

Smith, David F., and Jim Phillips. "Chapter 1: Food Policy and Regulation: A Multiplicity of Actors and Experts." In *Food, Science, Policy and Regulation in the Twentieth Century*, ed. David F. Smith and Jim Phillips, pp. 1–16. New York: Routledge, 2000.

CHAPTER 2

Food and Agriculture Security: An Historical Illustration of Contemporary Challenges

Justin Kastner

Ensuring food and agriculture security is, quite simply, a formidable task. In the 21st century, the task appears acutely daunting; indeed, it is overwhelming to consider how to ensure the security and safety of agriculture and the food supply while also maintaining the ongoing operation of a global food system upon which modern nation-states and societies have come to depend. At the same time, today's students and thought leaders in food and agriculture security should note that they are not the first human beings to face this dilemma. During the second half of the 19th century, a number of British, American, and Canadian officials in the transatlantic trading region grappled with a conspicuously similar set of quandaries. The episode—the subject of this chapter, a work in historical research—deserves special examination, as it offers a number of lessons for those who are called to make difficult decisions in the regulation of the agriculture and food trade. The historical case illustrates the inevitable interplay between food security (specifically, food supply) considerations, and regulation of disease threats (specifically, animal diseases) posed by the international agricultural and food trade. The case was influenced by several factors, but economic considerations were most influential; therefore, the case will be introduced with an acknowledgement of that context.

ECONOMIC BACKDROP TO THE DILEMMA, AND SYNOPSIS OF THE CASE

During the second half of the 19th century, Great Britain was well aware of the importance of international supplies of food, particularly those from the United States. In May 1867, the food committee of Britain's Society of the Arts illustrated this awareness in Britain during a session devoted to the prospect of further increasing imports of American meat, particularly bacon. The committee interviewed a businessman and a professor acquainted with the transatlantic trade in preserved American meat. While one noted quality concerns, both interviewees agreed that American meat could help supply Britain's working classes with nutritious, cheap food.[1] In the 1870s, British trade groups like the Liverpool Provision Trade Association promoted salt-preserved meat imports packed by Cincinnati- and Chicago-based firms like Armour & Co.[2] Salt-preserved meat, however, did not satisfy Britons' partiality for mild-tasting food, and businesspeople in the transatlantic region contemplated providing American meat in other forms.

This included livestock, which might be shipped alive across the Atlantic, imported into Britain, and slaughtered closer to meat markets. In the late 1860s and early 1870s, firms in Scotland and the United States conducted experiments in the transatlantic shipping of North American cattle.[3] Although the live cattle trade was not immediately successful, by the mid-1870s shipping entrepreneurs, most notably New York's Timothy Eastman, were regularly sending American cattle to Britain.[4] Initially, American cattle were allowed into Britain alive. These so-called store cattle, or stores, were fattened by British farmers, slaughtered, and sold as fresh beef. In addition to live store cattle, entrepreneurs tried shipping refrigerated fresh beef. Unlike the live cattle experiments, refrigerated beef shipments were immediately successful. In 1875, Eastman sent to London's Smithfield Meat Market the first-ever transatlantic shipment of chilled beef. A sample of the inaugural shipment was taken to Windsor Castle, where it met a declaration of approval from Queen Victoria. When American chilled beef reached the important port of Liverpool, customers bought up supplies by mid-afternoon. American beef was deemed superior to continental European beef, and some regarded it as equal in quality to British beef.[5]

While the aroma and flavor of American meat may have been inviting, it was not the main reason why Britons were interested in American agriculture. Britons were most intrigued by North America's vast agricultural resources and what they might mean in economic terms: if transported to the eastern seaboard and across the Atlantic Ocean, American and Canadian wheat and meat could be a bountiful source of inexpensive food for Britain.[6] Nineteenth-century British politicians and investors actively pursued this possibility, infusing capital into American railroads and transatlantic shipping. Strategically, the British did this to cheapen domestic food prices.[7] Significantly, however, railroad and shipping schemes were attractive for other reasons; they also offered new investment ventures in which to put Britain's excess capital to work.

During the second half of the 19th century, the United States was the most important recipient of British international investment. British investors first sought to put their capital to work in U.S. railroad enterprises; while a necessary part of Britain's strategy to ensure a cheap food supply, railroad schemes were attractive in that they were ventures where British capital could earn dividends. Both the British government and its people invested in American railroad securities, and after 1850 sales of British railroad securities subsided, giving way to a growing investment interest in U.S. railroads.[8] In addition to American railroads, transatlantic shipping received attention and money from British investors. "British bottoms" (that is, British ships) carried most transatlantic commerce.[9] By the 1870s, British transportation investment was paying off, and American food supplies arrived into British ports in increasing amounts.

Just as British investment in transportation aimed to secure access to American food supplies, British capital was devoted to a wide variety of American agricultural enterprises. These ventures ranged from wheat farming and milling to cattle ranching and meatpacking.[10] Journalists like James MacDonald, for *The Scotsman* in 1877–1878, would travel to North America and report favorably on agricultural investment opportunities there.[11] Other reports noted the industriousness of American farmers and America's growing expertise in the handling and transporting of food products,[12] and in 1878, an English businessman involved in the cattle trade highlighted in the pages of the *New York Times* the opportunity for business development on both sides of the Atlantic.[13] A special Parliamentary commission would report in 1880 that 33 percent profits were possible in the American ranching industry, prompting more British investment (and emigration). Scottish businessmen from Edinburgh and Dundee proceeded to buy up cattle ranches stretching from Texas to Saskatchewan. One company, the Matador Land and Cattle Company, represented over one million North American acres in British ownership.[14] Britain was in love with American ranching for both food-supply and financial-investment reasons.

British investment contributed to westward expansion and the rapid commercialization of North American agriculture.[15] As America expanded westward, so did ranching. In the 1870s, Kentucky and Illinois were the states from which Timothy Eastman sourced his export cattle, but by the mid-1880s 95 percent of American cattle raised for the British export market were sourced west of Chicago, Illinois.[16] British investment in railroad and steamship transportation helped pave the way for the conveyance of live cattle over these long distances. Fresh meat, however, presented unique transportation challenges. Agricultural education institutions, land grant universities and, later, agricultural experiment stations would help North America address some of these problems.[17] Progress, however, was slow. The success of U.S. chilled beef exports had prompted others to participate in the trade, but refrigeration technology was still in its infancy in the 1870s. Stitched in canvas, beef carcasses were hung and stored in ice- and fan-cooled chambers in the ships. By 1878, ice-salt mixtures and cooling pipes were being used.[18] By 1880, similar technologies had been adapted to many ocean-going vessels, but quality problems persisted and chilled meat arriving into Liverpool and London had to be sold within two weeks.[19] Until refrigeration technology further improved, salt-preserved pork and live cattle would remain the principal sources of American meat in Britain.

In Britain, increases in U.S. food imports (both meat as well as wheat) tended to push agricultural commodity prices down. However, it should be noted that during the late 19th century (1873–1896), the general level of all prices in Britain fell by 40 percent.[20] This great depression of prices, of which wheat and meat-price reductions were a part, contributed to a rise in real income in Britain, for money wages remained largely unchanged during the period.[21] Increased international competition in both meat and wheat markets also prompted an adjustment within the British economy between the agricultural and industrial sectors. During the second half of the 19th century, many landowners sold their landed assets and reinvested them in industrial projects. In an 1878 article regarding foreign food supplies, the *Economist* celebrated this intra-economy shift as part of Britain's commitment to free trade.[22] Due to increased competition and lower food prices, even the poor were able to improve their diets.[23]

These economic circumstances were of benefit to wage earners, investors, and consumers in Britain, but they were increasingly problematic for agriculturalists. While Britain in general prospered through cheaper food prices and attendant increases in real income, British farmers experienced hardships that prompted them to rethink their business. An agriculture depression struck British farmers during the last quarter of the century, prompting some to leave agriculture altogether and those capable of adjustment to diversify their production and perhaps boost efficiency. Wheat farmers suffered the most from international competition, as their prices dropped 11 percent more than the general level of prices, leaving them, in real terms, with increased labor costs. Meanwhile, prices in the livestock sector fell less than did the general level of prices; farmers noticed this and shifted their production to capture the more buoyant prices in animal products. While wheat farmers clearly suffered, livestock farmers were comparatively untroubled by the fall in prices. In fact, some livestock farmers benefited as cheaper cereals meant cheaper feedstuffs.[24] Nevertheless, British livestock producers were well acquainted with hardship. Late 19th-century Britain's love affair with cheap food prices, combined with its desire to use capital and labor for industrial ventures, did not bode well for the British farmer, including those in livestock and meat production. Livestock farmers were part of a larger British agricultural community that felt increasingly marginalized.

More significantly, livestock farmers were familiar with the economic pains of animal disease. The rinderpest or cattle plague outbreak of 1865–1867 had brought £5 million in losses. Foot and mouth disease (FMD), first imported into Britain in 1839, was problematic for owners of cattle, sheep, and pigs throughout the 19th century. Contagious bovine pleuro-pneumonia, a lung disease in cattle, was more troublesome and, like rinderpest, had a high mortality rate. Economic losses associated with these diseases prompted Britain to adopt disease-control legislation in the 1860s and 1870s and propelled a number of British politicians to wage campaigns against diseased animal imports. In challenging the prevailing economic ethos in Britain, veterinarians such as George Fleming and Thomas Walley proffered their own economic arguments. Both believed that guarding against animal diseases made economic sense because British stockowners still provided the lion's share of Britain's meat and milk.[25] Congruent with their and other veterinarians' wishes, British animal disease policy became increasingly stringent during the last quarter of the 19th century.

On the other side of the Atlantic, in the United States, appeals for the regulation of animal disease were slower in coming. This was partly because America's experience with animal disease had been less devastating than Britain's. Pleuro-pneumonia had invaded the United States in the 1840s, but it did not immediately become the kind of problem that pleuro-pneumonia posed in Britain's dairies. To be sure, pleuro-pneumonia was enough of a problem to spur state and business leaders in Massachusetts to raise disease-containment funds in the 1860s. However, it was not until the 1870s that animal diseases would become economically significant enough to win the serious attention of U.S. regulators. Referring to the prevalence of pleuro-pneumonia prior to 1878, the U.S. agriculture commissioner downplayed its importance and prevalence.[26] However, in the U.S., economic pressures would increase and compel America to take animal diseases more seriously. These pressures came in the form of an international trade dispute with Britain over contagious bovine pleuro-pneumonia.

As governmental intervention in the livestock trade came to be accepted, British veterinary authorities restricted livestock imports. Continental Europe, from where animal diseases had been brought to Britain since time immemorial, was the first to become subject to trade restrictions. By 1878, many European countries were either banned from importing livestock into Britain or permitted to do so only under a provision of immediate slaughter at ports of entry. Continental Europe's loss actually fuelled Britain's reliance on North American livestock and meat imports. However, livestock trading in the transatlantic region was complicated in 1879 when Britain discovered diseases—most notably, contagious bovine pleuro-pneumonia—among U.S. animals and extended the immediate-slaughter order to U.S. livestock. The trade in American store cattle ended, and American exporters feared an imminent reduction of livestock exports. Lest they lose their most important export market, the American livestock industry lobbied the federal government to adopt and enforce animal disease control regulations. U.S. action in animal health was initially undertaken for the objective of retaining access to the British export market. Economic pressures were evident from the very beginning of the trade dispute, when U.S. treasury secretary John Sherman and U.S. agriculture commissioner William G. Le Duc hastily (and separately) contrived export certification schemes and then pleaded with Congress to act. Britain never allowed resumption of the American store trade, but American livestock exporters and regulators remained optimistic that robust regulations would pave the way for its resumption. With its eye on the British export market, America improved its animal disease regulatory machinery during the 1880s, first with the Treasury Cattle Commission and later an actual regulatory body: the U.S. Department of Agriculture Bureau of Animal Industry. Later, domestic economic changes would join international trade forces in compelling American regulators to take a sober view of animal disease: with a growing human population, controlling livestock diseases increasingly became an issue of domestic food security, just as it had been in Britain for years.

While the economic devastation of animal disease justified government intervention in the livestock trade, Britain was still generally committed to the principles of free trade. Britain was economically invested in North American agriculture and the transatlantic food trade, and it was increasingly dependent on food imports. U.S. diplomats did not need to remind Britain of these economic realities, but they did anyway. In February 1879, when the British government moved closer to subjecting U.S. cattle to the immediate-slaughter policy, U.S. secretary of state William Evarts argued that such a restriction would be an unwise check on a food supply upon which Britain was increasingly dependent.[27] Evarts later argued that restrictions on the transatlantic cattle trade would raise British meat prices and were therefore not in the interests of the British working class.[28] A number of British politicians, including the outspoken Anthony Mundella in the British parliament, agreed with Evarts. While meat consumption increased in direct proportion to income, the British working classes nonetheless had benefited from cheap meat imports. Britain's reliance on imported sources of meat continued to increase during the last quarter of the 19th century, and at its eventual peak in the late 1890s, the United States provided a full 30 percent of Britain's meat supply.[29]

Although the uninhibited importation of live store cattle was disallowed, the transatlantic cattle trade continued. Indeed, Britain's immediate-slaughter regulation was a kind of compromise—between, on the one hand, an outright prohibition on American livestock imports and, on the other, completely unregulated importation. It was good sanitary trade policy for Britain because it guarded against the importation of pleuro-pneumonia while facilitating supplies of port-killed beef, which contributed to transatlantic commerce and kept domestic meat prices low. In order to accommodate this policy, Liverpool port authorities upgraded slaughtering facilities at the Liverpool docks.[30]

In 1887, the secretary of Britain's Central Chamber of Agriculture published a report on the growth of the meat trade. In the secretary's report, he noted that Britain's consumption of foreign meat had grown four-fold over 20 years. Over that time, meat from live animal imports had doubled, and meat arriving in preserved or chilled form grew six-fold.[31] Later, after 1900, a growing American population and a decline in domestic beef production made the United States a net importer of beef. American livestock producers and meatpackers became less preoccupied with access to British markets. As this preoccupation vanished, so did America's complaints of Britain's immediate-slaughter policy.[32]

Economic considerations were, arguably, the most influential in the transatlantic trade disputes over livestock disease. Generally loyal to free-trade principles, even unilateral trade liberalization, Britain was dependent upon American agriculture and the transatlantic livestock and meat trade for both investment and food-supply reasons. This economic dependence prevented an outright ban on American cattle imports. Britain's familiarity with the economic costs of animal disease had compelled it to subject American livestock to the immediate-slaughter policy, but this importation policy was an economically favorable compromise: Britain could continue to import American sources of meat, even if subject to immediate slaughter. While Britain's experiences with animal disease had propelled it to adopt animal disease controls, American agriculturalists and policymakers were propelled down the animal-disease regulatory path by international trade pressures, specifically the lure of the British store-cattle market. Throughout the dispute, American regulators held out hope that if the United States improved its sanitary regulatory controls and eradicated animal diseases, it would regain the lucrative privilege of exporting store cattle to Britain. While domestic economic considerations would also become important, export-market aspirations were the primary reason why the United States undertook animal-disease regulation. Eventually, new economic opportunities, assisted by refrigeration technologies in the chilled-meat trade, profoundly affected the dispute over diseased livestock; by exporting chilled meat rather than live animals, disease transmission was reduced, animal welfare complaints were assuaged, and the cattle trade dispute became increasingly unimportant.

REGULATORY DECISION MAKING IN THE CASE: THE IMMEDIATE-SLAUGHTER ORDER

In March 1878, the mayor of the British port city of Liverpool, the town clerk, the local medical officer of health, two members of parliament, and other prominent officials sought to persuade the Duke of Richmond, Lord

President of the Privy Council and staunch advocate for the agricultural interest in Great Britain, on a number of points regarding legislation then under consideration in parliament.[33] After reminding Richmond of the importance to Liverpool of the live-cattle trade, the mayor argued that existing animal-disease regulations were sufficient to guard against disease, that a large proportion of Liverpool's imports were disease-free by virtue of being from North America, that proposals for the immediate slaughter of all imported cattle were too rigid, and that the Privy Council should continue to enjoy flexibility in deciding from which countries live cattle could be imported.[34]

At issue was the Contagious Diseases (Animals) Bill, which proposed a fundamental shift in British trade policy. Previously, and in concert with the Contagious Diseases (Animals) Act of 1869, the free importation of live animals had been the norm, and import restrictions were applied only to specifically so-called scheduled countries. According to the 1869 law, scheduled countries were those where livestock diseases were known to be endemic or where outbreaks had recently occurred. Livestock from scheduled countries had to be slaughtered at the port of entry immediately (specifically, within 10 days of importation). Three of the livestock diseases that would trigger a scheduling order were especially familiar to British stockowners and dairymen. Rinderpest had ravaged the British livestock industry in 1865–1867 and was largely responsible for prompting the British government to adopt systematic slaughter and containment policies. The prevalence of FMD, which had been imported into Britain in 1839 and spread rapidly thereafter, was also justification for scheduling. Pleuro-pneumonia was even more problematic; pleuro-pneumonia had a high mortality rate and had been a menace for dairymen and livestock owners ever since its importation in 1840. All three scourges repeatedly plagued British livestock in the 1860s and 1870s.

Because animals from scheduled countries were subject to immediate slaughter at ports of entry, and because most continental European countries were in fact scheduled during the 1870s (although not always permanently), the lucrative business of importing European store cattle for inland fattening and slaughter diminished. As continental European countries were scheduled during the 1870s, traffic in London's chief port for scheduled animals, the Foreign Cattle Market at Deptford, grew. Meanwhile, dealings in live foreign stores declined at London's Metropolitan Cattle Market, at Islington.[35] The 1878 Contagious Diseases (Animals) Bill proposed to accelerate this trend by making immediate slaughter a general rule rather than an exception.[36]

The contemplated legislation had important implications for North American live cattle imports. The United States and Canada had both avoided scheduled status under the 1869 law and the trade in North American stores benefited as the British government scheduled continental European countries in the 1870s.[37] For example, Britain looked to North

American live-cattle supplies after it suspended imports from eastern Europe because of a pleuro-pneumonia outbreak in 1877.[38]

Those involved in the livestock trade at Liverpool and other ports responsible for receiving North American animals feared that the Contagious Diseases (Animals) Bill would require the immediate slaughter of their valued commodity. North American exporters and British salesmen argued that restrictions on live importation would reduce the home supply of meat and raise prices. The delegation from Liverpool, supported by shipping companies such as Messrs. Flinn, Main, & Montgomery,[39] pressed Richmond on whether or not the bill intended the immediate slaughter of North American cattle. Actually, the government, and Richmond as Lord President of the Privy Council, had deferred the question of North American cattle to a Select Committee of the House of Lords appointed to consider the Contagious Diseases (Animals) Bill.[40] During the next several months, the bill was the subject of much debate. Richmond continued to stress the importance of the immediate-slaughter restriction, if not for North America, then certainly for Europe. Richmond emphasized that the bill featured both domestic and foreign-trade restrictions. Meanwhile, livestock farming representatives from Scotland and Ireland visited Richmond; a Highland Society representative urged no compromise on the bill's immediate-slaughter provisions. Richmond, proudly alluding to his own Scottish roots, agreed that stock-raising regions such as Scotland deserved vigilant protection from the likes of rinderpest, pleuro-pneumonia, and FMD.[41]

However, reports of the slaughter of infected animals from abroad had become routine and seemed to affirm the existing policy whereby the Privy Council used discretion in scheduling countries. The *Economist* argued that the Contagious Diseases (Animals) Bill did little to control domestic sources of disease and feared discrimination against North American cattle supplies, upon which Britain was increasingly dependent.[42] Eventually, parliament affirmed immediate slaughter at the ports as a general principle. An amended version of the original bill came into force on October 1, 1878,[43] and regulatory orders issued by the Privy Council under the act would become effective on January 1, 1879. After the amendments, the Contagious Diseases (Animals) Act of 1878 made restricted entry into Britain the rule, thereby reversing the 1869 policy of free importation being the norm.[44] However, and significantly, free importation was provided for certain countries under conditions subject to Privy Council review. For Richmond, the passage of the act was a victory, even if he did not think it went far enough. He still held the reigns of discretionary power in the Privy Council, and it was no secret that he would continue to be vigilant in the exercise of that power. Richmond immediately initiated preparations for the reorganization of the Privy Council Veterinary Department and the enforcement of the act. An early example of such action was the Privy Council's Foreign Animals Order Number 452. This order was one of several promulgated under the act and effectively divided foreign livestock into three classes:

1. Animals from countries where one or more diseases were endemic. For these animals, importation was absolutely prohibited. The prohibition affected the following countries: Austria-Hungary, Greece, Italy, Montenegro, Romania, Russia, and the Ottoman Empire, including the provinces of Bosnia and Herzegovina.
2. Animals from countries where disease was common. Unless expressly prohibited (no. 1 above) or exempted (no. 3 below), countries were automatically included in this category. Animals from such countries (e.g., Germany, Holland, Belgium, France, Argentina, and Uruguay) were to be landed at designated Foreign Animals Wharves and slaughtered immediately (that is, within 10 days of importation).
3. Animals from countries where disease was uncommon or unknown. These animals were exempt from immediate slaughter but had to be held for at least 12 hours, examined, and certified as disease-free by an inspector of the Privy Council before being released inland. If suspected of disease, the animals were slaughtered and, in the case of pleuro-pneumonia suspicions, their lungs would be inspected. Countries exempted were Denmark, Norway, Sweden, Spain, Portugal, Canada, and the United States.[45]

Exemption for the North American live-cattle trade was significant. More significant were the conditions upon which that exemption would depend. After the adoption of the Contagious Diseases (Animals) Act, U.S. diplomats were told that the importation of livestock into Britain could continue without immediate slaughter but only if diseases were not detected among them and only if a government health certificate accompanied shipments. Britain also demanded that the U.S. government provide information on its efforts to prevent the importation and spread of contagious diseases in the U.S. Immediately, the U.S. assistant secretary of state, Frederick Seward, conferred with the secretary of the Treasury Department, who consulted with the commissioner of agriculture, to formulate a response.[46] Meanwhile, scientists, diplomats, and newspaper correspondents speculated whether U.S. animals would continue to be exempted from compulsory slaughter.

There were grounds for doubt. George Fleming, an outspoken veterinarian, had already argued the case against the free importation of live U.S. animals.[47] Fleming's warnings echoed those of James Law, a veterinary professor at New York's Cornell University who had previously taught in Britain. In a report noticed by both the American and British governments, Law explained that pleuro-pneumonia existed along the eastern seaboard (specifically, in eastern New York, New Jersey, Pennsylvania, Maryland, Delaware, Virginia, and the District of Columbia), and that the U.S. government needed to adopt domestic controls for the suppression of the insidious disease.[48] In his report, Law referred to an 1871 study by his former colleague John Gamgee who, among other things, had traced the epidemiological history of pleuro-pneumonia in the United States. Gamgee had discovered that while the western states had avoided the scourge, several eastern states were home to pleuro-pneumonia.[49] More troubling than Fleming's, Law's, and Gamgee's reports were recent episodes of disease; in the summer and autumn of 1878, there were outbreaks of pleuro-pneumonia in the District of Columbia, Maryland, Virginia, New Jersey, and New York.[50]

The U.S. State Department, in consultation with the Treasury and Agriculture Departments, continued to develop its response; and it is insightful to consider what animal disease control regulations were in fact available to showcase to the British government. An October 1878 appraisal of U.S. animal-health policy would have revealed an incoherent hodgepodge of federal and state laws and immature regulatory institutions. The U.S. State Department had little to offer the British government other than (a) federal laws restricting the importation of cattle and hides and (b) disease surveillance efforts that were underfunded and still in their infancy. On October 25, Assistant Secretary of State Seward formally responded to Sir Edward Thornton, the British minister in Washington. Seward explained that U.S. laws prohibiting cattle and hide imports were, at the moment, suspended for all countries provided that the imports were accompanied by a certificate, issued by a U.S. consular agent in the exporting country, declaring them to be disease-free. Citing Treasury Secretary John Sherman and Agriculture Commissioner Le Duc, Seward promised to convey to the British government any new disease information as it became available.[51]

Seward's communication did not put to rest speculation that the U.S. live-cattle trade was on the verge of becoming subject to Britain's immediate-slaughter provision. A month later, on November 27, New York's *Weekly Tribune* cited the prevalence of pleuro-pneumonia in neighborhoods around Washington, D.C. Agriculture Commissioner Le Duc sent one of his correspondents to investigate, and it was confirmed that pleuro-pneumonia prevailed in northern Virginia.[52] Finally convinced of Law's earlier warnings, Le Duc immediately wrote to Congress, asking for help. However, Congress was slow to respond.

On January 1, 1879, Britain's new Foreign Animals Order officially went into effect.[53] Richmond, as Lord President of the Privy Council, and Professor George T. Brown, head of the Privy Council Veterinary Department, set out to enforce the order. Two weeks later, Brown received word from Mr. Moore, the Privy Council inspector for Liverpool, that a Canadian bullock showing signs of pleuro-pneumonia had been slaughtered. As would become routine practice, Moore excised a diseased portion of a lung in the slaughtered animal and forwarded it to Professor Brown at the Veterinary Department in London. The sample signaled pleuro-pneumonia, but Brown wanted a second opinion. Aware that Canadian officials would vehemently contest the diagnosis on account of the absence of pleuro-pneumonia in Canada, Brown circulated the lung sample among at least seven other veterinarians, all of whom concurred that it was in fact pleuro-pneumonia. Later, Brown learned that the Canadian animal, while originally shipped from Quebec, was part of a cargo from the United States. Coupled with the recent reports of pleuro-pneumonia in America, the revelation absolved Canada and legitimized growing suspicions of American cattle shipments.[54]

By now the British Consul in New York was questioning agricultural leaders and government officials in New York, New Jersey, Connecticut, Delaware, and Rhode Island, about the prevalence of pleuro-pneumonia. Some denied that pleuro-pneumonia currently prevailed in their state, and others, conceding its existence, argued that the disease was contained. As U.S. exporters and Liverpool importers waited in suspense, Commissioner Le Duc continued to be inundated with advice and pleas for federal action. About that same time, Le Duc met with Duncan McEachran, a Canadian veterinary professor investigating pleuro-pneumonia along the U.S. eastern seaboard. After the meeting, McEachran persuaded one of Le Duc's correspondents to accompany him to New York, where they found several cases of pleuro-pneumonia in a dairy near Brooklyn.[55]

Two days later, Le Duc secured an opportunity, before the Senate Committee on Agriculture, to beg for help.[56] It was already too late. Earlier in January, the steamship *Ontario*, loaded with 265 cattle, had left Portland, Maine. The shipment, which had originated in Canada, was comprised of both American and Canadian cattle. On Sunday, January 26, the *Ontario* arrived at Liverpool. One hundred ninety-nine cattle, two of which were dead, were landed at the port. Mr. Moore, the Privy Council's inspector for Liverpool, examined the lungs of one of the dead carcasses and detected pleuro-pneumonia. According to standard procedure, Moore sent portions of the diseased lungs to the Privy Council Veterinary Department in London, where the diagnosis was confirmed. Professor Brown, head of the department, ordered the detainment of the remaining animals. Richmond, as Lord President of the Privy Council, told Brown to send his assistant inspector, Professor W. Duguid, to Liverpool to assist in the inspection and slaughter of the entire cargo. After slaughter, Moore and Duguid noticed that a considerable number of the cattle had respiratory inflammations as a result of exposure to cold, and diagnosed pleuro-pneumonia in the lungs of 12 animals.[57] The discovery of pleuro-pneumonia among the *Ontario* shipment had immediate ramifications. On Thursday, January 30, the British foreign secretary, Lord Salisbury, announced by telegram that, on account of detecting pleuro-pneumonia among the *Ontario* cargo, the British government was reconsidering its exemption of U.S. cattle from immediate slaughter. Salisbury's minister in Washington, Sir Edward Thornton, immediately conveyed the announcement to U.S. secretary of state William Evarts.[58] On Saturday, February 1, Richmond received British agricultural representatives urging the immediate slaughter of American cattle.[59]

Even though shipments of American cattle would arrive at Liverpool in healthy condition over the next several days, the diagnosis of pleuro-pneumonia in the *Ontario* shipment had initiated the unraveling of America's animal disease reputation. Several challenged the Privy Council's diagnosis, arguing that the *Ontario* cases were due to conventional bronchitis—not the more deadly and contagious pleuro-pneumonia. The argument was not far-fetched. The Privy Council itself admitted that a large number of the *Ontario* shipment suffered from respiratory ailments brought on by cold weather. Meanwhile, importers at Liverpool had invited down the principals of the three veterinary schools in Scotland: Principal McCall of the Glasgow Veterinary College, Principal Thomas

In 1879, British veterinary inspectors intensified scrutiny of U.S. livestock imports, and the diagnosis of contagious bovine pleuro-pneumonia presented new challenges to food and agriculture security thought leaders in the 19th-century, transatlantic trading region. (Image of an *American Agriculturalist* illustration reproduced with permission from a reprint on page 83 of Smithcors, J. F. (1975) *The Veterinarian in America 1625–1975*, American Veterinary Publications, Inc)

Walley of Edinburgh's Royal (Dick) Veterinary College, and Principal William Williams of Edinburgh's New Veterinary College. Walley, who was accompanied by McCall, noticed that several of the detained *Ontario* cattle were coughing and, after being shown the lungs of two recently slaughtered animals, found the lesions of pleuro-pneumonia. Williams also saw the animals before and after slaughter, but he identified conventional bronchitis, not pleuro-pneumonia. The transatlantic veterinary community was soon engrossed in a debate over the *Ontario* pleuro-pneumonia diagnosis. When the Privy Council detected additional cases of pleuro-pneumonia in American shipments, more disagreements followed. Williams, dubbed an international expert on pleuro-pneumonia by veterinarians in Canada and the United States, continued to receive lung-tissue samples from condemned cattle and challenge the diagnoses of the Privy Council authorities. The transatlantic trade dispute over pleuro-pneumonia would continue to be influenced by veterinary scientists, all of whom were imperfect human beings historically situated in an era with, historians can now see, incomplete information.[60]

On February 10, 1879, Richmond and the Privy Council decided that effective March 3, U.S. cattle would no longer be exempted from immediate slaughter. The decision—Foreign Animals Order Number 467—was promptly challenged by the United States. In Liverpool, agents squarely faced the reality that American cattle had to be slaughtered at the port. Lest it lose the growing American cattle trade to other British ports, the Cattle Trade Association of Liverpool volunteered to help install the requisite lairage and abattoirs. In late February, after last-minute improvements and just before Foreign Animals Order Number 467 went into effect, the Privy Council awarded Foreign Animals Wharf designation to the Wallasey landing stage, at Birkenhead just across the River Mersey from Liverpool. While movement inland of live cattle was prohibited, American cattle continued to be imported, and they were slaughtered at the port within 10 days.[61]

Foreign Animals Order Number 467 served to focus the minds of Canadian and U.S. government officials. Canadian authorities, acting to protect their country's disease reputation, immediately prohibited imports of U.S. cattle.[62] With little help from Congress over the next two years, Sherman, Le Duc, and other U.S. officials would try to hammer out a federal sanitary policy, if only in ad hoc fashion. Yet despite the recent pleuro-pneumonia diagnoses, the transatlantic trade in U.S. livestock and meat continued, as the immediate-slaughter order did keep trade alive, albeit in a restricted manner.

Paradoxically, while many feared that the 1879 requirements of immediate slaughter at the ports presaged a diminution of the livestock trade, trade actually grew. The value of U.S. live-cattle exports to Britain markedly increased from $2.4 million in 1878 to $6.6 million in 1879, and transatlantic dealings in livestock would continue to grow until the end of the century. Significantly, growth in the livestock trade was accompanied by the advent of the chilled and frozen meat trade. Between 1850 and 1870, the United States had exported to Britain preserved meat (chiefly salted pork and bacon but also dried, pickled, and cured beef). By the late 1860s, Chicago- and Cincinnati-based firms like Armour & Co. were sending to Britain tinned pork and beef.[63] In 1875, the British would be delighted when American meat would finally arrive in fresh, chilled form. By 1880, refrigeration technology had been successfully adapted to many ocean-going vessels, and chilled and frozen beef joined preserved pork (still the principal meat commodity) as key features of America's trade with Britain. Yet refrigeration technology was far from perfect in 1880, and chilled meat arriving into Liverpool and London had to be sold within two weeks. Fresh, port-killed beef remained popular, and the live-animal trade continued despite the immediate-slaughter order.[64]

Nevertheless, the United States lamented the immediate-slaughter policy because it prohibited participation in the more lucrative store trade. Yet still, U.S. interests did benefit in that they were never prohibited from landing cattle at British ports for slaughter; even subject to immediate slaughter, the export trade provided an important market for U.S. livestock raisers, and prices received for export cattle remained profitable until at least 1897.[65] Nevertheless, both American and British policymakers sought greener pastures by gravitating toward an even more lucrative trade arrangement that rendered unimportant the diseased-livestock trade dispute. This arrangement was the chilled-meat trade.

The transatlantic trade in chilled beef had grown steadily since Timothy Eastman first brought samples to England in 1875. However, technological accommodation of the trade was slow in coming. Eventually, improved refrigeration capabilities on steamers would enable transatlantic shipments of fresh beef to flourish and provide an alternative to live-cattle transatlantic enterprises. The benefits of trading in meat not only reduced the likelihood of animal disease spread but also appealed to humane societies and other social activist groups.[66] Livestock producers were aware of this, as the Chicago-based *Breeder's Gazette* explained in 1890 in its endorsement of the refrigerated beef trade.[67] Regulators also saw the meat trade as the panacea for the diseased-cattle trade dispute. By the early 1890s, both pork and beef could be sent to continental Europe and Britain. American diplomats would continue to rail against Britain's immediate-slaughter provision, but the meat trade had made it less of an American preoccupation. Eventually, the U.S. market would grow and make even the meat export trade relatively unimportant; after 1900, increasing demand for beef in the United States made British markets less critical for American traders.[68]

BILATERAL REGULATORY COOPERATION

A close examination of primary-source documents related to the case illuminates a remarkable degree of bilateral regulatory coordination between U.S. and British officials. Prior to the genesis of the animal disease dispute (in 1879, when British authorities condemned the *Ontario* shipment and imposed the immediate-slaughter order on American livestock), U.S.-British regulatory dialogue was rare. In the opening months of the dispute, transatlantic regulatory discussions became more frequent, and during the 1880s international trade pressures and a growing appreciation of the seriousness of animal disease risks gradually compelled the United States to adopt the kinds of sanitary regulations that had become commonplace in Britain. Assisted by transatlantic information sharing between veterinarians and regulatory officials, but delayed by the persistent debate about the accuracy of Britain's pleuro-pneumonia diagnoses, the U.S. animal disease regulatory regime had, by 1890, begun to mirror that of Britain.

In 1878, on the eve of the January 1879 condemnation of the *Ontario* shipment, Britain requested information from the United States as to its efforts to prevent the importation and spread of animal diseases. As explained earlier in this chapter, the United States had little to offer. Not only had the United States generally suspended its laws prohibiting cattle and hide imports, federal disease surveillance efforts were crude and in their infancy, having been inaugurated only one year before. Some U.S. officials, like Treasury Secretary John Sherman and Agriculture Commissioner William Le Duc, tried to reassure Britain with health certification schemes at the ports, but these were contrived too late for the January 1879 *Ontario* condemnation, an event that effectively shattered America's animal-disease reputation. By the summer of 1879, all American livestock had been made subject to immediate slaughter at British ports of entry. Still hoping to resume the lucrative store-cattle trade, the United States immediately put forth arguments that (a) its export livestock were sourced from west of the Allegheny Mountains, a region free from pleuro-pneumonia (the "disease-free west" argument) and (b) the British authorities had erred in their diagnosis of pleuro-pneumonia, a point enthusiastically made by Professor William Williams in Edinburgh. Both arguments fuelled and were fuelled by America's optimism that health certification schemes at the ports would compel Britain to cancel the immediate-slaughter order and restore the trade in American store cattle. While some, like Commissioner Le Duc and Secretary Sherman, understood that the U.S. was in a poor negotiating position as long as diseases existed anywhere, these same officials were nonetheless convinced that the British had erred in their diagnoses of pleuro-pneumonia in American cattle. If only they could win the pleuro-pneumonia diagnosis argument, they believed, then Britain would be obliged to permit the inland importation of live American animals.

Largely because of this belief, much of the early (1879–1884) transatlantic dialogue was devoted to the diagnosis debate and the "disease-free west" argument, rather than discussions about how to improve the domestic disease-control policies of America. During 1879 and 1880, the U.S.

surgeon-general, Secretary Sherman, and prominent veterinarians like Dr. James Law did talk about how to improve U.S. animal-disease policy, and many of these discussions were prompted by regulatory advice from the British minister in Washington.[69] However, these discussions were joined—and temporarily sidelined—by the U.S. government's preoccupation with exposing the error of the British pleuro-pneumonia diagnoses and winning Britain's acquiescence to the "disease-free west" argument. Eventually, in 1880, Le Duc commissioned Dr. Charles Lyman—based at Harvard, a well-connected veterinarian with ties to the British veterinary profession—to actually travel to Britain to confer with Professor Williams and meet with the British veterinary authorities. Le Duc's later recollection of the commissioning of Lyman confirms that the U.S. government was, at least for a time, more interested in proving the British wrong than in acquiring regulatory advice.[70]

Lyman's mission was unsuccessful, and he brought home a message for the U.S. government: as long as pleuro-pneumonia existed anywhere in the United States, and as long as no U.S. federal laws exist to control it, Britain would never relent in the immediate-slaughter order. Commissioner Le Duc, U.S. president Rutherford B. Hayes, and the U.S. Congress accepted Lyman's advice and in 1881 a regulatory body—the Treasury Cattle Commission—was created. The creation of the Treasury Cattle Commission opened the door to transatlantic harmonization of animal-disease regulation. Led by the British-educated Dr. James Law, the Treasury Cattle Commission understood that it needed to rectify many of America's regulatory shortcomings identified by British officials. Dr. Law and his colleagues acknowledged the futility of providing health certificates for export cattle in the absence of robust U.S. domestic-disease controls. Law and the commissioners therefore made domestic-disease control a priority and by 1883, the commission had won the right to regulate interstate commerce. Although the federal government was still not permitted to intervene and purchase diseased stock, clearer rules for quarantining imported cattle were in place, and the commission had elaborated rules for disinfecting cattle-conveyance ships. The Treasury Cattle Commission was called upon to participate in a separate U.S.-British dispute over the diagnosis of FMD in American cattle, and at least one of the commissioners travelled to Britain to participate in the discussions. More significant, however, was written correspondence between Dr. Law and Professor George Brown, the head of the British Privy Council Veterinary Department. By 1883, communication between the two officials had convinced Dr. Law that further regulatory improvements were still needed in the United States. Dr. Law's humble willingness to not argue with Brown but to rather focus on improving U.S. regulations was indeed helpful and, although not completely, it served to divert the U.S. government away from its fixation on debates related to the pleuro-pneumonia diagnosis and the "disease-free west" argument. Law's sincere desire to harmonize

America's domestic regulations with those of Britain is evident in a letter to Professor Brown dated July 24, 1883. The lengthy letter, written on the occasion of an upcoming meeting in Europe (an International Veterinary Congress in Brussels), provided Brown reassurance that Law—one of America's chief regulatory officials—took the pleuro-pneumonia issue seriously.[71] Importantly, Dr. Law was not the only American veterinarian aware of the degree to which U.S. animal-disease regulations needed to improve. At a November 1883 meeting in Chicago, several of America's livestock and veterinary leaders called for more federal animal-disease regulatory powers. During the two-day session, the leaders were reminded that the British government was well aware of where livestock diseases existed in the United States.[72] By December 1883, Dr. Law's campaign to improve America's animal-disease laws had won the favor of many in the U.S. agricultural community. Largely on the basis of his and Professor Brown's correspondence, Dr. Law urged Congress to bolster federal veterinary regulatory powers.

Although Dr. Law was denied the authority and money to purchase and slaughter infected livestock, Congress did create in May 1884 an official animal-disease control agency: the Bureau of Animal Industry. Two years later, the bureau was granted the authority to purchase and destroy diseased animals. The bureau's chief, Dr. Daniel Salmon, followed Dr. Law's practice of corresponding with the British veterinary authorities, and by 1889, the veterinary regulatory structures of Britain and America were noticeably similar. Dr. Salmon headed up the Bureau of Animal Industry and reported to the U.S. secretary of agriculture, and Professor Brown headed a Veterinary Department subordinate to the president of the British Board of Agriculture. Transatlantic information sharing became more routine and intentional as both countries made progress in eradicating pleuro-pneumonia. For example, rather than the ad hoc reports, letters, and visits characteristic of previous transatlantic correspondence, Dr. Salmon sent disease-eradication progress reports to Britain. Meanwhile, Professor Brown and his superior, Henry Chaplin, would keep American regulators apprised of British regulatory changes. British and American regulators also agreed to work together in the midst of their persistent disagreements. For example, when tensions over the pleuro-pneumonia dispute resurfaced in the early 1890s, veterinarians from the U.S. Bureau of Animal Industry were stationed at British ports alongside British inspectors, who sought to help the American officials trace the history of animals found to be infected.

Bilateral regulatory coordination proved an important dispute-resolution tool for the United States and Great Britain in other policy areas outside of pleuro-pneumonia. For example, U.S.-British veterinary cooperation efforts helped restore the live importation of American sheep.[73] Regulatory coordination also helped both countries successfully eradicate pleuro-pneumonia and (temporarily) FMD. Cooperation served the two countries well and, while complete resolution of the cattle dispute came only with new economic circumstances (i.e., the advent of the chilled-meat trade and the diminishment of the American export trade itself), one lesson is clear: bilateral regulatory cooperation is important in dealing with trade- and biosecurity-related dilemmas.

SUMMARY OF LESSONS LEARNED

This chapter—an in-depth exploration of an important episode in the history of food and agriculture security—offers several perspectives for those who will have to make decisions affecting food, agriculture, and global trade. First, tomorrow's decision makers should note that economic considerations were most influential in the U.S.-British trade dispute over animal disease. While regulatory cooperation was also important, only economic factors were sufficient to produce dispute resolution. Committed to free-trade principles for both food-supply and ideological reasons, and uniquely invested in both American agriculture and the transatlantic livestock and meat trade, Great Britain was motivated by economic considerations to reject an outright ban on American livestock imports despite pleuro-pneumonia, FMD, and other disease threats posed by them. At the same time, economic considerations—particularly the devastating costs of animal disease—also demanded that Britain adopt some sort of regulatory controls to guard against the importation of disease. The economically favorable compromise solution to Britain's dilemma was the immediate-slaughter policy, a regulatory tool that enabled Britain to continue to import American livestock, albeit slaughtered at ports of entry. Economic considerations also influenced American diplomats, regulators, shippers, and agriculturalists. On the basis of international trade hopes in the British store-cattle market, these Americans led—and at times, pushed—the U.S. government on the path toward improved animal-disease regulation. While the domestic economic cost of livestock diseases would also become important in America, export-market aspirations were the primary reason why the U.S. government initially undertook animal-disease regulation. However, U.S. regulatory improvements, even the eradication of pleuro-pneumonia from America, did not resolve the dispute. New economic realities—namely, innovation and investment in chilled-meat storage and transportation technologies—would bring the two countries closer to dispute resolution; by trading in chilled meat rather than live animals, disease transmission was reduced, and the diseased-livestock trade dispute waned in importance. Nevertheless, the dispute persisted as American officials continued to lament Britain's immediate-slaughter policy, a regulation that was never rescinded. Early in the 20th century, when economic circumstances dictated that the United States no longer needed to export livestock to Britain, the dispute finally ended.

In addition to economic considerations, regulatory cooperation amongst British and American veterinarians provides a helpful lesson for today's and tomorrow's food and agriculture security leaders. The eventual transatlantic coordination of regulatory institutions and laws, evident by the 1890s, brought the two countries closer to dispute resolution and helped them both improve their collective regulatory capacity.

Several other lessons emerge, and these are enumerated below:

1. *Economic considerations are influential in resolving food and agriculture security related trade disputes.* Perhaps the most valuable lesson to be gleaned from the 19th-century events over pleuro-pneumonia is the extent to which economic theories, policies, and dependencies dictated the outcome of the trade disputes. If still true today, this lesson means that dispute resolution is at the mercy of modern economic forces. These include economic realities such as globalization, western governments' agricultural economic protectionism, and western countries' financial and technological investment in foreign agricultural enterprises.

2. *While often decried, new technologies sometimes promote dispute resolution.* An important observation that may be taken from this analysis is how the advent of a new technology—refrigeration—brought a measure of peace to international trade tensions. Those involved in the livestock trade came to see the meat trade as a so-called win-win solution for all involved. British officials were optimistic that America could provide an ample supply of meat but only if it were properly refrigerated. Public health officials, American and British agriculturalists, and animal-welfare activists were also optimistic. However, while meat-refrigeration technologies were used on transatlantic steamships as early as 1875, chilling and freezing machinery was still in its infancy; innovation and investment were needed. Due in part to London's investment culture, many Britons would come to invest in transatlantic food systems, including refrigeration technologies for the meat trade. Because of this investment, capital was devoted to the much-needed technology of refrigeration. Application of refrigeration to transatlantic steamships was increasingly perfected, and by the 1890s the live-cattle trade became less important to both American and British traders. Animal-welfare activists, like Britain's Humanitarian League, were also pleased with the new technology. The story of meat refrigeration offers an important lesson for today's food and agriculture security policy discussions. While technology itself should not be deified, it must be remembered that novel technologies can help solve many of the food production, distribution, and safety issues often at the root of food and agriculture security problems. Scientific and technological innovation should be encouraged and embraced, not resisted.

3. *Officials should avoid "safety and security" claims that are not backed up by robust risk-management practices.* For a number of years, U.S. diplomats insisted on the healthfulness of American livestock despite the absence of any real regulatory or disease-surveillance infrastructure. When diseases were repeatedly discovered among U.S. livestock, America's animal-disease reputation was compromised. This loss of credibility delayed resolution of America's diseased-livestock dispute with Britain.

4. *Bilateral cooperation is essential in food and agriculture security.* While there were episodes of multilateralism (e.g., international veterinary conferences), dispute-resolution efforts in the U.S.-British case were almost always bilateral in nature. As this chapter has shown, U.S. and British authorities worked together, and this bilateral regulatory cooperation substantially helped.

5. *Food and agriculture security officials are real human beings who must work within the existing, available science.* Looking back at many of the personalities involved in the 19th-century disputes, it is tempting to accuse many of them of scientific ignorance of the risks posed by pleuro-pneumonia. Yet the veterinary regulators, microbiologists, and trade diplomats had to conduct their business according to the science of the day. During the last quarter of the 19th century, there were profound differences of opinion about the etiology of and diagnoses of pleuro-pneumonia, the causative organism for which was not discovered until 1898. These disagreements effectively delayed both America's focus on domestic veterinary risk management and U.S.-British transatlantic regulatory coordination. One hundred years later, similar phenomena are at work. As recent as the late 20th century, regulatory officials sat on the cusp of new science regarding sanitary risks like BSE, chronic wasting disease, and other transmissible spongiform encephalopathies, and they had to make difficult decisions based on new and unfolding science. Tomorrow's food and agriculture security decision makers will likely face the same situation: making tough decisions in the midst of incomplete information.

These historical perspectives and lessons are respectfully left at the door of today's and tomorrow's food and agriculture security officials. Thus equipped, these officials will, the author hopes, approach their important work with a kind of new, historically rooted wisdom.

NOTES

1. The committee was actually the meat subcommittee of the society's food committee. "Proceedings of the Society: Food Committee," *Journal of the Society of Arts* 15, no. 756 (1867): 414–17.

2. The Liverpool Provision Trade Association was formed in 1874 to manage the trade in packed meat, but it later expanded to include dairy products, eggs, and canned goods. Gordon Read and Michael Stammers, *Guide to the Records of Merseyside Maritime Museum* (St. John's, Newfoundland: Trustees of the National Museums and Galleries on Merseyside & International Maritime Economic History Association, 1995), p. 78. John Burnett, *Plenty and Want, a Social History of Diet in England from 1815 to the Present Day* (London: Thomas Nelson and Sons Ltd., 1966), pp. 100–101.

3. Pioneers were John Bell & Sons (Glasgow), Swan & Sons (Edinburgh), and Nelson Morris (Chicago). John Dyke conducted shipping experiments involving Canadian cattle in 1873. W. D. Zimmerman, "Live Cattle Export Trade between United States and Great Britain, 1868–1885," *Agricultural History* 36 (1962): 46. Fred Wilbur Powell, *The Bureau of Animal Industry: Its History, Activities and Organization,* ed. Institute for Government Research, Service Monographs of the United

States Government (Baltimore, MD: The Johns Hopkins Press, 1927), p. 4. "Cattle Diseases and the Meat Supply," *Times,* February 10, 1890.

4. Eastman was the largest U.S. exporter of live cattle between 1877 and 1885. Zimmerman, "Live Cattle Export Trade between United States and Great Britain, 1868–1885," p. 47.

5. Richard Perren, *The Meat Trade in Britain 1840–1914,* ed. F.M.L. Thompson, Studies in Economic History (London: Routledge & Kegan Paul Ltd, 1978), pp. 114, 126. James Troubridge Critchell and Joseph Raymond, *A History of the Frozen Meat Trade* (London: Constable & Company Ltd., 1912), p. 191. Zimmerman, "Live Cattle Export Trade between United States and Great Britain, 1868–1885," p. 48.

6. Britain, of course, was also interested in Canada providing part of its food. Lord Beaconsfield indicated this in a September 1879 speech to British agriculturalists; the speech is available in "Diplomatic Correspondence Paper No. 53: Mr. Hoppin to Mr. Evarts, September 19, 1879," *Papers Relating to the Foreign Relations of the United States* (1879).

7. W. W. Rostow, *British Economy of the Nineteenth Century* (Oxford: Oxford University Press, 1948; reprint, 1952), p. 231. P. L. Cottrell, *British Overseas Investment in the Nineteenth Century,* Studies in Economic and Social History (London: The MacMillan Press Ltd., 1975), p. 22.

8. Herbert Heaton, *Economic History of Europe,* ed. Guy Stanton Ford, rev. ed., Harper's Historical Series (New York: Harper & Row, 1948), p. 575.

9. According to U.S. Treasury Department statistics for 1879, less than 20 percent of American exports were carried by American ships; most of the rest were British bottoms. U.S. Bureau of Statistics, *Annual Report on the Foreign Commerce of the United States* (Washington, D.C.: Government Printing Office, 1879), p. xxix.

10. Cottrell, *British Overseas Investment in the Nineteenth Century,* p. 40.

11. MacDonald's North American tour was comprehensive; and the author notes that he visited both Guelph, Ontario, and Manhattan, Kansas, locales where the author has studied food science. James MacDonald, *Food from the Far West: American Agriculture with Special Reference to the Beef Production and Importation of Dead Meat from America to Great Britain* (London: William P. Nimmo, 1878).

12. Nineteenth-century North America was rapidly becoming the world expert in handling and transporting food. Gregory P. Marchildon, "Canadian-American Agricultural Trade Relations: A Brief History," *American Review of Canadian Studies* 28, no. 3 (1998): 237.

13. J.H.D., "Texas Live Stock: An Englishman's Opinion of Its Value for Exportation," *New York Times,* August 14, 1878.

14. The Matador Land and Cattle Company, consisting of Dundee investors familiar with animal husbandry, purchased a small ranch in Texas in 1882. This ranch eventually reached from Texas to Saskatchewan. There were other alien investments in Texas; by 1886, these totaled $15 million. W. M. Pearce, *The Matador Land and Cattle Company* (Norman: University of Oklahoma Press, 1964), pp. vii, 10. Jimmy M. Skaggs, *Prime Cut: Livestock Raising and Meatpacking in the United States, 1607–1983* (College Station: Texas A&M University Press, 1986), p. 59. For more on the Parliamentary commission, see Zimmerman, "Live Cattle Export Trade between United States and Great Britain, 1868–1885," pp. 47–48.

15. Marchildon, "Canadian-American Agricultural Trade Relations," p. 237.

16. Eastman exported cattle raised in Paris, Kentucky, and Macon County, Illinois. John Gillet, the Macon County farmer responsible for Eastman's inaugural

beef shipments, was visited by James MacDonald during his North American tour. MacDonald, *Food from the Far West*, pp. 143–47. Zimmerman, "Live Cattle Export Trade between United States and Great Britain, 1868–1885," p. 47.

17. Marchildon, "Canadian-American Agricultural Trade Relations," pp. 235–39. Douglas Hurt, *American Agriculture: A Brief History* (Ames: Iowa State University Press, 1994), pp. 192–94.

18. Critchell and Raymond, *A History of the Frozen Meat Trade*, pp. 25–26, 190–91. Perren, The Meat Trade in Britain, p. 130.

19. John P. Huttman, "British Meat Imports in the Free Trade Era," *Agricultural History* 52, no. 2 (1978): 254. Perren, *The Meat Trade in Britain*, p. 132.

20. While the years before 1873 and after 1896 were characterized by upward economic growth, the period 1873–1896 was downward. Heaton, *Economic History of Europe*, pp. 422, 653.

21. Richard Perren, *Agriculture in Depression, 1870–1940*, ed. Michael Sanderson for the Economic History Society, New Studies in Economic and Social History (Cambridge: Cambridge University Press, 1995), pp. 9–10.

22. "Our Foreign Food Supplies," *Economist*, July 20, 1878.

23. H.C.G. Matthew, "The Liberal Age (1851–1914)," in *The Oxford History of Britain*, ed. Kenneth O. Morgan (Oxford and New York: Oxford University Press, 1988), p. 540. Huttman, "British Meat Imports in the Free Trade Era," p. 247.

24. Perren, *Agriculture in Depression, 1870–1940*, pp. 9–12.

25. For example, see George Fleming, "Letter to the Editor of 27 June," *Times*, July 1, 1878.

26. 45th Congress (3rd Session), "Senate Misc. Doc. 71: Information On…Pleuro-Pneumonia among Cattle," *U.S. Serial Set*, no. 1833v.1 (1879), p. 2.

27. Great Britain (Parliament), "Correspondence Connected with the Detection of Pleuro-Pneumonia among Cattle Landed in Great Britain from the United States of America," *Sessional Papers* 58 (1878–1879), pp. 349–350.

28. "Diplomatic Correspondence Paper No. 264: Mr. Evarts to Mr. Welsh, April 2, 1879," *Papers Relating to the Foreign Relations of the United States* (1879).

29. Huttman, "British Meat Imports in the Free Trade Era," pp. 250, 254.

30. Perren, *The Meat Trade in Britain*, pp. 116–17. Richard Perren, "The North American Beef and Cattle Trade with Great Britain, 1870–1914," *Economic History Review*, 2d series, 24, no. 3 (1971): 435.

31. P. G. Craigie, "Twenty Years' Changes in Our Foreign Meat Supplies," *Journal of the Royal Agricultural Society of England*, 2nd ser., 23 (1887): 469.

32. Perren, *The Meat Trade in Britain*, pp. 157, 162–63.

33. Richmond himself had introduced the legislation. T. Duckham and G. T. Brown, "The Progress of Legislation against Contagious Diseases of Live Stock," *Journal of the Royal Agricultural Society of England*, 3rd. ser., 4 (1893): 284.

34. "The Importation of Foreign Cattle: Deputation to the Duke of Richmond from the Corporation of Liverpool (*Daily Mercury* Clipping of March 15th)," in *Cattle Trade Accommodation (General) Worked-up Papers*, vol. 1 (Liverpool: Mersey Docks and Harbour Board & Merseyside Maritime Museum Archives, 1878).

35. Perren, *The Meat Trade in Britain*, p. 111.

36. Ken McCarron, *Meat at Woodside: The Birkenhead Livestock Trade 1878–1981* (Birkenhead: Merseyside Port Folios and the National Museums and Galleries on Merseyside, 1991), p. 19.

37. Margaret Derry, *Ontario's Cattle Kingdom: Purebred Breeders and Their World, 1870–1920* (Toronto: University of Toronto Press, 2001), pp. 60–61.

38. Zimmerman, "Live Cattle Export Trade between United States and Great Britain, 1868–1885," p. 46.

39. In correspondence with the Mersey Docks and Harbour Board, the entity responsible for managing the ports of Liverpool, Messrs Flinn Main & Montgomery submitted a petition against the Contagious Diseases (Animals) Bill and requested that the board press for amendments. The board agreed that the lobbying efforts led by the mayor adequately addressed this company's concerns. "Docks & Quays Agenda: Letter from Messrs Flinn Main & Montgomery of March 27th," in *Cattle Trade Accommodation (General) Worked-up Papers*, vol. 1 (Liverpool: Mersey Docks and Harbour Board & Merseyside Maritime Museum Archives, 1878).

40. Duckham and Brown, "The Progress of Legislation against Contagious Diseases of Live Stock," p. 274.

41. "The Cattle Diseases Bill," *Times*, June 26, 1878.

42. "The Cattle Disease Bill," *Economist*, June 29, 1878. "Our Foreign Food Supplies."

43. Duckham and Brown, "The Progress of Legislation against Contagious Diseases of Live Stock," p. 274.

44. Perren, *The Meat Trade in Britain*, p. 113.

45. Extract from 1879 Annual Report of the Veterinary Department of the Privy Council Office of Great Britain in 46th Congress (3rd Session), "Senate Ex. Doc. 5: Documents...Relative to Contagious Diseases of Cattle," *U.S. Serial Set*, no. 1941v.1 (1880), pp. 20–21.

46. "Diplomatic Correspondence Paper No. 219: Mr. Seward to Sir Edward Thornton, October 25, 1878," *Papers Relating to the Foreign Relations of the United States* (1878).

47. Fleming, "Letter to the Editor of 27 June."

48. 45th Congress (2nd Session), "Senate Ex. Doc. 35: Message from the President of the United States Communicating...Information in Relation to the Disease Prevailing among Swine and Other Domestic Animals," *U.S. Serial Set*, no. 1780v.1 (1878), pp. 142–45.

49. The principal subject of Gamgee's investigation was the 1868 outbreak of Texas Fever in the American Midwest. Gamgee was hired by the U.S. government to make these investigations in Illinois, Kansas, and Texas. 41st Congress (2nd Session), "Diseases of Cattle in the United States: Report of the Commissioner of Agriculture, Including Reports from Professor Gamgee," *U.S. Serial Set*, no. 1430v.16 (1871).

50. See a report of the D.C. medical health officer, Smith Townshend, MD, in Great Britain (Parliament), "Correspondence," p. 360. New York and New Jersey accounts provided in James Law, *The Lung Plague of Cattle, Contagious Pleuro-Pneumonia* (Ithaca, NY: published by the author, 1879), pp. 8, 17–19.

51. "Diplomatic Correspondence Paper No. 219: Mr. Seward to Sir Edward Thornton, October 25, 1878."

52. 45th Congress (3rd Session), "Senate Misc. Doc. 71," p. 3. See also November 1878 report of Commissioner Le Duc, cited in 46th Congress (3rd Session), "Senate Ex. Doc. 5," p. 26.

53. That is, Foreign Animals Order No. 452.

54. 46th Congress (3rd Session), "Senate Ex. Doc. 5," pp. 5, 17.

55. McEachran clandestinely entered a dairy near Brooklyn, where he found several cases. Great Britain (Parliament), "Correspondence," p. 351.

56. "Fearing Cattle Disease," *New York Times,* February 1, 1879.

57. Extract from annual report of the Veterinary Department of the Privy Council of Great Britain, 1879, in 46th Congress (3rd Session), "Senate Ex. Doc. 5," pp. 18, 23–25.

58. Evarts had already received the news from the American minister in London. Great Britain (Parliament), "Correspondence," pp. 349–50.

59. "Fearing the Cattle Disease," *New York Times,* February 4, 1879.

60. For a detailed account of this episode in history, including William Williams's role in the diagnosis controversy, see Justin Kastner et al., "Scientific Conviction Amidst Scientific Controversy in the Transatlantic Livestock and Meat Trade," *Endeavour* 29, no. 2 (2005).

61. 45th Congress (3rd Session), "Senate Misc. Doc. 71," p. 9. 46th Congress (3rd Session), "Senate Ex. Doc. 5," pp. 20–21. McCarron, *Meat at Woodside,* p. 21.

62. "Fearing the Cattle Disease."

63. Preserved, tinned meat from American was one-half the price of locally sourced fresh meat. Burnett, *Plenty and Want,* p. 101.

64. Huttman, "British Meat Imports in the Free Trade Era," p. 254. Perren, *The Meat Trade in Britain,* p. 132.

65. For a glimpse at how American fatstock had become a regular feature of the British food supply, see "The American Fat Stock Show," *Times,* December 8, 1890.

66. A good example of humanitarians' support of the meat trade as an alternative to the live-animal trade is the following tract: I. M. Greg and S. H. Towers, "Cattle Ships and Our Meat Supply," *The Humanitarian League's Publications,* no. 15 (1894): 26–28.

67. April 2, 1890, issue of the *Breeder's Gazette,* cited in 1st Session 51st Congress, "Senate Rep. 829: Select Committee on the Transportation and Sale of Meat Products," *U.S. Serial Set,* no. 2705v.3 (1890), p. 30.

68. Perren, *The Meat Trade in Britain,* pp. 157, 162.

69. The U.S. surgeon-general believed that a newly created National Board of Health was the logical venue for combining animal- and human-disease-control policy. Dr. Law and his contemporaries at the U.S. Veterinary Medical Association also wanted a federal authority supervising animal disease control, but they wanted it to be run by veterinarians. Sherman therefore pushed for a veterinary sanitary commission in February 1880. In his request, Sherman mentioned the advice of the British minister, from a letter dated January 24,1880, available in 46th Congress (2nd Session), "House Ex. Doc. 53: Pleuro-Pneumonia in Neat Cattle," *U.S. Serial Set,* no. 1925v.24 (1880), p. 7.

70. See Le Duc's autobiography, published posthumously in 1963: William G. Le Duc and Augustine V. Gardner, *Recollections of a Civil War Quartermaster: The Autobiography of William G. Le Duc* (St. Paul, MN: North Central Publishing Company, 1963), p. 161.

71. See letter from Dr. James Law to Professor George Brown, Parliament (House of Commons), "Further Correspondence Relating to Diseases of Animals in the United States of America," *Sessional Papers* 74 (1884), pp. 227–29.

72. See statement of Dr. Gadsden, in ibid., p. 278.

73. During an April 1890 meeting with Brown and Chaplin, the U.S. minister in London learned that Britain was satisfied with American efforts to stamp out FMD and other diseases from sheep. U.S. officials were informed, and the U.S. minister noted that new legislation already proposed would further enhance American sheep's reputation in Britain. Correspondence over the next two years eventually brought removal of the British restrictions on sheep. "Diplomatic Correspondence Paper No. 208: Mr. Lincoln to Mr. Blaine, April 5, 1890," *Papers Relating to the Foreign Relations of the United States* (1896), p. 321. "Diplomatic Correspondence Paper No. 248: Mr. Blaine to Mr. Lincoln, April 28, 1890," *Papers Relating to the Foreign Relations of the United States* (1896). 54th Congress (2nd Session), "House Doc. 166: Restrictions on American Live Cattle in British Ports," *U.S. Serial Set*, no. 3524v.48 (1897), p. 19ff.

BIBLIOGRAPHY

41st Congress (2nd Session). "Diseases of Cattle in the United States: Report of the Commissioner of Agriculture, Including Reports from Professor Gamgee." *U.S. Serial Set*, no. 1430v.16 (1871).

45th Congress (2nd Session). "Senate Ex. Doc. 35: Message from the President of the United States Communicating…Information in Relation to the Disease Prevailing among Swine and Other Domestic Animals." *U.S. Serial Set*, no. 1780v.1 (1878).

45th Congress (3rd Session). "Senate Misc. Doc. 71: Information On…Pleuro-Pneumonia among Cattle." *U.S. Serial Set*, no. 1833v.1 (1879).

46th Congress (2nd Session). "House Ex. Doc. 53: Pleuro-Pneumonia in Neat Cattle." *U.S. Serial Set*, no. 1925v.24 (1880).

46th Congress (3rd Session). "Senate Ex. Doc. 5: Documents…Relative to Contagious Diseases of Cattle." *U.S. Serial Set*, no. 1941v.1 (1880).

51st Congress, 1st Session. "Senate Rep. 829: Select Committee on the Transportation and Sale of Meat Products." *U.S. Serial Set*, no. 2705v.3 (1890).

54th Congress (2nd Session). "House Doc. 166: Restrictions on American Live Cattle in British Ports." *U.S. Serial Set*, no. 3524v.48 (1897).

"The American Fat Stock Show." *Times*, December 8, 1890, 4, column c.

Burnett, John. *Plenty and Want, a Social History of Diet in England from 1815 to the Present Day*. London: Thomas Nelson and Sons Ltd., 1966.

"The Cattle Disease Bill." *Economist*, June 29, 1878, 764.

"The Cattle Diseases Bill." *Times*, June 26, 1878, 11, column b.

"Cattle Diseases and the Meat Supply." *Times*, February 10, 1890, 4, column b.

Cottrell, P. L. *British Overseas Investment in the Nineteenth Century*, Studies in Economic and Social History. London: The MacMillan Press Ltd., 1975.

Craigie, P. G. "Twenty Years' Changes in Our Foreign Meat Supplies." *Journal of the Royal Agricultural Society of England*, 2nd ser., 23 (1887): 465–500.

Critchell, James Troubridge, and Joseph Raymond. *A History of the Frozen Meat Trade*. London: Constable & Company Ltd., 1912.

Derry, Margaret. *Ontario's Cattle Kingdom: Purebred Breeders and Their World, 1870–1920*. Toronto: University of Toronto Press, 2001.

"Diplomatic Correspondence Paper No. 53: Mr. Hoppin to Mr. Evarts, September 19, 1879." *Papers Relating to the Foreign Relations of the United States* (1879): 453–63.

"Diplomatic Correspondence Paper No. 208: Mr. Lincoln to Mr. Blaine, April 5, 1890." *Papers Relating to the Foreign Relations of the United States* (1896): 319–21.
"Diplomatic Correspondence Paper No. 219: Mr. Seward to Sir Edward Thornton, October 25, 1878." *Papers Relating to the Foreign Relations of the United States* (1878): 356–57.
"Diplomatic Correspondence Paper No. 248: Mr. Blaine to Mr. Lincoln, April 28, 1890." *Papers Relating to the Foreign Relations of the United States* (1896): 322.
"Diplomatic Correspondence Paper No. 264: Mr. Evarts to Mr. Welsh, April 2, 1879." *Papers Relating to the Foreign Relations of the United States* (1879): 423–27.
"Docks & Quays Agenda: Letter from Messrs Flinn Main & Montgomery of March 27th." In *Cattle Trade Accommodation (General) Worked-up Papers*. Vol. 1. Liverpool: Mersey Docks and Harbour Board & Merseyside Maritime Museum Archives, 1878.
Duckham, T., and G. T. Brown. "The Progress of Legislation against Contagious Diseases of Live Stock." *Journal of the Royal Agricultural Society of England*, 3rd ser., 4 (1893): 262–86.
"Fearing Cattle Disease." *New York Times*, February 1, 1879, 5, column c.
"Fearing the Cattle Disease." *New York Times*, February 4, 1879, 5, column b.
Fleming, George. "Letter to the Editor of 27 June." *Times*, July 1, 1878, 11, column f.
Great Britain (Parliament). "Correspondence Connected with the Detection of Pleuro-Pneumonia among Cattle Landed in Great Britain from the United States of America." *Sessional Papers* 58 (1878–1879): 349–64.
Greg, I. M., and S. H. Towers. "Cattle Ships and Our Meat Supply." *The Humanitarian League's Publications*, no. 15 (1894).
Heaton, Herbert. *Economic History of Europe*, ed. Guy Stanton Ford. Rev. ed. Harper's Historical Series. New York: Harper & Row, 1948.
Hurt, Douglas. *American Agriculture: A Brief History*. Ames: Iowa State University Press, 1994.
Huttman, John P. "British Meat Imports in the Free Trade Era." *Agricultural History* 52, no. 2 (1978): 247–62.
"The Importation of Foreign Cattle: Deputation to the Duke of Richmond from the Corporation of Liverpool (*Daily Mercury* Clipping of March 15th)." In *Cattle Trade Accommodation (General) Worked-up Papers*. Vol 1. Liverpool: Mersey Docks and Harbour Board & Merseyside Maritime Museum Archives, 1878.
J.H.D. "Texas Live Stock: An Englishman's Opinion of Its Value for Exportation." *New York Times*, August 14, 1878, 3, column 3.
Kastner, Justin, Douglas Powell, Terry Crowley, and Karen Huff. "Scientific Conviction Amidst Scientific Controversy in the Transatlantic Livestock and Meat Trade." *Endeavour* 29, no. 2 (2005): 78–83.
Law, James. *The Lung Plague of Cattle, Contagious Pleuro-Pneumonia*. Ithaca, NY: published by the author, 1879.
Le Duc, William G., and Augustine V. Gardner. *Recollections of a Civil War Quartermaster: The Autobiography of William G. Le Duc*. St. Paul, MN: North Central Publishing Company, 1963.
MacDonald, James. *Food from the Far West: American Agriculture with Special Reference to the Beef Production and Importation of Dead Meat from America to Great Britain*. London: William P. Nimmo, 1878.

Marchildon, Gregory P. "Canadian-American Agricultural Trade Relations: A Brief History." *American Review of Canadian Studies* 28, no. 3 (1998): 233–52.

Matthew, H.C.G. "The Liberal Age (1851–1914)." In *The Oxford History of Britain*, ed. Kenneth O. Morgan. Oxford and New York: Oxford University Press, 1988.

McCarron, Ken. *Meat at Woodside: The Birkenhead Livestock Trade 1878–1981*. Birkenhead: Merseyside Port Folios and the National Museums and Galleries on Merseyside, 1991.

"Our Foreign Food Supplies." *Economist,* July 20, 1878, 854.

Parliament (House of Commons). "Further Correspondence Relating to Diseases of Animals in the United States of America." *Sessional Papers* 74 (1884): 187–367.

Pearce, W. M. *The Matador Land and Cattle Company*. Norman: University of Oklahoma Press, 1964.

Perren, Richard. *Agriculture in Depression, 1870–1940,* ed. Michael Sanderson for the Economic History Society, New Studies in Economic and Social History. Cambridge: Cambridge University Press, 1995.

Perren, Richard. *The Meat Trade in Britain 1840–1914,* ed. F.M.L. Thompson, Studies in Economic History. London: Routledge & Kegan Paul Ltd., 1978.

Perren, Richard. "The North American Beef and Cattle Trade with Great Britain, 1870–1914." *Economic History Review* 2d series, 24, no. 3 (1971): 430–44.

Powell, Fred Wilbur. *The Bureau of Animal Industry: Its History, Activities and Organization,* ed. Institute for Government Research, Service Monographs of the United States Government. Baltimore, MD: The Johns Hopkins Press, 1927.

"Proceedings of the Society: Food Committee." *Journal of the Society of Arts* 15, no. 756 (1867): 414–17.

Read, Gordon, and Michael Stammers. *Guide to the Records of Merseyside Maritime Museum*. St. John's, Newfoundland: Trustees of the National Museums and Galleries on Merseyside & International Maritime Economic History Association, 1995.

Rostow, W. W. *British Economy of the Nineteenth Century*. Oxford: Oxford University Press, 1948. Reprint, 1952.

Skaggs, Jimmy M. *Prime Cut: Livestock Raising and Meatpacking in the United States, 1607–1983*. College Station: Texas A&M University Press, 1986.

U.S. Bureau of Statistics. *Annual Report on the Foreign Commerce of the United States*. Washington, D.C.: Government Printing Office, 1879.

Zimmerman, W. D. "Live Cattle Export Trade between United States and Great Britain, 1868–1885." *Agricultural History* 36 (1962): 46–52.

CHAPTER 3

Food and Agriculture Security Along the Farm-to-Table Continuum

Kathryn Krusemark

Consumers in the United States have come to expect access to a variety of food and agricultural products on a year-round basis. Globalization and the importation of these products into the United States have allowed this.[1] A majority of products like bananas, coffee, chocolate, fish and shellfish, apple juice, cashew nuts, and spices are imported into the United States because they are produced in greater quantities or less at a lower cost abroad or, in some cases, simply cannot be produced domestically.[2] Whether produced domestically or abroad, food and agricultural products do not magically wind up in stores or in front of consumers; they are often part of a complex supply chain. The food and agriculture production system is commonly viewed on a "farm-to-table" or "farm-to-fork" continuum.

This continuum is complex and multifaceted. Students of food and agriculture security can observe this complexity in multiple commodities and sectors in the food and agriculture system. While chapter 4 explores particular cases that illustrate the vulnerability of multiple commodities and sectors, this chapter begins by acknowledging the many steps involved in their supply chains. Food and agriculture security thought leaders have found it helpful to categorize these steps into two broad categories: pre-harvest and post-harvest. In the plant and crop production realm, harvest occurs and then is followed by a number of post-harvest steps connected through transportation: storage, processing, packaging, additional storage, wholesale, distribution through retail or food-service systems, and final delivery to consumers. The pre-harvest livestock and animal-products activities in the continuum involve slaughter and a similar (and equally complex) set of transportation, processing, packaging, storage, wholesale, and distribution steps. [3]

REGULATORY COMPLEXITY

The safety and security of these complex supply chains are often the subject of conversations involving food and agriculture security scholars, and it is appropriate to clarify some of the terms used in these discussions. At the time of the publication of this chapter, the terms "food safety," "food defense," "food protection," and "food security" are commonly used. Food safety focuses on procedures and situations that protect food from incidental or unintentional contamination that can cause illness.[4] Food defense is used by U.S. government agencies—most notably, the Food and Drug Administration (FDA), U.S. Department of Agriculture (USDA), and U.S. Department of Homeland Security (DHS)—when describing activities related to protecting the food supply from deliberate or intentional contamination, including tampering as well as bioterrorism (BT).[5] Food protection encompasses the totality of efforts that address both food safety and food defense issues to more effectively ensure a safe and secure food supply.[6] Historically, food security has represented access to nutritious, adequate, and safe foods that meet the preferences and social standards of the consumer.[7] However, some confusion has arisen as the U.S. government and others began, in recent years, to use the term when referencing issues related to the intentional contamination of food (including bioterrorism).[8] For the purposes of this book, food security may be understood in broad, general terms and be seen to include both food protection as well as the ongoing operation of an agriculture and food system that society has come to depend on—that is, a global system that meets the social standards and preferences for nutritious and adequate food.

To observe the multiple regulatory actors involved in food and agriculture security, it is helpful to examine the state of affairs in the United States. Worldwide, the U.S. government plays a key role in food safety and food defense efforts. These efforts include instituting safety standards, inspecting products, enforcing regulations, determining root causes of problems faced by those in the agriculture and food industries, and defending the U.S. food supply.[9] The U.S. Government Accountability Office (GAO) has identified 15 federal departments or agencies responsible for governing 30 laws concerning food safety and related domains of food and agriculture security. The FDA, under the jurisdiction of the U.S. Department of Health and Human Services (HHS), and the Food Safety and Inspection Service (FSIS), under the jurisdiction of the USDA, receive the majority of their funding and staffing related to the regulatory oversight of food.[10]

The USDA FSIS ensures the safety of meat, poultry, and processed egg products. The USDA Animal and Plant Health Inspection Service (APHIS) protects and promotes the health of agricultural resources including plants and animals. USDA's Grain Inspection, Packers and Stockyards Administration (GIPSA) aids in the establishment of quality standards, inspection procedures, and marketing of grain and similar products. The Agricultural Marketing Service (AMS), also within USDA, assists in the efficient, fair marketing of American agricultural products, including food, fiber, and specialty crops. The USDA Agricultural Research Service (ARS) conducts research on the safety of food and agricultural products, and the USDA Economic Research Service (ERS) analyzes economic issues influencing the safety of food products in the United States. USDA also has an entity—the National Agricultural Statistics Service (NASS)—devoted to the development of statistical data regarding the safety of the U.S. food supply, and the National Institute of Food and Agriculture (NIFA, formerly the Cooperative State Research, Education and Extension Service) provides funding for food safety research, education, and extension programs in universities and other organizations. Within HHS, the FDA ensures the safety of all food products other than meat, poultry, and processed egg products. HHS's Centers for Disease Control and Prevention (CDC) oversees U.S. public health and monitors food-borne illness surveillance. The National Marine Fisheries Service within the U.S. Department of Commerce provides safety and quality examination of seafood products. The U.S. Environmental Protection Agency (EPA) establishes regulations regarding the use of pesticides and allowable levels of pesticide residues in animal feed and food products. The U.S. Department of the Treasury's Alcohol and Tobacco Tax and Trade Bureau implements laws regarding the production, use, and distribution of alcoholic beverages. The Federal Trade Commission enforces advertising laws regarding agricultural and food products. Finally, DHS oversees food defense and security efforts in the food and agriculture sector.[11] Many of these agencies have their regulatory eye on particular disease agents of concern, discussed in the next section.

COMMON FOOD-BORNE DISEASE AGENTS

Food and agricultural products can become contaminated at various stages along the farm-to-table continuum. The CDC estimates that food-borne diseases in the United States are responsible for 76 million sicknesses, more than 300,000 hospitalizations, and 5,000 deaths annually. Over 250 food-borne diseases have been described and are caused by consuming contaminated foods or beverages. The majority of these diseases are infections attributed to bacteria, viruses, and parasites. Other diseases are poisonings attributed to dangerous toxins or chemicals present in foods. Historically, food-borne diseases including typhoid fever (caused by *Salmonella* Typhi), tuberculosis (caused by *Mycobacterium tuberculosis*), and cholera (caused by *Vibrio cholerae*) were common in the United States. However, advances in food (including water) sanitation and agriculture production and processing have markedly reduced these diseases. The agents and microorganisms that cause food-borne diseases continually evolve. Various reasons may be cited to explain the evolving threat: microorganisms know no boundaries and easily move around the globe; microorganisms adapt to their surroundings and develop over time; environmental changes allow microorganisms to do the same; food and agriculture production and processing changes have enabled individuals' eating habits to change; and new laboratory techniques and tests have facilitated the discovery or identification of new microorganisms. The CDC has identified the following as common causes of food-borne disease: *Campylobacter, Salmonella, Escherichia coli* O157:H7, *Calicivirus, Shigella,* hepatitis A, *Giardia lamblia, Cryptosporidium, Staphylococcus aureus,* and *Clostridium botulinum.*[12] Each are briefly discussed below.

Campylobacter

C. jejuni and *C. coli* are often regarded as the most common causes of diarrheal disease around the globe. Symptoms of campylobacteriosis include abdominal cramps, nausea, vomiting, fever, headache, and chills.[13] *Campylobacter* is commonly found in the gastrointestinal tract of warm-blooded animals. It has been found in a variety of food products including raw meats (beef, pork, lamb, chicken, and turkey), milk, eggs, vegetables, mushrooms, and clams. Cooking to sufficient temperatures and the avoidance of cross-contamination can prevent infection with *Campylobacter.*[14]

Salmonella

Over 1.4 million cases of salmonellosis are reported annually in the United States, and over 2,400 serotypes of *Salmonella* have been identified.[15] Symptoms of salmonellosis include abdominal cramps, diarrhea, nausea, vomiting, chills, and fever. It can be especially dangerous (i.e., deadly) to immunocompromised individuals including infants and the elderly. Meat, milk, poultry, and eggs are common sources of the bacteria. *Salmonella* has also been isolated in produce (i.e., vegetables and fruits). Cooking to sufficient temperatures and the avoidance of cross-contamination can prevent infection with *Salmonella.*[16]

Escherichia coli O157:H7

E. coli O157:H7 was first recognized as a pathogen in the early 1980s. Since then, it has become more widespread and is frequently responsible for food-borne disease outbreaks and recalls in the United States.[17] The organism is often found in the gastrointestinal tract of animals, especially cattle. Foods that become contaminated with cow feces can then infect humans. Historically, products including ground beef, pork, poultry, lamb, and raw milk have been sources of *E. coli* O157:H7.[18] Lettuce, apple cider, unpasteurized apple juice, and alfalfa sprouts have also been sources of the organism.[19] Human infection is dangerous and can cause hemorrhagic colitis, hemolytic uremic syndrome (HUS), and thrombotic thrombocytopenic purpura (TTP). Symptoms of hemorrhagic colitis include abrupt abdominal cramps, watery and often bloody diarrhea, and vomiting. HUS is a disease that causes renal failure, a drop in the number of red blood cells (i.e., hemolytic anemia), and a reduction in the number of blood platelets (i.e., thrombocytopenia). TTP is similar to HUS, but symptoms also include fever and neurologic effects.[20] Cooking foods to adequate temperatures, avoiding unpasteurized milk and juices, and practicing adequate personal hygiene to prevent fecal-oral contamination can help control *E. coli* O157:H7.[21]

Calicivirus

The term norovirus is the official name for this group of viruses; however, other names include norwalk-like viruses (NLVs), caliciviruses (because they belong to the virus family *Caliciviridae*), and small round structured viruses.[22] Noroviruses are the most common and are estimated to cause 23 million cases of gastroenteritis annually. Illness often sets in after 10–50 hours and symptoms often include vomiting, watery diarrhea, abdominal cramps, and nausea. Symptoms often last one to three days. The virus is spread from one individual to another. Contaminated water, salads, sandwiches, raspberries, bakery items, and oysters can be a source of the virus. The virus can survive freezing, high temperatures, and 10 part-per-million chlorine-treated water. To prevent infection with noroviruses, individuals should practice proper hygiene (i.e., hand washing) and avoid work if experiencing illness.[23]

Shigella

Species of *Shigella* include *S. dysenteriae, S. flexneri, S. boydii,* and *S. sonnei*.[24] *S. flexceri* and *S. boydii* cause most cases of shigellosis in the United States. In the United States, nearly 14,000 cases are reported annually; however, the actual number of cases could likely be 20 times higher. In less developed countries, shigellosis is even more widespread. The majority of those infected with *Shigella* develop symptoms including diarrhea (often bloody), fever, and stomach cramps 24 to 48 hours after exposure to the organism and symptoms resolve 5 to 7 days later.[25] *Shigella* is found in the intestines of certain primates and humans. Humans carrying *Shigella* can shed it in their feces without exhibiting symptoms. Foods become contaminated with *Shigella* through fecal contamination. Individuals with shigellosis should not handle foods. Drinking and using only chlorinated water can also help prevent shigellosis.[26]

Hepatitis A

Hepatitis A is caused by hepatitis A virus (HAV), which is found naturally in primates. Human infection is caused by direct contact with individuals infected with HAV or by consuming foods or water contaminated with HAV. Symptoms including fever, loss of appetite, nausea, vomiting, diarrhea, and muscle pain and weakness may or may not develop after approximately four weeks of exposure. Abdominal and liver pain with jaundice, dark-colored urine, or light-colored stools can also occur. Symptoms commonly last for several weeks. Hepatitis A outbreaks are relatively unusual in the United States and the source of many reported cases goes unknown. Foods can become contaminated with HAV throughout the farm-to-table continuum including by food handlers; fresh produce including green onions, lettuce, and frozen strawberries have also caused HAV outbreaks in the United States. Shellfish have also been implicated as a source of HAV. To prevent infection and spread of food-borne HAV, individuals should frequently wash their hands. Control measures to prevent the spread of the virus by infected food handlers should also be utilized; vaccinations to protect against HAV are also available.[27]

Giardia lamblia

Giardia lamblia is a protozoa that causes giardiasis, which is the most common nonbacterial disease in North America. Individuals can develop giardiasis after consuming food or water contaminated with the organism (i.e., as a cyst). While in the gastrointestinal tract, the protozoa is activated (known as a trophozoite) causing disease. Symptoms including diarrhea, vomiting, and abdominal pain are common. Historically, *Giardia* cysts have been isolated on produce including lettuce and strawberries; however, the organism can be found on any food rinsed with contaminated water or handled by infected individuals who did not use adequate sanitary procedures.[28]

Cryptosporidium

At least nine species of the parasite *Cryptosporidium* have caused cryptosporidiosis in humans. Contaminated water is often the source of the parasite; more than 400,000 people became ill after consuming contaminated water in Milwaukee, Wisconsin, in 1993. However, food handled by individuals carrying the organism, food that was in contact with contaminated water, and food grown in soil contaminated with the organism can also be sources of *Cryptosporidium*. The parasite is common in animals, especially livestock. *Cryptosporidum* oocysts are hearty and can survive for long periods of time in water. Symptoms in humans include watery diarrhea, abdominal cramps, loss of appetite, weight loss, nausea, vomiting, tiredness, and low-grade fever. The disease commonly lasts one to two weeks in healthy individuals. Individuals with weakened immune systems can develop severe illnesses as a result of cryptosporidiosis.[29]

Staphylococcus aureus

Some strains of *S. aureus* can produce highly heat-stable enterotoxins that cause staphylococcal "staph" food poisoning. The organism is common in the environment and on the bodies of healthy individuals. Entertoxins are formed in contaminated foods not kept at proper temperatures (i.e., 140°F or above, or 45°F or below). Foods associated with *S. aureus* intoxication include meat and meat products; egg and poultry products; salads including egg, tuna, chicken, potato, and macaroni; bakery products including cream-filled pastries, cream pies, and éclairs; sandwich fillings; and milk and dairy products. Symptoms including nausea, vomiting, retching, and abdominal cramping can develop shortly after consuming contaminated foods. The severity of symptoms is dependent on the individual, their susceptibility to the toxin, the amount of contaminated food eaten, the amount of the toxin in the food, and the health of the individual. Symptoms often subside after two days; however, this can be longer in more severe cases. To prevent toxin development, foods should be kept at adequate temperatures and proper hygiene utilized when handling and consuming foods.[30]

Clostridium botulinum

C. botulinum is a spore-forming microbe capable of producing neurotoxins; types A, B, E, and F cause human botulism. *C. botulinum* and its spores are common in the environment including in cultivated and forest soils; bottom sediments in streams, lakes, and coastal waters; intestinal tracts of fish and mammals; and the gills and viscera of crabs and other shellfish. The spores are heat-resistant and can survive in foods that are not properly processed. The toxin can be destroyed if it is heated at 80°C for at least 10 minutes. The disease is infrequent; however, it is a major concern because it is deadly if not adequately treated. Symptoms often set in 18 to 36 hours after consuming food with the toxin and include marked lethargy, weakness, vertigo, double vision, and difficulty in speaking and swallowing. Other symptoms include difficulty breathing, weakness of muscles, abdominal distention, and constipation. Low-acid foods (i.e., those with a pH above 4.6) can support *C. botulinum* toxin production. Historically, canned corn, peppers, green beans, soups, beets, asparagus, mushrooms, ripe olives, spinach, tuna, chicken, chicken livers and liver pate, lunch meats, ham, sausage, stuffed eggplant, lobster, and smoked and salted fish have supported the growth of the toxin.[31]

HACCP: A FOOD SAFETY RISK MANAGEMENT TOOL

The agents discussed in the previous section, along with a host of other hazards, pose considerable risks to food safety. It is the responsibility of the food and agriculture industry—individuals and organizations at each step along the farm-to-table continuum—to provide consumers with wholesome, safe foods. In the United States and scores of other countries, Hazard Analysis Critical Control Point (HACCP) systems are widely utilized to prevent reasonably likely hazards from threatening the safety of food and agricultural products.[32]

In the 1960s, the Pillsbury Company, working with the National Aeronautics and Space Administration (NASA), U.S. Army Laboratories at Natick, and U.S. Air Force Space Laboratory Project Group, developed the HACCP system to ensure the microbiological safety of the foods intended for the U.S. space program. When HACCP was introduced in the early 1960s, it was a novel approach to food safety and food quality; most efforts focused on end-product testing, while HACCP offered a preventative program for the production of safe food.[33] In the United States, the National Advisory Committee on Microbiological Criteria for Foods (NACMCF) provides support and counsel to the secretary of agriculture and the secretary of health and human services regarding the microbiological safety of foods. NACMCF is chartered under the USDA and includes participants from FSIS, the FDA and CDC, the National Marine Fisheries Service, the Department of Defense, academia, industry officials, and state employees. The NACMCF endorses HACCP as a valuable method to identify, evaluate, and control food safety hazards.[34]

Since its inception and acceptance, HACCP has advanced and is applied in many forms. This section provides information on HACCP adapted from NACMCF materials. In the United States, HACCP is required for meat and poultry products; juices; and fish, shellfish, and fishery products.[35] Readers should note that there are many other resources available to aid in the development of a HACCP plan and many of these resources are industry- or commodity-specific. HACCP is widely utilized in the agriculture and food sector—from individual farms to organizations at each step along the farm-to-table continuum. Before the principles of HACCP can be applied to a specific product or process, five preliminary tasks must be completed by food and agriculture security professionals. These appear below.

Preliminary Task 1: Assemble the HACCP Team

The HACCP team should be made up of individuals who are familiar with the specific product and process being addressed. This can include people from engineering, production, sanitation, quality assurance, and food microbiology. Additionally, personnel who work directly with the products should be a part of the HACCP team; often, they have first-hand knowledge of the drawbacks and variability of the system. Experts, especially those who are experienced in identifying hazards associated with the specific product and process, should also participate or verify the hazard analysis and HACCP plan.

Preliminary Task 2: Describe the Food and Its Distribution

Next, the HACCP team should provide an accurate description of the food and its distribution. The HACCP team should describe the food, including its ingredients and how it is processed. The distribution method (i.e., frozen, refrigerated, or at room temperature) should also be documented.

Preliminary Task 3: Describe the Intended Uses and Consumers of the Food

The HACCP team should describe how the food is intended to be used. As part of this, the team should identify the intended consumers. Consumer groups might be differentiated demographically (e.g., the general public, children, or other possibly immunocompromised groups).

Preliminary Tasks 4 and 5: Develop a Flow Diagram Which Describes the Process, and Verify the Flow Diagram

The HACCP team should also develop a flow diagram that documents all steps in the production and processing of the product in the facility. The HACCP team should then verify the flow diagram through a review process. Verification ensures that the diagram accurately depicts the process. If necessary, modifications should be made.

Once the five preliminary tasks are accomplished, the seven principles of HACCP can be applied. The seven principles of HACCP include conducting a hazard analysis, determining the critical control points, establishing critical limits, establishing monitoring procedures, establishing corrective actions, establishing verification procedures, and establishing record-keeping and documentation procedures. Each principle is discussed below.

Principle 1: Conduct a Hazard Analysis

A hazard is a biological, chemical, or physical agent that would likely result in illness or injury. During a hazard analysis, the HACCP team first identifies potential hazards that would likely appear; to this end, the team would utilize information on ingredients, processing and handling steps, as well as hazards that have previously been linked to the product. Hazards can then be evaluated depending upon the severity of the potential hazards and the probability of them occurring. When considering the severity of a potential hazard, the HACCP team should take into account the resulting effects of being exposed to the hazard. When considering the probability of the potential hazard of occurring, the HACCP team should consider the current knowledge, epidemiological data, and scientific literature regarding the potential hazard. When the hazard analysis is completed, the hazard, its respective processing step, and control measure(s) should be recorded.

Principle 2: Determine the Critical Control Points

Using the information from the hazard analysis, the HACCP team can determine control points and critical control points (CCPs). A control point is a step at which a hazard can be controlled. A CCP is a point, step, or procedure where a control can be employed to prevent or eliminate a food-safety hazard, or reduce the hazard to an acceptable level. CCPs address food safety issues; CCPs identified by the HACCP team might, for example, include a heat treatment at a specified temperature for a designated period of time.

Principle 3: Establish Critical Limits

The HACCP team must then determine critical limits for all CCPs. A critical limit is a measureable minimum or maximum value that must be satisfied to achieve a CCP. If applied, critical limits prevent or eliminate a food safety hazard or reduce the hazard to an acceptable level; critical limits should not be confused with operational limits, which address issues other than food safety. Critical limits should be scientifically based upon factors such as time, temperature, water activity, and pH. The HACCP team should properly document (by citing regulatory resources, scientific literature, experimental results, and experts) the established critical limits.

Principle 4: Establish Monitoring Procedures

Monitoring procedures, such as observations or measurements, ensure that critical limits established for CCPs are met. Specifically, the HACCP plan should address what factors are monitored, where they will be monitored, how they will be monitored, when they will be monitored, and who is responsible for monitoring them. Monitoring procedures fulfill three purposes: (1) the tracking of the food processing operations, (2) the loss of control (i.e., not meeting established critical limits), and (3) the documentation of the operation used for verification. If possible, monitoring procedures should be carried out on a continuous basis; however, some monitoring procedures such as microbial testing can take time and their usefulness in detecting contaminants is limited. Therefore, adequate sampling plans and limitations of microbial testing must also be considered when determining monitoring procedures.

Principle 5: Establish Corrective Actions

The HACCP program aims to prevent or eliminate food safety hazards or reduce these hazards to acceptable levels. However, and quite simply, this does not always happen. Therefore, the HACCP team must establish corrective actions. Corrective actions should accomplish the following: (1) identify and rectify the reason why corrective action had to be taken, (2) identify what happened to the affected product, and (3) document the corrective actions taken. Those responsible for corrective actions should be familiar with the production process, product, and the HACCP plan.

Principle 6: Establish Verification Procedures

Verification procedures, in contrast to monitoring procedures, help confirm that the HACCP plan is valid and working effectively. Verification procedures include initial and subsequent validation of the HACCP plan, verification of CCP monitoring as explained in the HACCP plan, review of monitoring and correction action records to confirm alignment with the HACCP plan, and comprehensive HACCP system verification.

Principle 7: Establish Record-Keeping and Documentation Procedures

Record-keeping and documentation procedures are of considerable importance to a HACCP system. Records should include a summary of the hazard analysis, the HACCP plan (including the HACCP team and responsibilities; a description of the food, its distribution, intended use, and consumer; and the verified flow diagram), a HACCP summary table that addresses the seven HACCP principles, supporting documentation, and records created when the HACCP plan is carried out.

Food and agriculture security scholars recognize that HACCP is not a stand-alone food safety system; it requires prerequisite programs that provide environmental conditions and practices needed for the production of safe foods. These conditions and practices may be specified in federal, state, and local regulation and guidelines. Examples include current Good Manufacturing Practices (cGMPs) and the Food Code. Additional resources are available for foods destined for international trade. Successful implementation of a HACCP plan takes time and the plan must always be updated to accurately reflect the product and process. Additionally, educating and training employees on food safety and the role of HACCP is critical.

ACCIDENTAL VERSUS INTENTIONAL CONTAMINATION

Many food safety issues develop because of process, operator, or equipment malfunction. Food safety systems, like HACCP, have reduced the likelihood of food-safety issues from developing; however, no system is foolproof and issues still arise.[36] Consider the following scenarios that illustrate unfortunate realties that arise all too frequently: a thermometer is not properly calibrated, and consumers eat undercooked hamburgers; a leaky roof allows microorganisms to contaminate ready-to-eat products; or a food product is accidentally contaminated with metal fragments from processing equipment. However, such unintentional-contamination scenarios are not the only concerns along the farm-to-table continuum. In the past, food has actually been intentionally contaminated, sometimes with a view to gaining an advantage in times of war.[37] In its public definition, the World Health Organization (WHO) defines food terrorism as "an act or threat of deliberate contamination of food for human consumption with biological, chemical and physical agents or radionuclear materials for the purpose of causing injury or death to civilian populations and/or disrupting social, economic or political stability."[38] In the United States, concerns about food terrorism and biosecurity intensified after the terrorist attacks on September 11, 2001, but the vulnerability of the food and agriculture sector to intentional contamination was already documented.[39] In 2002, documents found by the U.S. military in an al Qaeda training camp in Afghanistan showed that the organization had contemplated using biological and chemical weapons to contaminate food and agricultural products in the United States.[40]

CRITICAL INFRASTRUCTURE PROTECTION AND FOOD AND AGRICULTURE SECURITY

In recent years, protecting the U.S. infrastructure and America's way of life has become a top priority and the focus of the Department of Homeland Security (DHS).[41] Former President George W. Bush issued Homeland Security Presidential Directives (HSPDs) in several areas associated with Homeland Security. Four HSPDs apply particularly to the Agriculture and Food Sector and each is discussed below.[42]

HSPD-5

Homeland Security Presidential Directive-5: Management of Domestic Incidents (HSPD-5) was issued on February 28, 2003, establishing a single National Incident Management System (NIMS) intended to prevent, prepare for, respond to, and recover from a terrorist attack, major disaster, or other crisis situation. This system allows for each sector of government to work together in an organized and constructive manner.[43] Additionally, NIMS is the foundation for the National Response Plan (NRP), an all-hazards approach to domestic incident response.[44] The National Response Framework (NRF) replaced the NRP on March 22, 2008. The NRF explains how communities, tribes, states, the federal government, private-sector organizations and actors, and nongovernmental partners can collaborate to manage national response and outlines specific authorities and best practices for managing incidents.[45]

HSPD-7

Homeland Security Presidential Directive-7: Critical Infrastructure Identification, Prioritization, and Protection (HSPD-7) was issued on December 17, 2003, creating a national policy to identify and defend the critical infrastructure and key resources (CIKRs) in the United States from terrorist attacks.[46] Critical infrastructure, as explained in the National Infrastructure Protection Plan (NIPP), refers to those systems and assets that, if incapacitated or destroyed, would have a debilitating impact on the security, economy, public health or safety, or environment of any federal, state, regional, territorial, or local jurisdiction in the United States.[47] Key resources, which are mentioned in the Homeland Security Act of 2002, include publicly and privately controlled resources necessary to the functioning of the economy and government.[48]

Government-based food and agriculture security officials are members of a larger community committed to the protection of a wide range of CIKRs. This community is spread across a number of sector-specific agencies. In the Agriculture and Food Sector, officials from USDA and HHS are actively engaged. In other sectors, other agencies are involved: Defense Industrial Base Sector (Department of Defense), Energy Sector (Department of Energy), Healthcare and Public Health Sector (HHS), National Monuments and Icons Sector (Department of the Interior), Banking and Finance Sector (Department of the Treasury), and Water Sector (EPA). Various DHS offices, divisions, and agencies seek to ensure the protection of additional CIKRs: Chemical, Commercial Facilities, Critical Manufacturing, Dams, Emergency Services, Information Technology, Communications, Postal and Shipping, Transportation Systems, and Government Facilities. DHS also oversees protection of the Nuclear Reactors, Materials, and Waste Sector.[49]

The NIPP—in accordance with HSPD-7—outlines how CIKR protection activities should be implemented, while recognizing and joining appropriate authorities, jurisdictions, and rights of these partners. The Agriculture and Food Sector is one of 18 identified CIKRs. USDA (with jurisdiction over meat, poultry, and eggs) and HHS (with jurisdiction over all other food products) share responsibility for overseeing their respective CIKRs.[50] Their plans, documented in May 2007, may be found in a multiagency document entitled "Agriculture and Food: Critical Infrastructure and Key Resources Sector-Specific Plan as input to the National Infrastructure Protection Plan."[51]

HSPD-8

Homeland Security Presidential Directive-8: National Preparedness (HSPD-8) was issued on December 17, 2003, establishing policies to enhance U.S. preparedness to prevent and respond to terrorist attacks, major disasters, and other crisis situations. HSPD-8 sets forth an all-hazards preparedness goal, with mechanisms for enhanced delivery of federal preparedness assistance to state and local governments. Procedures to improve preparedness capabilities of federal, state, and local entities are also included. HSPD-8 and HSPD-5 complement each other.[52] The final National Preparedness Guidelines (NPG)—released in September 2007—describe what all-hazards preparedness actually entails. The following four components of the NPG are noteworthy:

1. *National Preparedness Vision:* a concise description of the goal of U.S. preparedness.
2. *National Planning Scenarios:* a collection of 15 potential terrorist attack and national disaster scenarios intended for use in contingency planning by both the government and the private sector.
3. *Universal Task List (UTL):* a list of 1,600 distinctive tasks that can assist efforts in preventing, protecting against, responding to, and recovering from events exemplified in the National Planning Scenarios.
4. *Target Capabilities List (TCL):* a list of 37 capabilities needed by communities, the private sector, and the government in order to respond to disasters.[53]

HSPD-9

Homeland Security Presidential Directive-9: Defense of the United States Agriculture and Food (HSPD-9) was issued on January 30, 2004, creating a national policy to ensure the safety of the U.S. agriculture and food systems. Terrorist attacks, major disasters, and other emergencies affecting the U.S. Agriculture and Food Sector could have negative consequences on public health and the economy. Noting the extensiveness, openness, and complexity of the U.S. Agriculture and Food Sector, HSPD-9 notes that the U.S. agriculture and food systems are vulnerable to a number of threats—disease, pests, poisonous agents—that may occur naturally, be accidentally introduced, or be intentionally delivered through acts of terrorism.[54] HSPD-9 has legitimized concerns about food and agriculture security; indeed, the directive is frequently cited by thought leaders to justify the allocation of more time and money toward efforts to ensure the safety and security of agricultural and food products.

FOOD SAFETY VERSUS FOOD DEFENSE

To a casual reader, food safety and food defense may appear to be quite similar; however, they are distinctively different. Whereas food safety concerns the unintentional contamination of food, food defense is concerned with situations in which agents are chosen and used to contaminate food products.[55] Biological agents (e.g., microorganisms) that can potentially be used to intentionally contaminate food are diverse and each features its own set of concerns. These agents present different levels of stability, infective dosages, modes of transmission, symptoms, and degrees of morbidity and mortality. Chemical agents (e.g., pesticides, organic compounds, etc.) can seriously injure or even kill people, kill animals, and destroy crops. Their potential use in food products is especially concerning because some chemicals are odorless and tasteless—making detection even more problematic.[56] In the United States, the CDC and APHIS have identified agents that pose severe threat to public, animal or plant health, or to animal or plant products.[57] If successfully introduced into a food system, these agents could cause especially alarming damage. Agents or hazards identified in food safety systems (e.g., HACCP) are those that are reasonably likely and, at some level, expected to occur; the strategies to control them are well researched. In contrast, intentional attacks on the food supply are not commonly associated with certain foods and are thus not routinely tested for.[58] This situation is further complicated by the fact that, inherently, methods designed to determine contamination in food are themselves complicated; they must accurately identify the agent in question, identify the presence or absence of a certain level of the agent, be rapid, be affordable, and require minimal effort.[59]

The food supply is regarded as a potential target for intentional contamination for several reasons. At least four factors contribute to this susceptibility in higher risk foods; these include the following:

1. *Large batch size.* Large batch sizes typically result in a large number of servings. Large servings are needed to achieve high morbidity or mortality.
2. *Short shelf life and/or rapid turnaround at retail and rapid consumption.* Short shelf life and/or rapid turnaround at retail and rapid consumption minimize the amount of time public health officials have to determine the problem and adequately respond.
3. *Uniform mixing.* Uniform mixing after the contaminant is added allows all servings in the batch to be contaminated.
4. *Ease of access.* To be contaminated, a product must be accessible. The more accessible, the more likely it could be a target of intentional contamination.[60]

Aggressors (i.e., those who would likely intentionally contaminate the food supply) are commonly grouped into five different categories, principally according to their motives. Regardless of their motivation, aggressors need to be able to do the following: access products for a sufficient time, introduce an effective contaminant, and then contaminate the food product without being discovered. The categories of aggressors include the following:

1. *Disgruntled insiders.* These individuals act on personal feelings and interests. Their actions may be impulsive and have little or no planning. This group of aggressors is difficult to protect against, as they may have easy access to products.
2. *Criminals.* The level of sophistication possessed by criminals varies. Sophisticated criminals are often interested in high-value targets; unsophisticated criminals can lack expertise and resources. Regardless of their level of sophistication, criminals are often interested in targeting foods that are not likely to be detected.
3. *Protestors.* Protestors often act out to express frustration, discontent, or anger. They may seek publicity for their cause and do not intend to injure people. Nevertheless, their actions can be destructive. They are usually unsophisticated; but some protestors have adapted methods comparable to terrorists and can be dangerous.
4. *Subversives.* Subversives usually work in small groups and are well prepared. They aim to cause death and destruction and harm personnel, facility equipment, and business.
5. *Terrorists.* Terrorists can be politically or ideologically motivated. They often utilize extensive planning and employ highly intelligent individuals. Their goals include causing death and destruction, theft, and notoriety.[61]

CARVER PLUS SHOCK: A VULNERABILITY ASSESSMENT TOOL

There are various tactics used by aggressors to contaminate foods; these include insider compromise, exterior attack, forced entry, and covert entry. There are many ways those in the Food and Agriculture Sector can minimize the risk of intentional contamination.[62] This section discusses CARVER plus Shock—a vulnerability assessment tool commonly used in the industry.

While HACCP is used to control food safety hazards, CARVER plus Shock is used to prepare for a deliberate attack on the agriculture and food supply. CARVER plus Shock offers a way to evaluate the consequences, vulnerability, and threat faced by the Food and Agriculture Sector.[63] In utilizing the CARVER plus Shock methodology, those in the food and agriculture industries can conduct risk assessments to determine the most vulnerable points. In turn, appropriate intervention or countermeasure efforts can be developed. CARVER is an acronym for the following elements: Criticality, Accessibility, Recuperability, Vulnerability, Effect, and Recognizability. There are five steps to conducting a CARVER plus Shock analysis; each is summarized below.

Step 1: Establish Parameters

Prior to scoring each of the seven elements, it is imperative to establish the parameters of what the decision-makers are aiming to protect and what they are aiming to protect it from. These parameters include the precise food supply, agricultural chain, or facility that is going to be evaluated. Examples include a broad food supply chain from farm-to-fork such as that for milk, or a specific establishment such as facility that produces snack cakes. Next, an endpoint of concern is identified. Examples include food-borne illness or death in humans, plant or animal death, and economic impacts.

In addition, the type of attacker and attack must be acknowledged. Attackers could include disgruntled employees, terrorist organizations, or others wishing to harm a food supply, agricultural chain, or facility. In their vulnerability assessments, the FSIS and the FDA sometimes assume that terrorist organizations seek to cause a large number of deaths by contaminating food products. It may be helpful (conservative) to assume that an attacker has access to the facility (e.g., a trusted employee), as this individual is aware of all potential vulnerabilities. Another important parameter to establish concerns the agent that may be used. An attacker could use biological, chemical, or radiological agents. The properties (e.g., half-life, heat stability, lethal dose, etc.) of the specific agent can determine the impact of an attack on the food supply. Additionally, it can be helpful (conservative) if one selects an agent that can survive processing and remain toxic in the finished product, as this helps to identify all potential vulnerabilities for assigning ordered risks and planning.[64]

Step 2: Assemble Experts

In utilizing a CARVER plus Shock approach, a multidisciplinary team of subject matter experts should conduct the analysis. This may include production experts, food scientists, food toxicologists, epidemiologists, microbiologists, medical doctors, veterinarians, radiologists, risk assessors, intelligence or security professionals, and personnel or management directors. The team is then responsible for using the CARVER plus Shock method to assign a value for all elements of the food system's infrastructure, based on the parameters established in the previous step.[65]

Step 3: Detail the Food Supply Chain

The third step in conducting a CARVER plus Shock analysis involves detailing the food supply chain. This includes describing the system or facility that is being analyzed. A flow chart of the system and its subsystem, complexes, components, and nodes should be created. The following elements appear in hot dog production: live-animal production, slaughter/processing, and distribution (subsystem); slaughterhouse and processing facilities (complexes); raw materials receiving, processing, storage, and shipping areas (components); and individual pieces of equipment (nodes).[66]

Step 4: Assign Scores

Once the infrastructure is divided into components and nodes, they can be scored for each of the CARVER plus Shock elements and totaled to a score for the particular component or node. Those that have the highest overall score are those that are the most vulnerable. The logic behind the team's scoring should be documented. The following summary of elements, available from the USDA and FDA, are illustrative of how a multidisciplinary team might assign scores.[67]

With respect to the element of Criticality, a target is deemed critical when introduction of a threat agent into food at that location would have significant health or economic impact. Scores for Criticality are scored from 1 to 10. A team would score 1 or 2 if they perceived no loss of life or an economic loss of less than $100 million (or, if examining a particular company, an economic loss of less than 10 percent of the company's total value). A score of 3 or 4 would be appropriate for situations where loss of life is less than 100 or economic losses amount to between $100 million and $1 billion (or 10 to 30 percent of the total economic value of a single firm). Scores of 5 or 6 would be selected for when the loss of life is between 100 and 1,000 or the economic loss is estimated between $1 billion and $10 billion (or 31 to 60 percent of an individual company's value). A team would score Criticality as 7 or 8 if the loss of life is between 1,000 and 10,000 or if the economic costs were $10 billion and $100 billion (or 61 to 90 percent of an individual company's value). A score of 9 or 10 would be appropriate when the loss of over 10,000 lives is expected, or economic losses are forecasted to be more than $100 billion (or 90 percent of an individual company's value).

For the element of Accessibility, a target is understood to be accessible when an attacker can actually access the target to carry out the attack, and leave the target undetected. In this sense, Accessibility explains the openness of the target to the threat. Scores might be 1 to 2 (not accessible) if physical barriers, alarms, human observation, or defined means of intervention are in place, or if an attacker could access target for less than 5 minutes with all equipment carried in his or her pocket. A "Hardly Accessible" (score of 3 or 4) target would be one to which access is generally restricted to operators or other authorized personnel. Other scores might be "Partially Accessible" (5 or 6) or "Accessible" (7 or 8). An "Easily Accessible" target (score of 9 to 10) would be one with limited physical or human barriers or observation; possible attackers would have relatively unlimited access to the target, and attacks could be carried our using large volumes of contaminant without concern of being detected.

The element of Recuperability relates to the time required for the specific system to recover to a point of productivity; anticipated decreases in demand are to be taken into consideration. For example, specific systems' recovery times might, for example, be less than 30 days (score of 1 or 2), one to three months (score of 3 or 4), three months to a year (score of 5 to 8), or over one year (score of 9 or 10).

Vulnerability is the element that measures the ease with which threat agents can be introduced in quantities sufficient to achieve an attacker's purpose, once the target has been reached. This element is determined by the characteristics of the target (e.g., ease of introducing agents) as well as the characteristics of the environment (e.g., the ability to work unobserved). Vulnerability scores are to be chosen in light of what interventions are in place to thwart an attack. Scores might range from as low as 1 or 2 (when there is a less than 10 percent likelihood that sufficient agents could be introduced to achieve the attacker's aim) to as high as 9 or 10 (when the target's characteristics allow for the easy introduction of sufficient agents to achieve the attacker's aim).

The Effect element indicates the percentage of system productivity damaged by an attack at a single facility; it is inversely proportional to the total number of facilities producing the same product. Scores of 9 or 10 are appropriate when greater than 50 percent of the system's production is impacted. Lower scores (i.e., 1 to 4) would be selected when less than 10 percent of the system's production is compromised.

The element of Recognizability indicates the degree to which the target can be identified by an attacker, without confusion with other targets or components. Clearly recognizable targets would score high (i.e., 9 or 10), while others might be easily recognizable provided the attacker has received some training (e.g., score of 7 or 8). If the target is recognizable only by experts, and the target cannot otherwise be recognized, a score of 1 or 2 would be appropriate.

Shock is the final attribute in the methodology. Shock embodies the combined health, psychological, and collateral national economic impacts of a successful attack on a particular target. Evaluated on a national level, the Shock scores (e.g., 1 to 10) vary according to the extent of psychological impact (which would be exacerbated if there were a large number of deaths, or if the target was of historical, cultural, religious, or symbolic significance, or if victims of sensitive subpopulations such as children or the elderly were targeted). Mass casualties are not necessarily required to bring about widespread economic loss or psychological impact, and collateral economic damage (e.g., decreased national economic activity, increased unemployment in related industries, etc.) must also be considered included.

Step 5: Apply What Has Been Learned

Once the critical nodes are identified, countermeasures that lessen the attractiveness of the node should be instituted. Countermeasures are dependent upon the node but may include increased physical security, personnel security, and operational security.

One way to develop countermeasures is embodied in the FDA's ALERT initiative. ALERT is an acronym for: Assure, Look, Employees, Reports, and Threats.

This program can help illuminate potential hazards as well as countermeasures that can be applied throughout the farm-to-table continuum. Online training focusing on the ALERT principles is available (see the appendix of this book for details). The components of ALERT may be summarized in the following way:

1. *Assure.* Businesses must use supplies and ingredients from trusted vendors. Methods by which to ensure this include the following: establishing relationships with suppliers; requiring suppliers to institute measures to prevent intentional contamination; accepting only locked and sealed incoming shipments; and superintending the arrival of incoming materials such as ingredients, processing aids, packaging, and labels.
2. *Look.* Businesses must look at the measures used to ensure the security of ingredients and products in each step along the farm-to-table continuum. Methods to accomplish this include establishing procedures for product handling and processing; instituting methods that allow for the accurate tracking of materials, keeping product labels in a restricted area and discarding outdated or inaccurate product labels, tracking finished products, and requiring warehousing businesses to institute measures to prevent intentional contamination.
3. *Employees.* Individuals working for or visiting farms or facilities along the farm-to-table continuum should be there for legitimate reasons—and not there to inflict harm. Firms and farms can mandate background checks on all employees, supervise staff and visitor access, adopt a staff-identification system, restrict staff members' access to only those areas required for their jobs, and allow customers only limited access.
4. *Reports.* With a view to being able to report the safety of products under the company's control, the following activities could be adopted: sporadic checks on the effectiveness of security programs (e.g., by in-house or third-party organizations); periodic, unannounced food defense inspections; establishment and maintenance of record-keeping systems; and the intentional utilization of knowledge and lessons from past intentional contamination events (to prevent similar events from happening in the future).
5. *Threats.* All actors along the farm-to-table continuum must know what to do and who to notify if there is a threat, issue, or suspicious behavior. All stakeholders should be encouraged, in such situations, to hold the affected product and contact local law-enforcement personnel as well as the respective regulatory agency (e.g., the FDA or FSIS).[68]

Small Business Considerations and Available Software

Small businesses may not be able or willing to spend the money to carry out a CARVER plus Shock evaluation. With this understanding, the FDA pioneered the development of user-friendly CARVER plus Shock software. As the appendix details, this software is available for download and allows those in food and agriculture security to conduct their own, confidential evaluations. The software tool is also intended for use by state and local agencies, industrial providers, and other groups interested in food defense. The agents considered in the software-based evaluation include those that will survive most processes and therefore provide a worst-case (conservative) scenario. The software operates by modeling the thought processes common in an on-site CARVER plus Shock session; the software helps the user create a process flow diagram for the system being assessed. For each process flow diagram node, the software user answers questions for each of the seven CARVER plus Shock attributes. Based on these answers, the software calculates a score for each of the CARVER plus Shock attributes and totals them to produce an overall score for each node. Total scores range from 1 to 10 for each CARVER plus Shock attribute and, therefore, 7 to 70 for each node. The attribute scores and total for each node, the total scores for all nodes, and the attribute scores for all nodes can be seen individually.[69]

CONCLUSION

With an estimated 2.1 million farms, 30,000 processing sites, 19,000 packers, 224,000 retail food stores, and 565,000 retail food outlets in the United States alone, and scores of thousands of additional processing sites and packers abroad,[70] ensuring food and agriculture security is, indeed, a formidable challenge. Food and agriculture security scholars ought to view food and agricultural products along the farm-to-table continuum, and provide leadership to help ensure that they are free from both unintentional and intentional contaminants. Again, this is a daunting task. Intentional and unintentional contamination of food and agricultural products can have significant economic, public health, and psychological implications.[71] Regulatory guidance from departments and agencies within the U.S. government provide the Food and Agriculture Sector with information on food-safety and food-defense issues. However, it remains the responsibility of all stakeholders along the farm-to-table continuum to ensure that safe, wholesome products reach consumers. Food-safety programs (e.g., HACCP) are intended to prevent unintentional or inherent contamination of the food supply, while food-defense programs and tools (e.g., CARVER plus Shock) are available to help anticipate large-scale, intentional attacks. If food-safety or food-defense issues arise, those in the industry must be able to efficiently and effectively respond, thereby limiting the associated impacts.

NOTES

1. Geoffrey S. Becker, "U.S. Food and Agricultural Imports: Safeguards and Selected Issues," Congressional Research Service, December 16, 2009. Nearly 15

percent of the overall volume U.S. food was imported in 2005, which increased from 11 percent to 12 percent in 1995.

2. Andy Jerardo, "What Share of U.S. Consumed Food Is Imported?" *Amber Waves*, February 2008.

3. Department of Homeland Security: Office of Inspector General, "The Department of Homeland Security's Role in Food Defense and Critical Infrastructure Protection," Washington, D.C., February 2007, p. 123.

4. MedLine Plus, "Food Safety," U.S. National Library of Medicine and the National Institutes of Health, http://www.nlm.nih.gov/medlineplus/ency/article/002434.htm.

5. Food and Drug Administration, "Food Defense Acronyms, Abbreviations and Definitions," http://www.fda.gov/Food/FoodDefense/Training/ucm111382.htm. 1.

6. Food and Drug Administration, "Food Protection Plan," U.S. Department of Health and Human Services, http://www.fda.gov/Food/FoodSafety/FoodSafetyPrograms/FoodProtectionPlan2007/ucm132565.htm.

7. Economic Research Service, "Food Security in the United States: Measuring Household Food Security," United States Department of Agriculture, http://www.ers.usda.gov/Briefing/FoodSecurity/measurement.htm#what; J .R. Blanchfield, D. Lund, and W. Spiess, "Report on Food Security Forum," International Union of Food Science and Technology, Institute of Food Technologists, http://www.worldfoodscience.org/cms/?pid=1004507.

8. Barbara A. Rasco and Gleyn E. Bledsoe, *Bioterrorism and Food Safety* (Boca Raton, FL: CRC Press, 2005).

9. International Food Information Council, "2007–2009 Ific Foundation Media Guide on Food Safety and Nutrition. Backgrounder: Food Safety & Defense," http://www.ific.org/food/safety/upload/foodsafetybackgrounder.pdf.

10. Geoffrey S. Becker and Donna V. Porter, "The Federal Food Safety System: A Primer," Congressional Research Service, February 20, 2007.

11. Robert A. Robinson, "Overseeing the U.S. Food Supply: Steps Should Be Taken to Reduce Overlapping Inspections and Related Activities," Government Accountability Office, May 17, 2005.

12. Centers for Disease Control and Prevention, "Foodborne Illness," Department of Health and Human Services, http://www.cdc.gov/ncidod/dbmd/diseaseinfo/foodborneinfections_g.htm.

13. Bibek Ray, *Fundamental Food Microbiology* (Boca Raton, FL: CRC Press, Inc., 1996).

14. M. R. Adams and M. O. Moss, *Food Microbiology* (Cambridge, UK: The Royal Society of Chemistry, 1995); Ray, *Fundamental Food Microbiology*.

15. F. W. Brenner et al., "*Salmonella* Nomenclature," *Journal of Clinical Microbiology* 38, no. 7 (2000).

16. Adams and Moss, *Food Microbiology*; Ray, *Fundamental Food Microbiology*.

17. Paul S. Mead and Patricia M. Griffin, "Escherichia Coli O157: H7," *The Lancet* 352, no. 9135 (1998).

18. Ray, *Fundamental Food Microbiology*.

19. Mead and Griffin, "Escherichia Coli O157: H7."

20. Adams and Moss, *Food Microbiology*.

21. Ibid.

22. Centers for Disease Control and Prevention, "Norovirus: Q&A," http://www.cdc.gov/ncidod/dvrd/revb/gastro/norovirus-qa.htm.

23. Bonnie L. Gerald, "Foodborne Illness-Causing Pathogens," in *Food and Nutrition at Risk in America: Food Insecurity, Biotechnology, Food Safety, and Bioterrorism,* ed. Sari Edelstein et al. (Sudbury, MA: Jones and Bartlett Publishers, 2009).

24. Ray, *Fundamental Food Microbiology.*

25. Centers for Disease Control and Prevention, "Shigellosis," Division of Foodborne, Bacterial and Mycotic Diseases, http://www.cdc.gov/nczved/dfbmd/disease_listing/shigellosis_gi.html.

26. Ray, *Fundamental Food Microbiology.*

27. Anthony Fiore, "Hepatitis a Transmitted by Food," *Clinical Infectious Diseases* 38, no. 5 (2004).

28. Adams and Moss, *Food Microbiology*; Center for Food Safety and Applied Nutrition, "Bad Bug Book-Giardia Lamblia," http://www.fda.gov/Food/FoodSafety/FoodborneIllness/FoodborneIllnessFoodbornePathogensNaturalToxins/BadBugBook/ucm070716.htm.

29. N. E. Ramirez and Ramirez, "A Review of the Biology and Epidemiology of Cryptosporidiosis in Humans and Animals," *Microbes and Infection* 6, no. 8 (2004).

30. Center for Food Safety and Applied Nutrition, "Bad Bug Book-Giardia Lamblia."

31. Ibid.

32. Dane T. Bernard, "Hazard Analysis and Critical Control Point System Use in Controlling Microbiological Hazards," in *Food Microbiology: Fundamentals and Frontiers,* ed. Michael P. Doyle, Larry R. Beuchat, and Thomas J. Montville (Washington, D.C.: ASM Press, 1997).

33. American Public Health Association, "Proceedings of the 1971 National Conference on Food Protection," Washington, D.C.,1971; Pillsbury Company, "Food Safety through the Hazard Analysis and Critical Control Point System" (Minneapolis, MN: Pillsbury Company, Research & Development Department, 1973).

34. National Advisory Committee on Microbiological Criteria for Foods, "Hazard Analysis and Critical Control Point Principles and Application Guidelines," U.S. Food and Drug Administration, http://www.fda.gov/Food/FoodSafety/HazardAnalysisCriticalControlPointsHACCP/HACCPPrinciplesApplicationGuidelines/default.htm.

35. For legislation regarding each, see: "Part 417-Hazard Analysis and Critical Control Point (Haccp) Systems," in *9CFR17* (U.S. Government Printing Office, 2008); "Part 120-Hazard Analysis and Critical Control Point (Haccp) Systems," in *2CFR120* (U.S. Government Printing Office, 2009); "Part 123-Fish and Fishery Products," in *21CFR123* (U.S. Government Printing Office, 2009).

36. Shaun P. Kennedy and Frank F. Busta, "Biosecurity: Food Protection and Defense," in *Food Microbiology: Fundamentals and Frontiers,* ed. M. P. Doyle and L. R. Beuchat (Washington, D.C.: ASM Press, 2007).

37. Ibid.

38. Department of Food Safety, Zoonoses and Foodborne Diseases, *Terrorist Threats to Food—Guidelines for Establishing and Strengthening Prevention and Response Systems,* Geneva, Switzerland, World Health Organization Cluster on Health Security and Environment, May 2008.

39. Kennedy and Busta, "Biosecurity: Food Protection and Defense"; United States General Accounting Office, "Food Safety: Agencies Should Further Test Plans for Responding to Deliberate Contamination," Washington, D.C., October 1999.

40. John T. Hoffman and Shaun Kennedy, "International Cooperation to Defend the Food Supply Chain: Nations Are Talking; Next Step—Action," *Vanderbilt Journal of Transnational Law* 40 (2007).

41. Annette D. Beresford, "Homeland Security as an American Ideology: Implications for U.S. Policy and Action," *Journal of Homeland Security and Emergency Management* 1, no. 3 (2004).

42. Sharon R. Thompson et al., *Mgt 332: Agriculture and Food Vulnerability Assessment Training Course,* U.S. Department of Homeland Security, The University of Tennessee College of Veterinary Medicine, Western Institute for Food Safety and Security, New Mexico State University, Kirkwook Community College, Virginia-Maryland Regional College of Veterinary Medicine, The State of Tennessee, and Tennessee Office of Homeland Security, 2009.

43. Department of Homeland Security, "Homeland Security Presidential Directive 5: Management of Domestic Incidents," http://www.dhs.gov/xabout/laws/gc_1214592333605.shtm.

44. Ibid. An all-hazards approach covers all conditions that can cause injury, illness, or death; harm or destruction of equipment, infrastructure, or property; or cause functional damage to social, economic, or environmental aspects of life.

45. Federal Emergency Management Agency, "National Response Framework," Washington, D.C.: Department of Homeland Security, January 2008.

46. Department of Homeland Security, "Homeland Security Presidential Directive 7: Critical Infrastructure Identification, Prioritization, and Protection," http://www.dhs.gov/xabout/laws/gc_1214597989952.shtm.

47. Department of Homeland Security, "National Infrastructure Protection Plan," www.dhs.gov/xlibrary/assets/NIPP_Plan.pdf . 109.

48. Ibid., 110.

49. Adapted from Department of Homeland Security, "Homeland Security Presidential Directive 7: Critical Infrastructure Identification, Prioritization, and Protection."

50. Department of Homeland Security, "National Infrastructure Protection Plan."

51. Department of Homeland Security, Department of Agriculture, and Food and Drug Administration, "Agriculture and Food: Critical Infrastructure and Key Resources Sector-Specific Plan as Input to the National Infrastructure Protection Plan," May 2007.

52. Department of Homeland Security, "Homeland Security Presidential Directive 8: National Preparedness," http://www.dhs.gov/xabout/laws/gc_1215444247124.shtm#content.

53. Department of Homeland Security, "National Preparedness Guidelines," Washington, D.C., September 2007.

54. Department of Homeland Security, "Homeland Security Presidential Directive 9: Defense of United States Agriculture and Food," http://www.dhs.gov/xabout/laws/gc_1217749547663.shtm#1. 1.

55. Kennedy and Busta, "Biosecurity: Food Protection and Defense."

56. Rasco and Bledsoe, *Bioterrorism and Food Safety.*

57. Centers for Disease Control and Prevention and Animal and Plant Health Inspection Service, "Hhs and USDA Select Agents and Toxins," http://www.selectagents.gov/resources/List%20of%20Select%20Agents%20and%20Toxins_111708.pdf.

58. Kennedy and Busta, "Biosecurity: Food Protection and Defense."

59. Shaun Kennedy, "Why Can't We Test Our Way to Absolute Food Safety," *Science,* December 12, 2008.

60. Department of Homeland Security, Department of Agriculture, and Food and Drug Administration, "Agriculture and Food: Critical Infrastructure and Key Resources Sector-Specific Plan as Input to the National Infrastructure Protection Plan"; U.S. Food and Drug Administration and United States Department of Agriculture, "An Introduction to Food Security Awareness," http://www.fda.gov/downloads/Training/ForStateLocalTribalRegulators/UCM170564.pdf.

61. U.S. Food and Drug Administration and United States Department of Agriculture, "An Introduction to Food Security Awareness."

62. Ibid.

63. Department of Homeland Security, Department of Agriculture, and Food and Drug Administration, "Agriculture and Food: Critical Infrastructure and Key Resources Sector-Specific Plan as Input to the National Infrastructure Protection Plan," 69.

64. These parameters are adapted from: Thompson et al., *Mgt 332: Agriculture and Food Vulnerability Assessment Training Course*; United States Department of Agriculture and Food and Drug Administration, "An Overview of the Carver Plus Shock Method for Food Sector Vulnerability Assessment," www.fsis.usda.gov/PDF/CARVER.pdf.

65. Thompson et al., *Mgt 332: Agriculture and Food Vulnerability Assessment Training Course.*

66. See Thompson et al., *Mgt 332: Agriculture and Food Vulnerability Assessment Training Course*; and United States Department of Agriculture and Food and Drug Administration, "An Overview of the Carver Plus Shock Method for Food Sector Vulnerability Assessment."

67. See United States Department of Agriculture and Food and Drug Administration, "An Overview of the Carver Plus Shock Method for Food Sector Vulnerability Assessment."

68. Food and Drug Administration, "Alert: The Basics," U.S. Department of Health and Human Services, http://www.fda.gov/Food/FoodDefense/Training/ALERT/default.htm.

69. Food and Drug Administration, "Carver Software," Department of Health and Human Services, http://www.fda.gov/Food/FoodDefense/CARVER/default.htm.

70. Shaun Kennedy and Frank Busta, "Defending the Safety of the Food System through Research and Education," in *IFT Global Food Safety & Quality Conference,* Chicago, IL, August 1, 2007.

71. Food and Drug Administration, "Alert: The Basics."

BIBLIOGRAPHY

Adams, M. R., and M. O. Moss. *Food Microbiology.* Cambridge, UK: The Royal Society of Chemistry, 1995.

American Public Health Association. "Proceedings of the 1971 National Conference on Food Protection." Washington, D.C., 1971.

Becker, Geoffrey S. "U.S. Food and Agricultural Imports: Safeguards and Selected Issues." Congressional Research Service, December 16, 2009.

Becker, Geoffrey S., and Donna V. Porter. "The Federal Food Safety System: A Primer." Congressional Research Service, February 20, 2007.

Beresford, Annette D. "Homeland Security as an American Ideology: Implications for U.S. Policy and Action." *Journal of Homeland Security and Emergency Management* 1, no. 3 (2004): article 301.

Bernard, Dane T. "Hazard Analysis and Critical Control Point System Use in Controlling Microbiological Hazards." In *Food Microbiology: Fundamentals and Frontiers,* ed. Michael P. Doyle, Larry R. Beuchat and Thomas J. Montville. Washington, D.C.: ASM Press, 1997.

Blanchfield, J. R., D. Lund, and W. Spiess. "Report on Food Security Forum." International Union of Food Science and Technology, Institute of Food Technologists, http://www.worldfoodscience.org/cms/?pid=1004507.

Brenner, F. W., R. G. Villar, F. J. Angulo, R. Tauxe, and B. Swaminathan. "*Salmonella* Nomenclature." *Journal of Clinical Microbiology* 38, no. 7 (2000): 2465–67.

Center for Food Safety and Applied Nutrition. "Bad Bug Book-Giardia Lamblia." http://www.fda.gov/Food/FoodSafety/FoodborneIllness/Foodborne IllnessFoodbornePathogensNaturalToxins/BadBugBook/ucm070716.htm.

Centers for Disease Control and Prevention. "Foodborne Illness." Department of Health and Human Services. http://www.cdc.gov/ncidod/dbmd/disease info/foodborneinfections_g.htm.

Centers for Disease Control and Prevention. "Norovirus: Q&A." http://www.cdc. gov/ncidod/dvrd/revb/gastro/norovirus-qa.htm.

Centers for Disease Control and Prevention. "Shigellosis." Division of Foodborne, Bacterial and Mycotic Diseases. http://www.cdc.gov/nczved/dfbmd/ disease_listing/shigellosis_gi.html.

Centers for Disease Control and Prevention, and Animal and Plant Health Inspection Service. "Hhs and USDA Select Agents and Toxins." http:// www.selectagents.gov/resources/List%20of%20Select%20Agents%20 and%20Toxins_111708.pdf.

Department of Food Safety, Zoonoses and Foodborne Diesases. *Terrorist Threats to Food—Guidelines for Establishing and Strengthening Prevention and Response Systems*. Geneva, Switzerland: World Health Organization Cluster on Health Security and Environment, May 2008.

Department of Homeland Security. "Homeland Security Presidential Directive 5: Management of Domestic Incidents." http://www.dhs.gov/xabout/laws/ gc_1214592333605.shtm.

Department of Homeland Security. "Homeland Security Presidential Directive 7: Critical Infrastructure Identification, Prioritization, and Protection." http:// www.dhs.gov/xabout/laws/gc_1214597989952.shtm.

Department of Homeland Security. "Homeland Security Presidential Directive 8: National Preparedness." http://www.dhs.gov/xabout/laws/gc_12154 44247124.shtm#content.

Department of Homeland Security. "Homeland Security Presidential Directive 9: Defense of United States Agriculture and Food." http://www.dhs.gov/ xabout/laws/gc_1217449547663.shtm#1.

Department of Homeland Security. "National Infrastructure Protection Plan." www.dhs.gov/xlibrary/assets/NIPP_Plan.pdf

Department of Homeland Security. "National Preparedness Guidelines." Washington, D.C., September 2007.

Department of Homeland Security, Department of Agriculture, and Food and Drug Administration. "Agriculture and Food: Critical Infrastructure and Key Resources Sector-Specific Plan as Input to the National Infrastructure Protection Plan." May 2007.

Department of Homeland Security: Office of Inspector General. "The Department of Homeland Security's Role in Food Defense and Critical Infrastructure Protection." Washington, D.C., February 2007.

Economic Research Service. "Food Security in the United States: Measuring Household Food Security." United States Department of Agriculture. http://www.ers.usda.gov/Briefing/FoodSecurity/measurement.htm#what.

Federal Emergency Management Agency. "National Response Framework." Washington, D.C.: Department of Homeland Security, January 2008.

Fiore, Anthony. "Hepatitis a Transmitted by Food." *Clinical Infectious Diseases* 38, no. 5 (2004): 705–15.

Food and Drug Administration. "Alert: The Basics." U.S. Department of Health and Human Services. http://www.fda.gov/Food/FoodDefense/Training/ALERT/default.htm.

Food and Drug Administration. "Carver Software." Department of Health and Human Services. http://www.fda.gov/Food/FoodDefense/CARVER/default.htm.

Food and Drug Administration. "Food Defense Acronyms, Abbreviations and Definitions." http://www.fda.gov/Food/FoodDefense/Training/ucm111382.htm.

Food and Drug Administration. "Food Protection Plan." U.S. Department of Health and Human Services. http://www.fda.gov/Food/FoodSafety/FoodSafetyPrograms/FoodProtectionPlan2007/ucm132565.htm.

Gerald, Bonnie L. "Foodborne Illness-Causing Pathogens." In *Food and Nutrition at Risk in America: Food Insecurity, Biotechnology, Food Safety, and Bioterrorism*, ed. Sari Edelstein, Bonnie Gerald, Tamara Crutchley Bushell and Craig Gundersen, pp. 15–40. Sudbury, MA: Jones and Bartlett Publishers, 2009.

Hoffman, John T., and Shaun Kennedy. "International Cooperation to Defend the Food Supply Chain: Nations Are Talking; Next Step—Action." *Vanderbilt Journal of Transnational Law* 40 (2007): 1169–78.

International Food Information Council. "2007–2009 Ific Foundation Media Guide on Food Safety and Nutrition. Backgrounder: Food Safety & Defense." http://www.ific.org/food/safety/upload/foodsafetybackgrounder.pdf.

Jerardo, Andy. "What Share of U.S. Consumed Food Is Imported?" *Amber Waves*, February 2008, 36–37.

Kennedy, Shaun. "Why Can't We Test Our Way to Absolute Food Safety." *Science*, December 12, 2008, 1641–43.

Kennedy, Shaun, and Frank Busta. "Defending the Safety of the Food System through Research and Education." In *IFT Global Food Safety & Quality Conference*. Chicago, IL, August 1, 2007.

Kennedy, Shaun P., and Frank F. Busta. "Biosecurity: Food Protection and Defense." In *Food Microbiology: Fundamentals and Frontiers*, ed. M. P. Doyle and L. R. Beuchat, pp. 87–102. Washington, D.C.: ASM Press, 2007.

Mead, Paul S., and Patricia M. Griffin. "Escherichia Coli O157: H7." *The Lancet* 352, no. 9135 (1998): 1207–12.
MedLine Plus. "Food Safety." U.S. National Library of Medicine and the National Institutes of Health. http://www.nlm.nih.gov/medlineplus/ency/article/002434.htm.
National Advisory Committee on Microbiological Criteria for Foods. "Hazard Analysis and Critical Control Point Principles and Application Guidelines." U.S. Food and Drug Administration. http://www.fda.gov/Food/FoodSafety/HazardAnalysisCriticalControlPointsHACCP/HACCPPrinciplesApplicationGuidelines/default.htm.
"Part 120—Hazard Analysis and Critical Control Point (Haccp) Systems." In *2CFR120*, 293–303: U.S. Government Printing Office, 2009.
"Part 123—Fish and Fishery Products." In *21CFR123*, 303–11: U.S. Government Printing Office, 2009.
"Part 417—Hazard Analysis and Critical Control Point (Haccp) Systems." In *9CFR17*, 634–38: U.S. Government Printing Office, 2008.
Pillsbury Company. "Food Safety through the Hazard Analysis and Critical Control Point System." Minneapolis, MN: Pillsbury Company, Research & Development Department, 1973.
Ramirez, N. E., and Ramirez. "A Review of the Biology and Epidemiology of Cryptosporidiosis in Humans and Animals." *Microbes and Infection* 6, no. 8 (2004): 773.
Rasco, Barbara A., and Gleyn E. Bledsoe. *Bioterrorism and Food Safety*. Boca Raton, FL: CRC Press, 2005.
Ray, Bibek. *Fundamental Food Microbiology*. Boca Raton, FL: CRC Press, Inc., 1996.
Robinson, Robert A. "Overseeing the U.S. Food Supply: Steps Should Be Taken to Reduce Overlapping Inspections and Related Activities." Government Accountability Office May 17, 2005.
Thompson, Sharon R., Fred M. Hopkins, Matthew G. Welborn, David K. Smelser, F. Ann Draughon, John Jared, Bob Linnabary, F. William Pierson, Francois C. Elvinger, Jeff Witte, Billy Dictson, Jerry Gillespie, Ron Snyder, Mike Fagel, J. Howard Murphy, and Larry Cunningham. *Mgt 332: Agriculture and Food Vulnerability Assessment Training Course*: U.S. Department of Homeland Security, The University of Tennessee College of Veterinary Medicine, Western Institute for Food Safety and Security, New Mexico State University, Kirkwook Community College, Virginia-Maryland Regional College of Veterinary Medicine, The State of Tennessee, and Tennessee Office of Homeland Security, 2009.
United States Department of Agriculture, and Food and Drug Administration. "An Overview of the Carver Plus Shock Method for Food Sector Vulnerability Assessment." www.fsis.usda.gov/PDF/CARVER.pdf.
United States General Accounting Office. "Food Safety: Agencies Should Further Test Plans for Responding to Deliberate Contamination." Washington, D.C., October 1999.
U.S. Food and Drug Administration, and United States Department of Agriculture. "An Introduction to Food Security Awareness." http://www.fda.gov/downloads/Training/ForStateLocalTribalRegulators/UCM170564.pdf.

CHAPTER 4

Historical and Contemporary Cases Illustrating the Vulnerability of Specific Commodities and Sectors

Kathryn Krusemark and Cobus Block

While not the only country or government to do so, the United States has played a visibly intentional role in food and agriculture security efforts. These efforts include instituting safety standards, inspecting products, enforcing regulations, determining root causes of problems faced by those in the agriculture and food industries, and defending the U.S. food supply.[1] As chapter 3 explained, Homeland Security Presidential Directive-9: Defense of the United States Agriculture and Food (HSPD-9) created a national policy to ensure the safety and security of the U.S. Food and Agriculture Sector. Terrorist attacks, major disasters, and other emergencies affecting U.S. agriculture and food systems could have negative consequences on public health and the economy.[2]

In the U.S. and elsewhere, the food and agricultural industries are diverse and complex. Past outbreaks and incidents caused by unintentional contamination showcase just a few of the challenges in protecting agriculture and the food supply. Many in the food and agriculture industries approach food defense (i.e., intentional or deliberate) issues with an awareness that if food-safety issues can significantly impact public health and the economy, so too can issues caused by intentional or deliberate contamination. Industry personnel are not the only group concerned with these issues; to be sure, the public shares their concerns. Researchers have found that the public would hold both the government and food manufacturers responsible if a food terrorism incident were to occur.[3]

This chapter explores additional historical and contemporary cases that illustrate the vulnerability of specific commodities and sectors including those related to produce, food processing, retail, and milk. The broad spectrum of commodities and sectors helps paint a picture of the common vulnerability of the global agriculture and food system, and while the cases are primarily drawn from the United States, one involves international trade, and another is situated in the context of China's agricultural and food systems. Significantly, the cases paint a picture of history and of reality; if these types of vulnerabilities have appeared in the past, similar challenges are likely to emerge in the future.

PRODUCE

The produce industry once thought that using triple-wash technology with chlorinated water or a permitted sanitizing agent would ensure the microbiological safety of their products. However, outbreaks associated with fresh and fresh-cut fruits and vegetables have proved otherwise. Some attribute the increase in outbreaks to the increase in consumption of fresh produce as advocated by nutritionists and health officials. Additionally, increased consumption has resulted in increased production, increased distribution, and the expansion of processing facilities. Produce can be contaminated at any point along the farm-to-table continuum. Studies have identified the following as potential contamination sources in the pre-harvest stage: farms coupled with animal production, fecal contamination from wildlife, composted manure, soil, runoff, irrigation water, and the hands of packing workers. Produce can also be contaminated during packing; if not adequately sanitized and maintained, equipment can harbor dangerous microorganisms. Lastly, produce can be contaminated during processing.

Green salads and lettuces and tomatoes have been implicated in recent outbreaks.[4] This section explores the *Salmonella* serotype Saintpaul outbreak of 2008.

On May 22, 2008, the CDC was notified by the New Mexico Department of Health that four people were infected with the same strain of *Salmonella*—*Salmonella* serotype Saintpaul. Texas and Colorado public health officials followed suit on May 23, 2008, and reported cases of *S*. Saintpaul with matching pulsed-field gel electrophoresis (PFGE) patterns (i.e., matching genetic fingerprints). The New Mexico Department of Health fronted a multistate investigation and communicated a link between *S*. Saintpaul and tomato varieties including red plum, red Roma, and red round tomatoes on May 31, 2008.[5] On June 2, 2008, the CDC announced their investigation of the outbreak of infections caused by *S*. Saintpaul, as 40 individuals in Texas and New Mexico were infected with *S*. Saintpaul with the same PFGE pattern. Reported cases of *S*. Saintpaul from states across the country were also being investigated. Immunocompromised individuals, including infants and the elderly, in New Mexico and Texas were urged to avoid red plum, red Roma, and red round tomatoes.[6] On June 3, 2008, the FDA warned consumers in New Mexico and Texas to avoid certain types of raw red tomatoes (i.e., red plum, red Roma, and round red tomatoes) and products containing them. The FDA announced that cherry tomatoes, grape tomatoes, tomatoes sold with the vine still attached, and home-grown tomatoes were still safe.[7] Using traceback technology and distribution information, the FDA provided consumers a list of states, territories, and countries where tomatoes were grown and harvested that were not associated with the present outbreak. On June 7, 2008, the FDA issued a warning to consumers to not eat certain raw red plum, red Roma, and red round tomatoes, and products containing them (i.e., tomatoes that were harvested in an area not on the FDA's list).[8]

On June 30, 2008, the CDC announced plans to broaden their outbreak investigation to include foods that are commonly consumed with tomatoes, as several restaurant-associated clusters of illnesses were identified.[9] A week later, on July 7, 2008, the CDC alerted consumers that fresh cilantro and fresh hot chili peppers (e.g., jalapeños) could also be the source of the recent outbreak.[10] Two days later, the CDC suggested that immunocompromised consumers avoid raw jalapeño and raw serrano peppers and all consumers follow the recommendations regarding tomato consumption designated by the FDA.[11] The Minnesota Department of Health, through a case-control study, was also able to significantly associate illness with eating raw, jalapeño peppers.[12]

On July 17, 2008, the FDA lifted its consumer warning about eating certain types of raw red tomatoes. In its statement, the FDA acknowledged raw jalapeño and raw serrano peppers as a potential source of the outbreak. The FDA also encouraged immunocompromised individuals to follow the CDC's recommendation in avoiding these products.[13] Product testing by the FDA revealed the outbreak strain in jalapeño peppers distributed by a firm in McAllen, Texas. On July 21, 2008, the company recalled jalapeño peppers distributed after June 30, 2008, to states including Texas and Georgia.[14] FDA officials determined that the firm was not the original source of contamination.[15] This was later reiterated when the FDA released a statement on July 30, 2008, detailing laboratory results confirming the presence of the outbreak strain of $S.$ Saintpaul in serrano pepper and irrigation water samples collected by investigators on a farm in Tamaulipas, Mexico. Consumers were urged to avoid raw serrano and jalapeño peppers in Mexico and foods containing them.[16]

The outbreak of $S.$ Saintpaul ended in August 2008 and ultimately resulted in 1,442 cases with 286 hospitalizations. Infections possibly contributed to two deaths. The illnesses occurred between April 16 and August 11, and most individuals became ill in May or June. On July 21, 2008, the FDA reported isolation of the outbreak strain from a jalapeño pepper sample obtained, and it was deduced that this pepper was probably grown on a farm in Tamaulipas, Mexico (farm A). This farm also grew serrano peppers and Roma tomatoes. The FDA did not isolate the outbreak strain from environmental samples from farm A, but did isolate the outbreak strain from a sample of serrano peppers and a sample of irrigation water from another farm (farm B) in Tamaulipas. Farm B also grew jalapeño peppers, but not tomatoes. Farms A and B provided produce to a common packing facility in Mexico that exports to the United States.[17]

The tomato industry suffered significant economic losses—estimated at $250 million—as a result of the outbreak. Many in the tomato industry criticized the government because tomatoes were initially implicated as the source of the outbreak, and the implication was based on insubstantial evidence.[18] For years, thought leaders have argued about the North American food-safety system and modifications that could improve it. The complexity and difficulty surround S. Saintpaul case drew additional attention to this issue.

The S. Saintpaul outbreak revealed the complexity of a supply chain that crossed borders and involved an interconnected group of farms and packing and distribution companies. This complexity, along with the inherent risks posed, in this case, by a microorganism, illustrate the vulnerability of the produce sector to contamination—contamination which can cause both loss of life and financial hardship. Some have proposed factors that contributed to the complexity of and difficulty in this particular outbreak; these included delayed responses to resource and expertise differences at state and local levels of government, poor communication between stakeholders and various agencies, and poor traceability.[19] As produce safety continues to be a contentious issue, the FDA plans to issue a proposed rule to establish safety standards for the production and packing of fresh produce by the end of 2010. The agency is allowing stakeholders to submit comments before the proposed rule is written—allowing the rule to accurately reflect the challenges and real-world environments common to the produce industry. The goal of such regulation is to reduce the risk of foodborne illness attributed to fresh produce and prevent outbreaks—much like the S. Saintpaul outbreak—from happening.[20]

FOOD PROCESSING

The average consumer often fails to recognize the complexity of food processing and what goes into many foods. Take for example, a pepperoni pizza. At least seven of the U.S. agencies identified in chapter 3 have, at some point, regulatory oversight over some aspect of the production and processing of such a pizza. These steps include on-farm inputs (e.g., chemicals, seed, and animal feed); production and harvest (of wheat, tomatoes, cattle, and swine); first-level processing (e.g., of flour, tomato sauce, meat, and cheese); second-level processing (e.g., frozen pizza manufacturing); and retail activities (i.e., sale of the pizza to an actual consumer, who then eats it).[21] Such a simplified, rudimentary example (which does not detail all the sundry ingredients actually used in pizza processing) illustrates the multiple dimensions—and potential points of vulnerability—in pizza

Historical and Contemporary Cases

processing. The complexity of processed foods becomes more pronounced if one further explores the details of a pepperoni pizza. A real, albeit still basic, pizza crust would likely contain water, flour, yeast, salt, and sugar. A basic tomato sauce contains tomatoes, spices, and other vegetables (e.g., onions). Cheese is produced using milk, enzymes, salt, and starter cultures. Pepperoni is produced using meat (i.e., beef and pork), spices, water, sugar, preservatives, as well as a starter culture. This example illustrates a common food product which, as readers can see, is complex and multifaceted.

In today's world, food processors strive to meet the ever-changing and complex demands of consumers, while producing products that are themselves complex. Hundreds and thousands of new food products are introduced each year on store shelves, and many fail to meet consumers' expectations. Regardless of the food product, safety and security are of paramount importance in food processing. To illustrate this in the food-processing realm, this chapter explores the 2006–2007 *Salmonella* serotype Tennessee outbreak that occurred in peanut butter.

Throughout 2005 and most of 2006, PulseNet—a CDC-run organization of public health and food regulatory agency laboratories responsible for subtyping bacteria using PFGE—received one to five reports of *S.* Tennessee a month. However, 30 reports were received in October 2006. Noticeably more reports of *S.* Tennessee led the CDC to investigate further. OutbreakNet—a CDC team including local, state, and federal epidemiologists and public health officials that investigate food-borne illnesses—conducted interviews from November to December 2006; however, a common food exposure could not be identified. In January 2007, OutbreakNet officials across the United States interviewed 26 patients using a standard survey instrument and found that 85 percent of patients had eaten peanut butter and 48 percent of patients had eaten turkey in the week prior to the onset of illness.

A multistate investigation—carried out from February 5 to February 13, 2007, with 65 patients and 124 controls—was used to determine the food responsible for the illnesses. A case was defined as infection with *S.* Tennessee matching the outbreak strain in a person age 18 years or older with a history of diarrhea. Individuals from the extended neighborhood of patients served as controls. Investigators associated illnesses with eating peanut butter with the product code 2111.[22] The CDC notified ConAgra Foods—producer of the implicated peanut butter brands—and they stopped production, destroyed remaining product, and on February 14, 2007, recalled all peanut butter with the product code 2111. ConAgra worked with the FDA to ensure the safety of their products and offered full refunds to consumers.[23] Reports of illnesses decreased after the recall was enacted.[24] On February 22, 2007, ConAgra confirmed that peanut butter manufactured in their Sylvester, Georgia, plant had tested positive for *Salmonella*.[25] Additionally, the outbreak strain of *S.* Tennessee was found in open and unopened jars of ConAgra-produced peanut butter brands and in environmental samples from the Sylvester, Georgia, plant.[26] The outbreak resulted in 714 cases in 48 states.[27]

The recall—including the cost of the peanut butter, recovering it, and disposing of it—cost ConAgra between $50 million and $60 million.[28] In a news release on April 5, 2007, ConAgra announced upcoming plans (in August) to renovate their Sylvester, Georgia, plant; the company assured consumers that renovations, including modern machinery, technology, and design, would address all possible causes of the *Salmonella* outbreak. A plant investigation led ConAgra to believe that moisture, which accidentally entered the production line, provided conditions suitable for low levels of *Salmonella,* probably introduced from raw peanuts or peanut dust, to grow. Additionally, ConAgra created a position—a vice president of Global Food Safety—and established a Food Safety Advisory Committee. To increase inventory, ConAgra contracted an approved co-manufacturer who produced a common brand of peanut butter.[29]

ConAgra reopened its Sylvester, Georgia, plant in August 2007 and the top 30 grocery-store chains restocked their products.[30] ConAgra faced class action lawsuits that claimed injury and damages from eating tainted peanut butter.[31] A 2005 report prompted some consumers to question whether the outbreak was preventable. The report indicated that FDA inspectors investigated a suspected outbreak of *Salmonella* in peanut butter in October 2004 produced at ConAgra's Sylvester, Georgia, plant. ConAgra acknowledged that it destroyed certain products in that time period; however, the company did not provide a reason why. ConAgra asked FDA inspectors for a written request for documentation to protect proprietary information; the written request was not provided and ConAgra dismissed the case. The FDA defended its actions and assured consumers that further action would have been taken if inspectors had found serious problems.[32]

This particular case highlights the complexity and environment associated with the food- processing industry. There are an estimated 124,000 food-processing sites worldwide, and ensuring the safety of food products produced at all of these sites is a daunting task.[33] The risks and hazards faced by businesses at these sites continually evolve, and it is important for food processors to strive to prevent contamination and outbreaks to protect public health. Food and agriculture security scholars ought to note the vulnerabilities and challenges that occur in the food-processing sector.

RETAIL

The retail food sector is anything but simple. In the United States alone, more than 3,000 state, local, and tribal agencies are responsible for regulating the retail food and food-service industries. This includes inspecting and overseeing more than one million food establishments (i.e., restaurants and grocery stores; vending machines; cafeterias; and other outlets in health care facilities, schools, and correctional facilities). To assist in these efforts, the FDA provides these outlets a model Food Code, scientifically based guidance, training, program evaluation, and technical assistance.[34] This section explores the *Salmonella typhimurium* outbreak, the result of an intentional contamination event that occurred in a retail establishment in 1984.

Patrons, employees, and owners of Shakey's Pizza in The Dalles, Oregon, unsuspectingly dined from the restaurant's salad bar on Sunday, September 9, 1984. Later that day, Dave Lutgens—an owner of Shakey's Pizza—developed symptoms that included stomach cramping, nausea, diarrhea, and vomiting. Within the next week, Lutgens's wife, 13 of the restaurant's 28 employees, and dozens of customers reported similar illnesses.[35] On September 17, 1984, the Wasco-Sherman Public Health Department began receiving reports of individuals who developed gastroenteritis after eating at one of two different restaurants in The Dalles, Oregon.[36] Within two days, a pathologist at the Mid-Columbia Medical Center analyzed a patient's stool sample and determined that bacteria from the genus *Salmonella* was responsible for the illness. On September 21, the Oregon State Public Health Laboratory identified *S.* Typhimurium as the etiological agent. However, the specific strain of *S.* Typhimurium surprised public health officials, as it was not a common food poisoning agent.[37] Reports of individuals who worked at or ate at other restaurants in The Dalles suffering from gastroenteritis increased. Carla Chamberlain, head of the county public health office, and her staff interviewed restaurant owners, employees, and those struck ill; many of those suffering from gastroenteritis reported eating food from salad bars.[38] All salad bars in The Dalles temporarily closed beginning on September 25, 1984.[39] Additionally, the Oregon Health Division requested assistance from the CDC and its Epidemic Intelligence Service (EIS).[40]

Salmonellosis, an infection resulting from bacteria of the *Salmonella* genus, causes thousands of illnesses each year in the United States.[41] Individuals suffering from salmonellosis often experience diarrhea, fever, and abdominal cramping 12 to 72 after ingesting the bacteria; symptoms often subside within 4 to 7 days.[42] Immunocompromised individuals, including newborns, infants, and elderly individuals, are more inclined to develop salmonellosis than healthy adults.[43] Research suggests that ingesting as few as 1 to 10 cells can cause infection.[44]

Public health officials investigated The Dalles outbreak; the investigation involved interviewing patients and their families, checking water supplies, testing foods sold at restaurants, and using scores of other approaches to determine the source of the outbreak. *Salmonella* was found in coffee creamers at one restaurant and in the blue cheese salad dressing at another. However, *Salmonella* was not found in dry mix used to make the salad dressing.[45] Outbreak-associated cases included those where the appearance of symptoms or collection of *S.* Typhimurium occurred between September 9 and October 10, 1984, and the affected person lived in or visited The Dalles during that period. Restaurant-associated cases included cases in which individuals ate at a restaurant in The Dalles within seven days of the appearance of symptoms or worked at a restaurant in The Dalles. Secondary infections included those that occurred in individuals who did not eat or work at a restaurant in The Dalles seven days before the appearance of symptoms, but were exposed to a case patient between September 9 and October 10, 1984.[46]

Judge William Hulse suspected that a local religious commune caused this outbreak. The commune, led by Bhagwan Shree Rajneesh, lived on a remote ranch in Wasco County. In 1982, a group of his followers, referred to as Rajneeshees, moved into the adjacent town of Antelope where they gained control of the town council. With control of the town council, they developed the city of Rajneeshpuram—a community complete with modern infrastructure. However, they faced zoning issues. Hulse, head of the county commission, was tasked with settling these zoning issues. Nearly a year before the outbreak, Hulse and another county commissioner visited the Rajneesh ranch for a routine inspection. When they returned to their car, they found one of their tires was flat. Several Rajneeshees changed the tire, and the commissioners drank water in paper cups offered to them by other Rajneeshees. Eight hours later, both commissioners were struck ill with symptoms that included stomach cramping, nausea, diarrhea, and vomiting. They suspected that the Rajneeshees tainted their water; however, they did not have proof and did not bother to further pursue the matter.[47]

Upon hearing about the outbreak, Hulse became suspicious and related the story to Chamberlain. Chamberlain was aware that the Rajneeshees' medical laboratories were more sophisticated and better-equipped than those of the county; the Rajneeshees had access to the resources and facilities necessary to cause this outbreak. Hulse and Chamberlain concluded that it would be complicated to convince federal disease investigators that the outbreak was a result of intentional contamination by the Rajneeshees.[48] Over 1,000 people reported symptoms; however, it is likely that more were affected because of The Dalles' location on a major interstate with high traffic.[49] The outbreak investigation identified 751 cases with 388 (51.7 percent) culture-confirmed cases and 363 (48.3 percent) clinical cases. Investigators discovered two different phases of illnesses: 88 cases (13 percent) from September 9 through September 18, peaking on September 15, and 586 cases (87 percent) from September 19 through October 10, peaking on September 24.[50] Additionally, 692 (92 percent) cases were restaurant-associated, 11 (1 percent) cases were secondary, and 48 (6 percent) cases were of unknown origin because of inadequate information on restaurant exposure. Most cases were linked to 10 restaurants, and epidemiological studies concluded that eating from a salad bar was the major risk factor for infection. Foods affected on the salad bars varied between restaurants. Investigators did not identify a particular water supply, foodstuff, supplier, or distributor common to affected restaurants. Infected employees could have unintentionally spread the bacteria to food, but there was no indication that they were the source of the outbreak. Furthermore, improper chilling temperatures and food rotation could have favored the growth of S. Typhimurium but did not directly cause the outbreak.[51]

The outbreak strain of S. Typhimurium was compared to other strains from national surveys and results indicated that the outbreak strain was not commonly found prior to the current outbreak. A strain from an animal isolate matched the current outbreak strain, but public health officials were not able to link it to The Dalles salad bars. Additionally, researchers matched the current outbreak strain to three other 1984 Oregon outbreaks, but officials were not able to find a relationship to The Dalles salad bars.[52] Preliminary reports from the CDC and Oregon state officials concluded that the outbreak was caused by improper food handling; evidence failed to suggest that the outbreak was a result of intentional contamination. However, The Dalles residents and local law enforcement thought the Rajneeshees were responsible and questioned the conclusions of public health officials.[53]

On September 16, 1985, Bhagwan Shree Rajneesh held a press conference in which he accused Ma Anand Sheela—his personal secretary and acting Rajneeshee leader—and her partners of poisoning locals and other attempts to sicken individuals. Bhagwan Shree Rajneesh requested a government investigation, and state and federal police formed a task force with the Federal Bureau of Investigation (FBI), local and state police forces, sheriffs' offices, Immigration and Naturalization Service (INS), and the National Guard.[54] The Rajneesh ranch served as headquarters for the investigation; however, Rajneeshees secretly tapped phone lines and destroyed relevant evidence. On October 2, 1985, search warrants were executed and investigators explored Pythagoras Medical Clinic and the Rajneesh Medical Corporation—both located on the Rajneesh ranch. Inside a laboratory, investigators found vials filled with *Salmonella* disks. Ma Anand Puja, a nurse, ordered the disks that were intended for use in diagnostic testing. Further analysis determined that this strain matched the strain from The Dalles salad bar outbreak the previous year. After this discovery, CDC scientist Robert V. Tauxe explained that investigators in the outbreak were fearful of wrongly accusing the Rajneeshees, and evidence had not suggested intentional contamination. In the past, investigators had seen *Salmonella* cause larger outbreaks and were doubtful that anyone would deliberately harm the small town of The Dalles, Oregon.[55]

As the investigation unfolded, David Berry Knapp (known as Krishna Diva or K. D.) and Ava Kay Avalos (known as Ma Ava) cooperated with prosecutors and provided insider information about the Rajneeshees' biological capacity and efforts. Records showed that Puja made orders to biologic companies and received bacterial cultures including *Salmonella* serotype Typhi, *Salmonella* serotype Paratyphi, *Francisella tularensis,* and *Shigella dysenteriae*. During court hearings in the fall of 1985, K. D. and Ma Ava provided juries with a description of the Rajneeshees' activities from the past year. Rajneeshees tainted the lettuce at a local Albertson's grocery store with their blend of bacteria. Additionally, the two testified that other members went to restaurants and put *Salmonella* in coffee creamers, in blue cheese dressing, and over fruits and vegetables at some salad bars. In their testimonies, K. D. and Ma Ava revealed that Shree and Sheela assured the Rajneesh community that sickening The Dalles community members would help protect the Rajneesh vision; this was a trial run and the real run would happen later that year when enough voters would be struck ill and the Rajneeshees could gain control of local government. Attempts to register homeless people to vote for similar purposes failed; consequently, their candidates lost the election.[56]

Sheela and Puja, who had fled to Germany, were extradited back to the United States and pled no contest to charges including attempted murder, illegal wiretapping, the poisoning of Judge Hulse, and causing the *Salmonella* outbreak in The Dalles. The two were sentenced to a maximum of 20 years in federal prison, and Sheela was fined $400,000 and instructed to pay Wasco County $69,353.31 in restitution. Both served less than four years in prison and were released early for good behavior. Oregon wanted to seek additional charges against the two, but they fled to Europe before the charges could be brought up. Bhagwan Shree Rajneesh received a 10-year suspended prison sentence, paid $400,000, and fled the United States.[57]

This case—even though it occurred more than 25 years ago—remains as a reminder to those involved in food and agriculture security just how vulnerable food and agricultural products are to intentional contamination. The case is not the only historical event in which food or agricultural products have been intentionally targeted;[58] however, the case in The Dalles, Oregon, is the most frequently referenced case of food bioterrorism as it validates concerns for the safety of food and agriculture products.

MILK

In September 2008, reports surfaced that melamine had been discovered in Chinese dairy products. In China, adulterated milk content was blamed for the deaths of at least six children and widespread health problems among infants.[59] The resulting scandal was a major setback for China's dairy industry and raised concerns worldwide about the implications of importing food from China. The melamine incident should not be seen as damning proof of China's inability to produce safe food but rather as an example of what can go wrong in food-supply chains. Food and agriculture security scholars in all regions of the world ought to heed the lessons from the case.

Background Regarding China's Dairy Industry and Influential Factors

Increased milk consumption in China is a trend that reflects a larger dietary shift among Asian consumers away from grain-based carbohydrates and toward animal-based fats and proteins.[60] Urban Chinese consumers were already consuming 11.9 kilograms of fresh milk products per capita in 2001. By 2007, that number rose to 17.75 kilograms. Consumption of yogurt, milk powder, and related products also increased substantially over the same time.[61] China's government made use of this trend to push development in the dairy industry. The government relaxed the dairy pricing system—a remnant from the controlled market—and also identified the dairy sector as 1 of 11 superior agricultural industries that should receive government support. Perhaps most significantly, the government launched a National School Milk Program in order to promote student health and increase milk consumption among China's youth.[62] In response to friendly government policies and a growing market, Chinese milk production boomed. From 1980 to 1995, production grew by an average of 14 percent every year.[63] In 2007, China produced 36.33 million metric tons of milk—up 10.4 percent from the previous year. The dairy boom catapulted local companies onto the national stage. Those that had a history in milk processing sought to expand their businesses and take advantage of the growing market. They met fierce competition from other expanding firms and new startup companies eager to join the race. By 2007, there were 735 processing companies wrangling over China's very limited milk resources.[64]

Many processing companies (in 2007, the precise number was 255 out of 735) have been located in China's four largest cities and the south, which, with large populations, also have featured a major portion of the market for dairy products. Meanwhile, the north has produced nearly 87 percent of China's milk.[65] In 2006, around 60 percent of raw milk was supplied by farms with less than 20 head of cattle. Small producers scattered throughout the countryside may not have been an ideal source of raw milk but processing companies had few other options. In order to deal with the vast distances, milk companies built collection stations at central locations where farmers could deposit their milk. At set intervals, transportation units arrived, retrieved the milk, and then shipped it to processing plants. In some cases, two levels of collection stations began to appear. One county in Hebei Province had 210 milk stations and 154 milking facilities.[66]

Since there were no restrictions on who could build and operate collection facilities, many local entrepreneurs—hoping to make a profit on the resale of raw milk—built their own. Research indicates that 55 percent of milk collection facilities were individually owned, while the companies directly operated only 16 percent. The privately owned collection facilities were built at the operator's expense, or in joint venture with the milk companies.[67] Because station operators were paid for the amount of milk they supplied to the company, there was an incentive to accept poor quality milk and make additions in order to ensure the protein levels at collection facilities met company standards. One such operator confessed to adding hydrogen peroxide to each load of milk he delivered to the processing plant; this was added in addition to albumen powder, vitamin C, whey powder, fatty oil, and, on occasion, alkali and sulfuric acid.[68]

While a number of different factors played a role in the melamine case, it was wildly fluctuating prices that catalyzed the tremendous increase in the amount of melamine in milk products discovered in 2008. Intense competition among companies caused milk prices to alternatively rise and fall between 2000 and 2007. In 2006, prices fell by such a drastic amount that many farmers chose to slaughter their animals instead of continue producing milk. The following year, rapidly rising prices set off a scramble for resources that were no longer available. Safety and health considerations became even less of a priority than before.[69] Another factor that may have played an indirect role in the increased amount of melamine-adulterated milk was a rise in the cost of feed; feed prices soared in 2007 and remained high through 2008, forcing farmers to use poor quality fodder, which in turn led to thin milk and a more pronounced "need" for protein-enhancing additives such as melamine.[70]

Discovery of the Problem and Reaction

The Sanlu Group's milk was by far the worst tainted. The heads of the Sanlu Group were warned of possible contamination as early as December 2007; however, it was not until June of the next year (2008) that they began running tests on their dairy products.[71] Fonterra Cooperative Group, a New Zealand company that owned 43 percent of Sanlu shares, urged Sanlu's chairwoman to recall products on August 13, 2008, yet once again Sanlu stalled. It was not until September 12, 2008, that production was halted. By that time, thousands of infants had already suffered the effects of melamine poisoning, and a public scandal had ensued.[72] The dairy industry in China had once been considered a model for development,[73] but the discovery of melamine and other dangerous additives in products from 22 different companies sullied the entire industry. The Sanlu Group was hardest hit and was forced to declare bankruptcy later in 2008, as a substantial percentage of customers indicated their unwillingness to purchase Sanlu products. Other companies are still attempting to win back customer trust. In contrast, one firm that managed to stay clear of any connection to melamine-tainted milk actually gained a boost in popularity at Chinese supermarkets and later moved to take over its one-time competitor: Sanlu.[74]

What Can Be Learned from the China Melamine Incident

Food and agriculture security scholars can learn a great deal from the China case involving melamine in milk products. The industry's structure—with its complex, diffuse network of production, transportation, collection, and processing—was problematic. The problems discovered in China

Historical and Contemporary Cases

arose during the transfer of milk from the producer to the processor. As a possible solution, some might propose to streamline the supply chain and involve only larger producers. This would, theoretically, cut out the need for collection stations and potentially give milk-processing companies access to milk of better quality, which might lessen the temptation to add dangerous substances. However, the large proportion of small producers is a reality that is unlikely to change; collection stations will continue to be a necessity in China's dairy industry. Other issues arose with individually owned milk stations; these challenges will likely remain as it is not economically feasible to force milk companies to run milk stations and prohibit individual ownership. Nevertheless, it is apparent that a fragmented supply chain can be especially vulnerable to contamination—in this case, economically motivated adulteration. The fact that milk passes through so many hands on its way to Chinese markets creates a potential veil of security for those interested in compromising safety and security for the sake of profit. Indeed, the milk-station operators understood that adulterated milk could not be traced back to them individually.

Food and agriculture security scholars might note the role that enhanced quality of production might play in situations like that of China and its dairy industry. Some have noted Chinese farmers' need for technical training and better equipment; they note that additives reached critical levels because the milk quality was poor. Helping farmers breed better animals and access better fodder and shelter might, in fact, help. The private and public sectors should continue to provide assistance to farmers and collection facility operators but not assume such actions will completely solve the problem. In the early 2000s, companies took similar steps, yet failed to ensure food safety.[75]

The single most important issue from the China case is that of inspection. Chinese regulators failed to properly inspect collection facilities and allowed economically motivated adulteration to occur at one of the most critical points in the milk supply chain. Fortunately, the Chinese government has recognized these failings and is taking steps to rectify them.[76] Such steps will be welcomed by China's milk consumers, who tend to be in the urban middle class and expect the products they purchase to be safe. One study (prior to the melamine scare in China) found Beijing customers willing to pay significantly more for food brands that had acquired HACCP certification, such as that described in chapter 3.[77]

CONCLUSIONS: PREPARING FOR DECISION MAKING IN THE REAL WORLD

Regardless of the commodity area or sector involved, there are many resources, training programs, and tools available for industry members to utilize to prevent, prepare for, respond to, and recover from either food-safety or food-defense issues. Some of these—such as HACCP and CARVER plus Shock—were identified in chapter 3. While these programs and tools are useful, food and agriculture security scholars will notice from the cases above that food-safety and food-defense environments—where they may one day themselves be making decisions—are often fraught with unpredictable, dynamic, stress-filled, and fast-paced problems and challenges. One behavioral science framework—in particular, the theory of naturalistic decision making (NDM)—explores this very issue: how experienced individuals and groups of people make decisions in dynamic, uncertain, fast-paced environments.[78] The field of NDM, which describes the tasks and settings faced by real-world decision-makers, provides a good overview of the types of environment in which food and agriculture security decision makers must operate: a world filled with ill-structured problems; uncertain, dynamic environments; shifting, ill-defined, or competing goals; action/feedback loops; time constraints; outcomes with high stakes; multiple players; and organizational goals and norms. These factors complicate decision making in food safety and food defense and need to be considered when dealing with any issue in food and agriculture security.[79]

NOTES

1. International Food Information Council, "2007–2009 Ific Foundation Media Guide on Food Safety and Nutrition. Backgrounder: Food Safety & Defense," http://www.ific.org/food/safety/upload/foodsafetybackgrounder.pdf.

2. Department of Homeland Security, "Homeland Security Presidential Directive 9: Defense of United States Agriculture and Food," http://www.dhs.gov/xabout/laws/gc_1217449547663.shtm#1. 1.

3. Thomas F. Stinson et al., "Defending America's Food Supply against Terrorism: Who Is Responsible? Who Should Pay?" *Choices*, 2007.

4. Gerald Sapers and Michael Doyle, "Scope of the Produce Contamination Problem," in *The Produce Contamination Problem: Causes and Solutions*, ed. Gerald M. Sapers, Ethan B. Solomon, and Karl R. Matthews (Burlington, MA: Elsevier, Academic Press, 2009).

5. Ethel Taylor, Justin Kastner, and David Renter, "Challenges Involved in the Salmonella Saintpaul Outbreak and Lessons Learned," *Journal of Public Health Management and Practice* 16, no. 3 (2010).

6. Centers for Disease Control and Prevention, "Investigation of Outbreak of Infections Caused by Salmonella Saintpaul," http://www.cdc.gov/salmonella/saintpaul/jalapeno/archive/060208.html.

7. U.S. Food and Drug Administration, "FDA Warns Consumers in New Mexico and Texas Not to Eat Certain Types of Raw Red Tomatoes," http://www.fda.gov/NewsEvents/Newsroom/PressAnnouncements/2008/ucm116904.htm.

8. U.S. Food and Drug Administration, "FDA Warns Consumers Nationwide Not to Eat Certain Types of Raw Red Tomatoes," http://www.fda.gov/NewsEvents/Newsroom/PressAnnouncements/2008/ucm116908.htm.

9. Centers for Disease Control and Prevention, "Investigation of Outbreak of Infections Caused by Salmonella Saintpaul," http://www.cdc.gov/salmonella/saintpaul/jalapeno/archive/063008.html.

10. Centers for Disease Control and Prevention, "Investigation of Outbreak of Infections Caused by Salmonella Saintpaul," http://www.cdc.gov/salmonella/saintpaul/jalapeno/archive/070708.html.

11. Centers for Disease Control and Prevention, "Investigation of Outbreak of Infections Caused by Salmonella Saintpaul," http://www.cdc.gov/salmonella/saintpaul/jalapeno/archive/070908.html.

12. Taylor, Kastner, and Renter, "Challenges Involved in the Salmonella Saintpaul Outbreak and Lessons Learned"; Morbidity and Mortality Weekly Report, "Outbreak of Salmonella Serotype Saintpaul Infections Associated with Multiple Raw Produce Items—United States, 2008," ed. Centers for Disease Control and Prevention (August 29, 2008).

13. U.S. Food and Drug Administration, "FDA Lifts Warning About Eating Certain Types of Tomatoes," http://www.fda.gov/NewsEvents/Newsroom/PressAnnouncements/2008/ucm116923.htm.

14. U.S. Food and Drug Administration, "Agricola Zaragoza, Inc. Recalls Jalapeno Peppers Because of Possible Health Risk," http://www.fda.gov/Safety/Recalls/ArchiveRecalls/2008/ucm112471.htm.

15. U.S. Food and Drug Administration, "U.S. Grown Jalapeño and Serrano Peppers Not Connected to Salmonella Saintpaul Outbreak," http://www.fda.gov/NewsEvents/Newsroom/PressAnnouncements/2008/ucm116926.htm.

16. U.S. Food and Drug Administration, "FDA Extends Consumer Warning on Serrano Peppers from Mexico," http://www.fda.gov/NewsEvents/Newsroom/PressAnnouncements/2008/ucm116929.htm.

17. Morbidity and Mortality Weekly Report, "Outbreak of Salmonella Serotype Saintpaul Infections Associated with Multiple Raw Produce Items—United States, 2008."

18. Ricardo Alonso-Zaldivar, "CDC: Salmonella Outbreak Appears to Be Over," Associated Press, *USA Today,* http://www.usatoday.com/money/economy/2008-08-28-261734902_x.htm.

19. Taylor, Kastner, and Renter, "Challenges Involved in the Salmonella Saintpaul Outbreak and Lessons Learned."

20. Ibid.

21. Testimony Before the Subcommittee on Oversight of Government Management, Restructuring and the District of Columbia, Committee on Governmental Affairs, U.S. Senate, *U.S. Needs a Single Agency to Administer a Unified, Risk-Based Inspection System,* 1999, p. 6.

22. Centers for Disease Control and Prevention, "Multistate Outbreak of *Salmonella* Serotype Tennessee Infections Associated with Peanut Butter-United States, 2006–2007," *Journal of the American Medical Association* 298, no. 1 (2007).

23. ConAgra Foods Inc., "Peter Pan Peanut Butter and Great Value Peanut Butter Products Beginning with Product Code 2111 Recalled for Possible *Salmonella* Contamination," http://media.conagrafoods.com/phoenix.zhtml?c=202310&p=irol-newsArticle&ID=1008647&highlight=.

24. Centers for Disease Control and Prevention, "Multistate Outbreak of *Salmonella* Serotype Tennessee Infections Associated with Peanut Butter-United States, 2006–2007."

25. ConAgra Foods Inc. "Conagra Foods Announces Test Finds *Salmonella* in Its Peanut Butter," Omaha, NE, http://media.conagrafoods.com/phoenix.zhtml?c=202310&p=irol-newsArticle&ID=1008642&highlight=.

26. Centers for Disease Control and Prevention, "Multistate Outbreak of *Salmonella* Serotype Tennessee Infections Associated with Peanut Butter-United States, 2006–2007."

27. Robert V. Tauxe, "Real Burden and Potential Risks from Foodborne Infections: The Value of Multijurisdictional Collaborations," *Trends in Food Science and Technology* 19 (2008).

28. Marc Longpre and Hamilton Nolan, "Conagra Bolster Comms Amid Peanut Butter Recall," *PR Week*, February 26, 2007.

29. ConAgra Foods Inc., "Conagra Foods Announces the Renovation of Its Peanut Butter Plant and Enhanced Food Safety Measures," http://media.conagrafoods.com/phoenix.zhtml?c=202310&p=irol-newsArticle&ID=1008473&highlight=.

30. Jen Haberkorn, "Peter Pan Tries to Recover from *Salmonella*," *Washington Times*, April 9, 2007; Brad Dorfman, "Peter Pan Gets a Facelift," *Montreal Gazette*, August 8, 2007.

31. "Class Action Lawsuit Filed Vs. Conagra over *Salmonella* in Peanut Butter," Progressive Grocer, http://www.progressivegrocer.com/progressivegrocer/esearch/article_display.jsp?vnu_content_id=1003567768.

32. Elizabeth Williamson, "FDA Was Aware of Dangers to Food; Outbreaks Were Not Preventable, Officials Say," *Washington Post*, April 23, 2007.

33. Shaun Kennedy and Frank Busta, "Defending the Safety of the Food System through Research and Education," in *IFT Global Food Safety & Quality Conference* (Chicago, IL: August 1, 2007).

34. Food and Drug Administration, "Retail Food Protection," http://www.fda.gov/Food/FoodSafety/RetailFoodProtection/default.htm.

35. Judith Miller, Stephan Engelberg, and William Broad, *Germs: Biological Weapons and America's Secret War* (New York: Simon & Schuster, 2001); T. J. Török et al., "A Large Community Outbreak of Salmonellosis Caused by Intentional Contamination of Restaurant Salad Bars," *Journal of the American Medical Association* 278, no. 5 (1997).

36. Miller, Engelberg, and Broad, *Germs: Biological Weapons and America's Secret War*.

37. Ibid; F. W. Brenner et al., "*Salmonella* Nomenclature," *Journal of Clinical Microbiology* 38, no. 7 (2000). *Salmonella* nomenclature is complicated and different systems are used. The formal name of the bacteria, using CDC nomenclature, is *Salmonella* serotype Typhimurium—abbreviated S. Typhimurium.

38. Miller, Engelberg, and Broad, *Germs: Biological Weapons and America's Secret War*.

39. Török et al., "A Large Community Outbreak of Salmonellosis Caused by Intentional Contamination of Restaurant Salad Bars."

40. Miller, Engelberg, and Broad, *Germs: Biological Weapons and America's Secret War*. EIS was established during the Cold War to assist in the detection of a microbial attack on the United States. At the time of this outbreak, EIS was made up of 70 doctors trained in epidemiology.

41. CDC Division of Foodborne Bacterial and Mycotic Diseases, "Salmonellosis," http://www.cdc.gov/nczved/dfbmd/disease_listing/salmonellosis_gi.html#2. Roughly 40,000 cases of salmonellosis are reported annually; however, some

speculate that this number is possibly 30 times greater as less severe cases are not diagnosed or reported.

42. Ibid.

43. Jean-Yves D'Aoust, "*Salmonella*," in *Foodborne Bacterial Pathogens*, ed. Michael P. Doyle (New York: Marcel Dekker Inc., 1989); Jean-Yves D'Aoust, "*Salmonella* Species," in *Food Microbiology Fundamentals and Frontiers*, ed. Michael P. Doyle, Larry R. Beuchat, and Thomas J. Montville (Washington, D.C.: ASM Press, 1997).

44. Jean-Yves D'Aoust, D. W. Warburto, and A. M. Sewell, "*Salmonella* Typhimurium Phage-Type 10 from Cheddar Cheese Implicated in a Major Canadian Foodborne Outbreak," *Journal of Food Protection* 48(1985); G. Kapperud et al., "Outbreak of *Salmonella* Typhimurium Infection Traced to Contaminated Chocolate and Caused by a Strain Lacking the 60-Megadalton Virulence Plasmid," *Journal of Clinical Microbiology* 28, no. 12 (1990).

45. Miller, Engelberg, and Broad, *Germs: Biological Weapons and America's Secret War*.

46. Török et al., "A Large Community Outbreak of Salmonellosis Caused by Intentional Contamination of Restaurant Salad Bars," 390.

47. Miller, Engelberg, and Broad, *Germs: Biological Weapons and America's Secret War*.

48. Ibid. Laurence R. Foster, then Oregon's most senior epidemiologist, was from the area and firmly believed that the Rajneeshees were being unduly tormented because of their unfamiliar religious conventions. Foster served as a mentor to Thomas Török, a lead EIS officer in the case.

49. Barbara A. Rasco and Gleyn E. Bledsoe, *Bioterrorism and Food Safety* (Boca Raton, FL: CRC Press, 2005).

50. Török et al., "A Large Community Outbreak of Salmonellosis Caused by Intentional Contamination of Restaurant Salad Bars." The date of symptom onset was known in 674 cases (90%); thus, those cases were included in the two waves of illness.

51. Ibid.

52. Ibid.

53. Miller, Engelberg, and Broad, *Germs: Biological Weapons and America's Secret War*.

54. Ibid. Dave Fohnmayer, Oregon Attorney General, headed the task force.

55. Ibid.

56. Ibid.

57. Ibid.

58. James Martin Center for Nonproliferation Studies, "Agriculture Related Cbw Activity," http://cns.miis.edu/cbw/agromain.htm.

59. Staff, *Weisheng Bu: Jieshi Baobao Peichang Lunzheng Zhong Mianfen Zhengbaiji Youwang Jinyong* [MOH: Proving the Infant Kidney Stone Case and Prohibition of Whitener Use in Flour] (Nanfang Dushi Bao, 2008). David Barboza, "China Says Complaints About Milk Began in 2007" *New York Times*, September 23 2008.

60. P. Pingali, "Westernization of Asian Diets and the Transformation of Food Systems: Implications for Research and Policy," *Food Policy* 32(2006).

61. D. Xu, "Nian Zhongguo Naiye Fazhan Qingkuang [Situation of China's Dairy Development in 2007]" in *Zhongguo Naiye Nianjian 2008* [2008 China

Dairy Yearbook], ed. C. Liu and M. Dou (Beijing: China Agriculture Press, 2008), pp. 54–58

62. J. Yang, T. G. MacAulay, and W. Shen, "The Dairy Industry in China: An Analysis of Supply, Demand and Policy Issues," in *Annual Conference of the Australian Agricultural and Resource Economics Society* (Melbourne: 2004).

63. Frank H. Fuller et al., "Got Milk? The Rapid Rise of China's Dairy Sector and Its Future Prospects," *Food Policy* 31(2006).

64. D. Xu, "Nian Zhongguo Naiye Fazhan Qingkuang [Situation of China's Dairy Development in 2007]."

65. The north is comprised of three areas: Northeast (Manchuria), Huabei (north central China) and Northwest (mainly Xinjiang and Inner Mongolia). Ibid.

66. F. Gale and D. Hu, "Supply Chain Issues in China's Milk Adulteration Incident," in *International Association of Agricultural Economists' Conference* (Beijing: 2009).

67. Ibid.

68. N. Xu, "Luanxiang Huisu: 'Tiaonairen', 'Guanxi Nai' He 'Shazi Niu' [Recalling Chaos: 'Milk Adjusters', 'Relationship Milk', and 'Fool Cows']," *Nanfang Zhoumo* 30 (2008).

69. Gale and Hu, "Supply Chain Issues in China's Milk Adulteration Incident."

70. D. Xu, "Nian Zhongguo Naiye Fazhan Qingkuang [Situation of China's Dairy Development in 2007]"; Gale and Hu, "Supply Chain Issues in China's Milk Adulteration Incident."

71. J.-M. Chaumet and F. Desevedavy, "Food Consumption and Food Safety in China," *Asia Visions* 21(2009).

72. Z. Zhu and X. Cui, "Sanlu Ex-Boss Was Aware of Tainted Milk," *China Daily*, January 1, 2009.

73. There are a number of academic articles dealing with the Chinese dairy industry's spectacular rise. For a sample, see Fuller et al., "Got Milk? The Rapid Rise of China's Dairy Sector and Its Future Prospects."

74. Staff, *Sanlu in Bankruptcy Proceeding* (Beijing, China: Caijing: 2008).

75. Fuller et al., "Got Milk? The Rapid Rise of China's Dairy Sector and Its Future Prospects."

76. *Zhonghua Renmin Gonghe Guo Shipin Anquan Fa* [People's Republic of China Food Safety Law] (China: Xinhua, 2009).

77. H-H. Hsu, W. S. Chern, and F. Gale, *How Will Rising Income Affect the Structure of Food Demand, in China's Food and Agriculture: Issues for the 21st Century* (Washington, D.C.: Economic Research Service, 2002).

78. Caroline E. Zsambok, "Naturalistic Decision Making: Where Are We Now?," in *Naturalistic Decision Making*, ed. Caroline E. Zsambok and Gary Klein (Mahwah, NJ: Lawrence Erlbaum Associates, 1997). 5.

79. Kathryn S. Krusemark, "Decision-Making Applications in Food Safety and Food Defense" (Kansas State University, 2009).

BIBLIOGRAPHY

Alonso-Zaldivar, Ricardo. "CDC: Salmonella Outbreak Appears to Be Over." Associated Press, *USA Today*. http://www.usatoday.com/money/economy/2008–08–28–261734902_x.htm.

Barboza, David. "China Says Complaints About Milk Began in 2007." *New York Times*, September 23, 2008.

Brenner, F. W., R. G. Villar, F. J. Angulo, R. Tauxe, and B. Swaminathan. "*Salmonella* Nomenclature." *Journal of Clinical Microbiology* 38, no. 7 (2000): 2465–67.

CDC Division of Foodborne Bacterial and Mycotic Diseases. "Salmonellosis." http://www.cdc.gov/nczved/dfbmd/disease_listing/salmonellosis_gi.html#2.

Centers for Disease Control and Prevention. "Investigation of Outbreak of Infections Caused by Salmonella Saintpaul." http://www.cdc.gov/salmonella/saintpaul/jalapeno/archive/060208.html.

Centers for Disease Control and Prevention. "Investigation of Outbreak of Infections Caused by Salmonella Saintpaul." http://www.cdc.gov/salmonella/saintpaul/jalapeno/archive/063008.html.

Centers for Disease Control and Prevention. "Investigation of Outbreak of Infections Caused by Salmonella Saintpaul." http://www.cdc.gov/salmonella/saintpaul/jalapeno/archive/070708.html.

Centers for Disease Control and Prevention. "Investigation of Outbreak of Infections Caused by Salmonella Saintpaul." http://www.cdc.gov/salmonella/saintpaul/jalapeno/archive/070908.html.

Centers for Disease Control and Prevention. "Multistate Outbreak of *Salmonella* Serotype Tennessee Infections Associated with Peanut Butter-United States, 2006–2007." *Journal of the American Medical Association* 298, no. 1 (2007): 33(3).

Chaumet, J.-M., and F. Desevedavy. "Food Consumption and Food Safety in China." *Asie Visions* 21 (2009).

"Class Action Lawsuit Filed Vs. Conagra over *Salmonella* in Peanut Butter." Progressive Grocer. http://www.progressivegrocer.com/progressivegrocer/esearch/article_display.jsp?vnu_content_id=1003567768.

ConAgra Foods Inc. "Conagra Foods Announces Test Finds *Salmonella* in Its Peanut Butter." Omaha, NE. http://media.conagrafoods.com/phoenix.zhtml?c=202310&p=irol-newsArticle&ID=1008642&highlight=.

ConAgra Foods Inc. "Conagra Foods Announces the Renovation of Its Peanut Butter Plant and Enhanced Food Safety Measures." http://media.conagrafoods.com/phoenix.zhtml?c=202310&p=irol-newsArticle&ID=1008473&highlight=.

ConAgra Foods Inc. "Peter Pan Peanut Butter and Great Value Peanut Butter Products Beginning with Product Code 2111 Recalled for Possible *Salmonella* Contamination." http://media.conagrafoods.com/phoenix.zhtml?c=202310&p=irol-newsArticle&ID=1008647&highlight=.

D'Aoust, Jean-Yves. "*Salmonella*." In *Foodborne Bacterial Pathogens*, ed. Michael P. Doyle, 327–445. New York: Marcel Dekker Inc., 1989.

D'Aoust, Jean-Yves. "*Salmonella* Species." In *Food Microbiology Fundamentals and Frontiers*, ed. Michael P. Doyle, Larry R. Beuchat, and Thomas J. Montville, 129–58. Washington, D.C.: ASM Press, 1997.

D'Aoust, Jean-Yves, D.W. Warburto, and A. M. Sewell. "*Salmonella* Typhimurium Phage-Type 10 from Cheddar Cheese Implicated in a Major Canadian Foodborne Outbreak." *Journal of Food Protection* 48 (1985): 1062–66.

Department of Homeland Security. "Homeland Security Presidential Directive 9: Defense of United States Agriculture and Food." http://www.dhs.gov/xabout/laws/gc_1217449547663.shtm#1.

Dorfman, Brad. "Peter Pan Gets a Facelift." *Montreal Gazette*, August 8, 2007, A3.

Food and Drug Administration. "Retail Food Protection." http://www.fda.gov/Food/FoodSafety/RetailFoodProtection/default.htm.

Fuller, Frank H., Jikun Huang, Hengyun Ma, and Scott Rozelle. "Got Milk? The Rapid Rise of China's Dairy Sector and Its Future Prospects." *Food Policy* 31 (2006): 201–15.

Gale, F., and D. Hu. "Supply Chain Issues in China's Milk Adulteration Incident." In *International Association of Agricultural Economists' Conference*. Beijing, 2009.

Haberkorn, Jen. "Peter Pan Tries to Recover from *Salmonella*." *Washington Times*, April 9, 2007, C08.

Hsu, H-H., W. S. Chern, and F. Gale. *How Will Rising Income Affect the Structure of Food Demand, in China's Food and Agriculture: Issues for the 21st Century*. Washington, D.C.: Economic Research Service, 2002.

International Food Information Council. "2007–2009 IFIC Foundation Media Guide on Food Safety and Nutrition. Backgrounder: Food Safety & Defense." http://www.ific.org/food/safety/upload/foodsafetybackgrounder.pdf.

Kapperud, G., S. Gustavsen, I. Hellesnes, A. H. Hansen, J. Lassen, J. Hirn, M. Jahkola, M. A. Montenegro, and R. Helmuth. "Outbreak of *Salmonella* Typhimurium Infection Traced to Contaminated Chocolate and Caused by a Strain Lacking the 60-Megadalton Virulence Plasmid." *Journal of Clinical Microbiology* 28, no. 12 (1990): 2597–2601.

Kennedy, Shaun, and Frank Busta. "Defending the Safety of the Food System through Research and Education." In *IFT Global Food Safety & Quality Conference*. Chicago, IL, August 1, 2007.

Krusemark, Kathryn S. "Decision-Making Applications in Food Safety and Food Defense." Kansas State University, 2009.

Longpre, Marc, and Hamilton Nolan. "Conagra Bolster Comms Amid Peanut Butter Recall." *PR Week*, February 26, 2007, 2.

Miller, Judith, Stephan Engelberg, and William Broad. *Germs: Biological Weapons and America's Secret War*. New York Simon & Schuster, 2001.

Morbidity and Mortality Weekly Report. "Outbreak of Salmonella Serotype Saintpaul Infections Associated with Multiple Raw Produce Items—United States, 2008," ed. Centers for Disease Control and Prevention, August 29, 2008.

Pingali, P. "Westernization of Asian Diets and the Transformation of Food Systems: Implications for Research and Policy." *Food Policy* 32 (2006): 261–98.

Rasco, Barbara A., and Gleyn E. Bledsoe. *Bioterrorism and Food Safety*. Boca Raton, FL: CRC Press, 2005.

Sapers, Gerald, and Michael Doyle. "Scope of the Produce Contamination Problem." In *The Produce Contamination Problem: Causes and Solutions*, ed. Gerald M. Sapers, Ethan B. Solomon and Karl R. Matthews. Burlington, MA: Elsevier, Academic Press, 2009.

Staff. *Sanlu in Bankruptcy Proceeding*. Caijing, 2008.

Staff. *Weisheng Bu: Jieshi Baobao Peichang Lunzheng Zhong Mianfen Zhengbaiji Youwang Jinyong* [MOH: Proving the Infant Kidney Stone Case and Prohibition of Whitener Use in Flour]: Nanfang Dushi Bao, 2008.

Stinson, Thomas F., Jean Kinsey, Dennis Degeneffe, and Koel Ghosh. "Defending America's Food Supply against Terrorism: Who Is Responsible? Who Should Pay." *Choices*, 2007, 67–71.

Studies, James Martin Center for Nonproliferation. "Agriculture Related Cbw Activity." http://cns.miis.edu/cbw/agromain.htm.

Tauxe, Robert V. "Real Burden and Potential Risks from Foodborne Infections: The Value of Multijurisdictional Collaborations." *Trends in Food Science and Technology* 19 (2008): S18-S25.

Taylor, Ethel, Justin Kastner, and David Renter. "Challenges Involved in the Salmonella Saintpaul Outbreak and Lessons Learned." *Journal of Public Health Management and Practice* 16, no. 3 (2010): 221–31.

Testimony Before the Subcommittee on Oversight of Government Management, Restructuring and the District of Columbia, Committee on Governmental Affairs, U.S. Senate. *U.S. Needs a Single Agency to Administer a Unified, Risk-Based Inspection System*, 1999.

Török, T. J., R. V. Tauxe, R. P. Wise, J. R. Livengood, R. Sokolow, S. Mauvais, K. A. Birkness, M. R. Skeels, J. M. Horan, and L. R. Foster. "A Large Community Outbreak of Salmonellosis Caused by Intentional Contamination of Restaurant Salad Bars." *Journal of the American Medical Association* 278, no. 5 (1997): 389–95.

U.S. Food and Drug Administration. "Agricola Zaragoza, Inc. Recalls Jalapeno Peppers Because of Possible Health Risk." http://www.fda.gov/Safety/Recalls/ArchiveRecalls/2008/ucm112471.htm.

U.S. Food and Drug Administration. "FDA Extends Consumer Warning on Serrano Peppers from Mexico." http://www.fda.gov/NewsEvents/Newsroom/PressAnnouncements/2008/ucm116929.htm.

U.S. Food and Drug Administration. "FDA Lifts Warning About Eating Certain Types of Tomatoes." http://www.fda.gov/NewsEvents/Newsroom/PressAnnouncements/2008/ucm116923.htm.

U.S. Food and Drug Administration. "FDA Warns Consumers in New Mexico and Texas Not to Eat Certain Types of Raw Red Tomatoes." http://www.fda.gov/NewsEvents/Newsroom/PressAnnouncements/2008/ucm116904.htm.

U.S. Food and Drug Administration. "FDA Warns Consumers Nationwide Not to Eat Certain Types of Raw Red Tomatoes." http://www.fda.gov/NewsEvents/Newsroom/PressAnnouncements/2008/ucm116908.htm.

U.S. Food and Drug Administration. "U.S. Grown Jalapeño and Serrano Peppers Not Connected to Salmonella Saintpaul Outbreak." http://www.fda.gov/NewsEvents/Newsroom/PressAnnouncements/2008/ucm116926.htm.

Williamson, Elizabeth. "FDA Was Aware of Dangers to Food; Outbreaks Were Not Preventable, Officials Say." *Washington Post*, April 23, 2007, A01.

Xu, D. "Nian Zhongguo Naiye Fazhan Qingkuang [Situation of China's Dairy Development in 2007]." In *Zhongguo Naiye Nianjian 2008* [2008 China Dairy Yearbook], ed. C. Liu and M. Dou, pp. 54–58. Beijing: China Agriculture Press, 2008.

Xu, N. "Luanxiang Huisu: 'Tiaonairen', 'Guanxi Nai' He 'Shazi Niu' [Recalling Chaos: 'Milk Adjusters', 'Relationship Milk', and 'Fool Cows']." *Nanfang Zhoumo* 30 (2008).

Yang, J., T. G. MacAulay, and W. Shen. "The Dairy Industry in China: An Analysis of Supply, Demand and Policy Issues." In *Annual Conference of the Australian Agricultural and Resource Economics Society*. Melbourne, 2004.

Zhonghua Renmin Gonghe Guo Shipin Anquan Fa [People's Republic of China Food Safety Law], China: Xinhua, 2009.

Zhu, Z., and X. Cui. "Sanlu Ex-Boss Was Aware of Tainted Milk." *China Daily*, January 1 2009.

Zsambok, Caroline E. "Naturalistic Decision Making: Where Are We Now?" In *Naturalistic Decision Making*, ed. by Caroline E. Zsambok and Gary Klein, pp. 3–16. Mahwah, NJ: Lawrence Erlbaum Associates, 1997.

CHAPTER 5

Import Security: U.S. and Global Approaches

Edward Nyambok

Food and agriculture security scholars may be aware that the United States has some of the most stringent food policies and regulations in the world, resulting in one of the safest food and drug supplies in the world; however, even the most robust systems, including that of the United States, have their own weaknesses. The United States has been working to identify weaknesses in its regulations and infrastructure, particularly those issues that compromise the safety of food. In recent years, the United States has encountered significant sanitary (food-safety- and/or animal-health-related) and phytosanitary (plant-health-related) problems (collectively, SPS-related problems). Many of the SPS-related problems have originated from food imports. SPS-related problems that stem from food imports are complex; as a result, scholars of food and agriculture security should adopt multidisciplinary approaches to better understand them. This book chapter focuses on the SPS-related import security problems encountered by the United States, while addressing the systems that are being developed, considered, or implemented to prevent future problems.

BACKGROUND

The Centers for Disease Control and Prevention (CDC) estimates that 76 million people fall ill each year from food-borne illnesses; an estimated 5,000 people die each year from illnesses resulting from the presence of microbial pathogens in food.[1] The CDC's data on the results of food contamination indicates that much still needs to be done to secure the safety of locally produced food as well as imported food. Most of the food and drug laws currently enforced by the Food and Drug Administration (FDA) were enacted in the 1900s.[2] While there have been considerable changes in food production techniques and technological advancement in food processing, changes in the food and drug laws under which the FDA operates have been slow. However, significant changes were made in the U.S. food laws in the post–September 11, 2001, era; a good number of these changes were geared toward strengthening the safety and security of the nation's food supply from the intentional contamination of food.

As mentioned earlier, the United States has one of the safest food and drug supplies in the world; nevertheless, the country has often experienced food-safety problems stemming from both imported food and domestically produced food. In 2007, a large number of pets in the United States died after consuming pet food contaminated with melamine—an industrial chemical. The pet food was manufactured by a U.S.-based company using contaminated wheat gluten which had been imported from China.[3] This incident triggered the largest pet-food recall in U.S. history. In the same year, large quantities of Chinese aquaculture products were seized by the FDA due to violative levels of unapproved veterinary drugs. The year 2007 also witnessed the largest recall of imported Chinese toothpaste from the U.S. stores; the toothpastes were contaminated with diethylene glycol—a chemical used in the manufacture of antifreeze. In the same year, contaminated blood thinner exported by China to various countries around the world caused heightened public health concerns over the safety of Chinese products.[4]

Critics of the U.S. regulatory system emphasize that the current food-safety systems were developed in the early- and mid-1900s, during which most of the food and drugs consumed in the United States were locally produced; therefore, they argue, the systems are inadequately designed and poorly funded to deal with the current surge in imported products.[5] The United States has several agencies responsible for the safety of imported food and drugs. The FDA, an agency within the Department of Health and Human Services (HHS), regulates all food and drugs produced locally and those imported. The FDA derives its authority from Title 21 of the Federal Food, Drugs, and Cosmetic Act (FD&C Act). The FDA is responsible for all food products except meat, poultry, and egg products—which are under the exclusive jurisdiction of the U.S. Department of Agriculture (USDA). Section 21 of the FD&C Act gives the FDA statutory authority to ensure the safety of all food and drugs offered for commerce within the country.[6] FDA-regulated products may be deemed adulterated for different reasons: if they contain poisonous or deleterious substances; if they contain unsafe food additives; if they were prepared, packaged, or held under unsanitary conditions leading to the product's contamination or its becoming injurious to health; if they lack the necessary constituents; if their necessary constituents have been substituted; if any of their constituents have been added; if they contain unsafe color additives; or if they contain filthy, putrid, and so on, matter. Confectioneries that have alcohol or non-nutritive substances are also considered to be adulterated. Misbranded products include the following: those that have false or misleading labels, products that are offered for sale in another name, products that imitate other foods, and products packaged in misleading containers.[7] Title 21 part 110 of the Code of Federal Regulations allows the FDA to require all foreign and domestic food facilities to adhere to Good Manufacturing Practices (GMP), which addresses safe food handling and plant sanitation.[8] Section 801 of the FD&C Act authorizes the FDA to "refuse entry" of any item of food that "appears"—based on physical examination or otherwise—to be adulterated, misbranded, or in violation of the law.

The 2002 Public Health Security and the Bioterrorism Preparedness Act (or 2002 Bioterrorism Act), instituted after the 2001 terrorism attacks against the United States, outlined a new requirement: prior notice for importers. The prior-notice regulation requires importers to provide, in advance, information about any shipments of food destined for the United States. The information must be provided to the FDA not more than five days before the shipment arrives at a U.S. port of entry. Food imports that have inadequate prior notice are subject to refusal and must be held at the ports of entry.[9] The FDA has a notification system—the Operational and Administrative System for Import Support (OASIS), which enables it to rank products in terms of the risk they pose. This helps the FDA to determine which imports are to be isolated for further inspection.[10] If imported products are found to not be in compliance with import regulations, the FDA is authorized to refuse entry of the products into the country, seize the products, or order the destruction of the products. The FDA may also detain imports without physical examination based on a previous history of violation, or if the FDA has reason to believe that the imports pose serious or adverse health risks, including the risk of death, to consumers.[11]

FUNDING AND SCOPE OF INSPECTIONS

The United States has more than 300 ports of entry; meanwhile, as of 2007, there were 450 FDA inspectors working to cover all of these entry points. Some have argued that the FDA's ability to operate effectively has often been limited by insufficient funds and shortage of manpower. In addition to inspection of imports at the ports of entries, the FDA often conducts in-plant inspections in domestic and foreign food processing facilities.[12] The FDA carries out biennial inspections of domestic food and drug facilities. This inspection frequency is not typically seen with foreign food and drug facilities, in part because of insufficient manpower and monetary resources dedicated to foreign-inspection services. In 2007, the FDA received a budgetary allocation of $10 million for foreign-inspection services; in 2008, the agency received $11 million for foreign inspections. The funds and manpower under which the FDA operates have often been insufficient to carry out even a one-time inspection of all foreign food and drug facilities; under the resources with which the FDA operated in 2009, it was estimated that it would take 13 years to conduct a one-time inspection of all foreign food and drug facilities.[13] Congressional hearings, testimonies before Senate committees, and various subcommittees studying the safety of the U.S. food supply have occasionally identified several challenges facing the FDA in conducting inspections. A number of hearings were conducted after the United States encountered significant safety problems with imported foods and drugs from foreign countries, mostly from China. The Congress, in 2010, increased the FDA's budget from approximately $649 million for the fiscal year 2009 to approximately $783 million for the fiscal year 2010.[14] The increase in the FDA's operating budget provided the agency with resources to hire more inspectors, thereby improving its inspection capability. The FDA increased its inspection capabilities by opening new offices in foreign countries, expanding its presence in regions that export large amounts of food to the United States. This move is considered to be a way of "pushing the borders backward," so to speak, so that unsafe goods are intercepted at the countries of origin before they arrive at the U.S. ports of entry.

In a new approach to enhance the safety and security of the U.S. food supply, the FDA, in agreement with foreign countries' governments, started opening offices in foreign countries. In 2008, the FDA collaborated with the Chinese government to open three offices in China.[15] In January 2009, the FDA opened its first offices in Latin America—in Costa Rica (San Jose). The Latin American offices were opened to facilitate trade, while improving the safety and security of food and drug products originating from Latin American countries destined for U.S. markets.[16] On January 16, 2009, the FDA opened offices in New Delhi and Mumbai, India. India is the fourth largest exporter, by volume, of prescription drugs—especially prescription generic drugs and biologics—to the United States. In 2008, Indian companies exported $7.4 billion worth of drugs including prescription drugs to the United States.[17] Indian firms are an important source of prescription drugs and food for the United States. The FDA opened offices in India to provide technical advice and to conduct inspection of facilities that export food and drugs to the United States. The FDA's officers stationed in India work with the Indian government to develop certification programs to enable the smooth flow of goods destined for the U.S. markets. As of January 2010, the FDA was considering opening offices in the Middle East, Mexico, Chile (Santiago), Belgium (Brussels), the United Kingdom (London), and Italy (Parma). The FDA's foreign offices work with the foreign governments to strengthen the inspection of food and drugs destined for the U.S. markets, develop the capacity of the foreign governments to perform sufficient inspections for goods destined for the United States, and harmonize national inspection standards. These efforts help ensure that the inspection standards of the countries where the United States sources its foods and drugs provide equivalent levels of protection as U.S. standards.

U.S. IMPORT SECURITY AND THE MULTILATERAL TRADING SYSTEM

The U.S. government has also instituted agencies and systems to ensure that food products presented at the U.S. entry ports are safe for consumption. The USDA FSIS conducts inspections at 150 import houses located at approximately 35 ports of entry. At the ports of entry, FSIS agents use an automated computerized system—the Automated Import Information System (AIIS)—to generate lists of imports that are to be subjected to inspection based on the level of risks associated with the products and/or the country of origin of the imports. During inspections, the inspectors look for various issues such as the eligibility of the country (from which the products originate) to ship products to the United States, the general condition of the imports, proper labeling, presence of defects, and so forth. Samples may also be collected for further laboratory analysis for contaminants.[18] While the United States exerts every effort to ensure the safety of the food and drugs it receives from its trading partners, it must do so within the confines of multilateral rules regarding international trade. The United States is a signatory to a number of multilateral trade rules; the Agreement on the Application of Sanitary and Phytosanitary Measures (SPS Agreement) encourages countries to adopt measures necessary to protect human, animal, and plant life and health, provided the measures adopted are not unjustifiable, discriminatory against other members, or being used as a disguised form of protectionism.[19] The SPS agreement also allows countries to adopt higher SPS measures than would otherwise be achieved by international standards, guidelines, or recommendations, provided the measures are based on scientific principles and are consistent with the relevant provisions of the SPS Agreement. Through its involvement in the multilateral trading system and its participation in various international standard-setting organizations such as the Codex Alimentarius Commission (Codex), the International Plant Protection Convention (IPPC), and the World Organization for Animal Health (OIE), the United States along with other World Trade Organization (WTO) members play an important role in formulating and shaping global SPS standards. Developing countries occasionally receive technical assistance from the WTO to develop their SPS standards. The United States actively participates in the WTO's standard setting bodies (Codex, IPPC, and OIE); consequently, it indirectly contributes to the improvement of the safety and inspection standards and procedures for goods exported from developing countries.

INSPECTIONS OF FACILITIES, RECALL AUTHORITY, AND ACCESS TO RECORDS

Domestic food processing facilities except those that handle meat, poultry, eggs, and their products must comply with the FDA's regulations. Failure of a domestic food-processing facility to comply with FDA's regulations often carries stiff penalties, which may include fines, litigation, or closure of the facility. As already mentioned in this chapter, while the FDA conducts biennial inspection of domestic food facilities, this is not the same for foreign food processing facilities; the FDA does conduct inspection of foreign food and drug facilities, albeit occasionally. As already discussed, increasingly these foreign inspections are often done in collaboration with foreign governments and foreign food-processing facilities. Foreign-processing facilities may, in some cases, actually refuse to allow the FDA's officials to inspect their facilities. To increase the volume of food imports that are both targeted and inspected, the FDA uses computer-based tools including, but not limited to, the Predictive Risk-Based Evaluation for Dynamic Import Compliance Targeting (PREDICT) program. The program assists the FDA in conducting targeted sampling of food imports, based on the risks associated with the imports and the history of previous violations, and to evaluate their compliance with import regulations.[20] Tools such as PREDICT help the FDA to prevent adulterated, misbranded, or violative imports from entering the country; at the same time, these tools can help facilitate the entry of non-violative imports.

The FDA's regulatory approach relies on voluntary guidelines for most food industries; some argue this is inadequate for ensuring the safety of diverse food supplies. Recall or withdrawal of defective or unsafe food products from the market has often been at the discretion of food facilities; indeed, food facilities often withdraw or recall unsafe food products upon request by the FDA. The FDA has historically not possessed the authority to recall products from the market when firms were unwilling to voluntarily recall or withdraw products. In a new approach to give the FDA more muscle to protect consumers from unsafe products, new proposed policies—including, for example, H.R. 2749 (the Food Safety Enhancement Act), and S. 510 (the Food Safety Modernization Act)—propose that mandatory recall authority be granted to the FDA. This would, proponents argue, enable the agency to conduct recalls if needed, in a timely manner, to protect the public from potential unsafe products in the market. The new proposed regulations would also give the FDA more access authority to production records in emergency situations. There are also other legislative proposals, currently under consideration, that seek to reward producers who continuously maintain best production practices. The proposed policies would allow producers who uphold high standards of production to participate in a voluntary program that would allow for the expedited entry of food imports.

Import Security

Following increased problems encountered with imports in 2006 and 2007, former president George W. Bush issued an executive order establishing an Interagency Working Group on Import Safety. The working group was charged with the task of reviewing import safety problems and making recommendations for actions to resolve the safety problems associated with imported food. The working group came up with 14 recommendations. Recommended approaches included the following:

- Establishing new incentives for importers who follow strong safety practices and demonstrate a good track record;
- Increasing the training of inspectors in foreign countries so they can stop unsafe food products at their borders before they arrive at U.S. ports of entry;
- Working for higher and more uniform standards for high-risk foods and consumer goods; and
- Working to increase penalties for those who violate U.S. import laws.

Based on the report by the Interagency Working Group, the president unveiled a *Food Protection Plan* for the FDA. The plan addressed both imported and domestically produced food. The plan had an objective of increasing the capacity of the FDA to coordinate with other federal agencies, to protect the U.S. food supply chain, to prevent safety problems from arising, to respond effectively if safety problems do arise, and to facilitate communication with the industry and the public.[21]

The action plan developed by the Interagency Working Group contained 50 action steps that provide a road map for improved protection of consumers. It provided a means for enhancing the safety of the high volume of imports in the country. The plan proposed a strategy aimed at risk-based prevention with a verification model that allocates import safety resources based on risks associated with the imports or history of previous violations.[22] It also recommended steps to replace so-called snapshot safety inspections done at the ports of entry with less expensive models that focus on the risks associated with imported products and the history of previous import violation by importers. The new inspection models would increase impacts of inspections by identifying and targeting points with greatest risks and directing resources to these areas. The proposed management approach to safety problems in food imports was designed to prevent contaminated products from reaching consumers. Additional recommendations from the Interagency Working Group on import safety included the following:

- Authorize the FDA to require producers of high-risk foods from certain countries to certify that their products conform to regulations;
- Introduce voluntary certification for foreign manufacturers, to help U.S. inspectors expeditiously clear for importation products from certified importers;
- Provide incentives to importers who uphold higher safety practices for high-risk products;

- Establish information sharing agreements with foreign governments to facilitate the timely exchange of imports and recall-related data;
- Publicize names of certified producers and importers in order to increase transparency, and enlighten consumers and distributors so they are able to make informed decisions on the safety of products; and
- Require the FDA to recall adulterated or contaminated products from the market.

A major historical change in the manner in which the United States conducts business with the world came in the wake of the September 11, 2001, terrorist attacks; largely in response to these events, the United States enacted the 2002 Bioterrorism Act. The act contained key provisions for protecting the U.S. food supply; these included permitting the secretary of health and human services to require the establishment and maintenance of records, registration of food facilities, prior notice of imported shipments of food, and administrative detention of food. These four provisions are discussed below.

Establishment and Maintenance of Records

The 2002 Bioterrorism Act authorizes the secretary of health and human services to require all persons (excluding farms, restaurants, and certain other entities) who manufacture, process, pack, transport, distribute, receive, hold, or import food to establish and maintain records. For non-transporters of food, the records kept must identify the immediate previous source (foreign or domestic) of all food items received (i.e., "one step backward") and the immediate subsequent recipient of the food items released (i.e., "one step forward"). The records to be kept must include details such as the name, address, telephone number, and e-mail address of the firm. Other details, such as the type of food, the brand name of the food, the specific variety of the food, the date the food item was received or released, and the quantity and type of packaging used, must also be kept. Records that can reasonably identify the specific sources of ingredients used in the processing of finished products should also be kept in accordance with the new regulations.[23]

For transporters, records must be kept of the immediate previous source of the food item or immediate subsequent recipient of the food item, where applicable. Transporters also need to keep records of the origin of the food items, destination of the food, the date the food shipment is received, the date the shipment is released, the number of packages, the description of the freight, the route of movement, the time of transportation, and the points through which the food shipment is moved.

The 2002 Bioterrorism Act specifies the period of time for which records must be kept; the period of time for which records must be kept depends upon the shelf life of the food. For food with a high risk of spoilage and food that can undergo significant loss of value or palatability within 60 days, records must be retained for a period of six months. For food items with significant risk of spoilage, loss of value, or loss of palatability after a minimum of 60 days but not exceeding six months, records must be retained for one year. For food featuring a significant risk of spoilage, loss of value, or loss of palatability occurring after 60 months, non-transporters must retain records for a period of two years while transporters or persons keeping records on their behalf must retain the records for a period of one year. Records for animal food (including pet food) must be retained for one year. All records kept must be made available to the FDA inspectors upon request; failure to produce records if and when required may warrant civil action or prosecution in a federal court.[24] Keeping of records is important as it facilitates the ease with which food can be traced back—and, therefore, assists authorities carrying out recalls in a timely manner.

Registration of Food Facilities

The 2002 Bioterrorism Act permits the secretary of health and human services to require registration of all domestic and foreign food facilities that manufacture, process, pack, or hold food for human or animal consumption. All food facilities must register with the FDA. The purpose of registration is to enable the FDA to establish the location and origin of potential bioterrorism incidents or any outbreaks of food-borne illness; registration also allows the FDA to quickly notify facilities that may be affected by any bioterrorism incident or illnesses resulting from intentional or unintentional food contamination. The FDA requires a one-time registration of domestic and foreign food manufacturers or processors, domestic and foreign packers, and domestic and foreign-storage operations. Domestic food facilities are required to register regardless of whether or not their products actually enter interstate commerce. If any information provided during registration of a food facility changes, an updated registration must be provided. If a food is handled by more than one foreign facility (e.g., if a foreign facility processes, packages, or holds food and then sends it to another foreign facility for further manufacturing, processing, packaging, or holding) before being exported to the United States, the second food facility that holds food prior to being exported to the United States must register with the FDA. If a food is handled by more than one foreign food facility, before being sent to the U.S., and the second food facility carries out even seemingly minimal activities (e.g., labeling), both facilities must still register with the FDA. Those exempted from the registration requirements include, but are not limited to, restaurants, retail food establishments, fishing vessels that harvest and transport fish, facilities within the United States that are regulated by the USDA, transport vehicles that serve as food carriers, charitable or nonprofit food facilities, and non-bottled water/drinking water collection and distribution facilities and structures (e.g., municipal water systems).[25] Any entity that fails to register a food facility is liable to civil action or prosecution by the federal government. Food imports from foreign facilities that fail to register with the FDA are subject to refusals or holds.

Prior Notice of Imported Food Shipments

The 2002 Bioterrorism Act requires the FDA to take extra steps to protect the U.S. food supply from potential terrorist attack and other food-safety threats involving the intentional contamination of food. The act requires advanced notice of import shipments destined to the United States. These regulations came into force on December 12, 2003.[26] Under the prior notice requirement, the FDA must be informed, in advance, of any food shipment before it arrives at a U.S. port of entry. This regulation is important as it enables the FDA to review and assess shipment-related information before the food shipments actually arrive into ports of entry; in addition, it enables the FDA to more effectively deploy its limited inspection resources while increasing its ability to intercept contaminated products before they enter the country. The regulation affects the following:

- U.S. and foreign entities involved in cross-border transportation of food through rail, trucks, ship, and air;
- Entities, domestic and foreign, that import food into the United States;
- Foreign entities that export food to the United States;
- U.S. and foreign food manufacturers and growers; and
- U.S. and foreign filers and brokers.

For the purpose of prior notice, the FDA defines what constitutes food: articles used for food or drink for humans or animals; chewing gum; and articles used as components in food, drinks, or chewing gum. Interestingly, the FDA's definition of food excludes food contact materials as well as pesticides. There are some exceptions to the application of the prior-notice requirements, and these exceptions have been extended to food imported for personal use, storage, or distribution in the United States (e.g., gifts) and food samples intended for trade, quality assurance/quality control, and market research. Exceptions have also been given to food trans-shipped through the United States to other countries, food shipments intended for future export, and food intended for use in Foreign Trade Zones. Prior notice is not required for food that is under the exclusive jurisdiction of the USDA as defined in the Federal Meat Inspection Act, the Poultry Products Inspection Act, and the Egg Products Inspection Act.

Electronic submission of prior notice related information is required before food shipments arrive at any U.S. port of entry; the FDA must receive and confirm the notification within five days unless the food is arriving by international mail. The deadlines for submitting prior notice information vary depending on the mode of transportation. For food shipments arriving by road, the FDA must be notified at least two hours before arrival at a U.S. port; for food shipments arriving by rail and air, notification must be submitted at least four hours before arrival; and for shipments arriving by water, notification must be submitted at least eight hours before arrival at a U.S. port of entry.[27] Notifications for food sent by mail must be made before the food is sent.

Administrative Detention of Food

The 2002 Bioterrorism Act authorizes the FDA to take steps necessary to protect the public from threats or actual terrorist attack on the U.S. food supply. The act authorizes any qualified FDA official to order the detention of any article of food deemed to have the potential to cause serious or adverse health consequence or death to humans or animals. This particular regulation came into effect on June 12, 2002, immediately following the enactment of the 2002 Bioterrorism Act. The administrative detention procedure was added to the 2002 Bioterrorism Act as a precautionary measure to enhance the safety of the U.S. food supply. The act also called upon the FDA to develop regulations on how to deal with, in an expedited manner, enforcement actions on perishable products which are subject to detention orders. Consequently, the FDA issued a final rule covering procedures on how the FDA conducts detention, the procedures for appealing against detention orders, and expedited procedures for handling detention on perishable food items.

The FDA may issue a detention order if it has credible evidence or information indicating that the article of food presents serious or adverse health consequence or death to human or animal. As with prior notice, foods under the exclusive jurisdiction of the USDA are not subject to the FDA's detention order rules. The detention order must be approved by the director of the FDA district or any senior official located where the food item has been detained. The detention order issued should include, among other things, the detention order number, the hour and date of the detention, the identification of the detained article of food, the detention period, the reason for detention, the name of the authorized FDA official who orders and approves the detention, the location of the detained article of food, and the conditions under which the detained food is held. Under the detention order rule, an article of food cannot be detained for more than 30 days. Regulations also stipulate that detained articles of food must be held at a secure location and under conditions specified in the FDA's detention order. Movement of food which is under detention order without authorization from the FDA (or before the detention order expires) is prohibited; therefore, an article of food that is under detention may not be delivered to another individual. For a detained article of food to be moved (e.g., for the purpose of preserving the integrity or the quality of the food, for re-labeling, for moving it to a secure facility, etc.), a specific request for modification of the detention order must be made. When the FDA initiates seizure actions against perishable products, it provides for a facilitated process for handling such perishable food products. The FDA also provides procedures by which importers or any interest groups can appeal for detentions orders imposed against their imports.

IMPORTATION OF ANIMAL AND PLANT SPECIES: U.S. AND EU APPROACHES

Scholars of food and agriculture security should note that both animal and plant species imported from other countries can be carriers of diseases into the importing country. This can have devastating effects on the countries whose major economic activity is agriculture; indeed, it can actually affect countries' capacity to produce food and, therefore, their food security. Various countries have developed and implemented means by which to protect themselves from the importation of foreign animal and plant diseases. Some of these systems are reviewed in this section.

U.S. Approach to Managing Imports of Animal and Plant Species

In the United States, a number of agencies have been involved in the regulation of the importation of animals that are capable of causing diseases in humans (e.g., dogs, cats, turtles, and certain species of birds).[28] USDA, in particular, regulates plants and animal species that are used as food, but several agencies (described below) are involved. Agriculture is a major economic activity in the United States; an outbreak of a so-called foreign animal disease in the United States could have devastating effects on the health and lives of animals, the quantity and quality of the U.S. food supply, and the nation's ability to sustain international trade in animal and animal products.

There are two vital principles that the United States employs in excluding exotic animal diseases; these include:

- Exclusion to prevent transmission of disease-causing agents through direct or indirect contact of animal disease or contact with a vector, and
- Enforcement of regulations to prevent the introduction of foreign animal diseases.

The United States has employed the exclusion principle, which has helped prevent the entry, establishment, and spread of exotic animal diseases in the country. Inspections of imported animal species in the United States are conducted by different federal agencies. These agencies work together to ensure efficiency in protecting the country from foreign animal diseases. The following federal agencies, in collaboration with each other,

Import Security

participate in the inspection of imported plant and animal species and their products:

- The Agricultural Marketing Service (AMS) regulates the commercial importation of shell eggs; AMS has offices at strategic locations in the country, which enhance its ability to regulate these imports.
- Customs and Border Protection (CBP), an agency under the Department of Homeland Security (DHS), regulates commercial and noncommercial shipments at U.S. ports of entry. The CBP has agricultural specialists located at U.S. ports of entry; agricultural specialists regulate animal products by conducting identification and classification of imports, thereby determining if entry requirements are met. The CBP agricultural specialists review documentation accompanying imports to ensure that they are compliant, and the CBP is authorized to take any regulatory action according to regulations developed by APHIS, an agency within the USDA. CBP agricultural specialists work in consultation with local USDA officers to address concerns arising during importation.
- The Fish and Wildlife Service (FWS) is nested in the Department of the Interior; it regulates the following: all nonfarm animals including birds, animal by-products (e.g., pelts' coats, skins, game, trophies, ivory products, and tortoise shell products), the eggs of endangered or threatened birds, and abandoned pets.
- The FDA inspectors work in collaboration with the CBP to regulate drugs, medication, and animal feed; commercial importation of food products; wild fowl meat; and wild ruminant meat.
- The USDA FSIS regulates meat and poultry products offered for both importation and for export. The FSIS often provides certification to exporters for exporting meat and meat products from the United States to other countries. FSIS regulates the importation of meat and meat products to ensure that they are safe, wholesome, and fit for human consumption. However, as indicated above, wild ruminants and fowl are regulated by the FDA. Foreign countries interested in exporting meat and meat products to the U.S. are often required to demonstrate that their inspection standards are equivalent to those set by the FSIS. After a foreign country demonstrates equivalency of their standards to U.S. standards, they obtain FSIS approval. The foreign country is then allowed to issue certificates for the commercial importation of meat and meat products into the United States. The FSIS also inspects and samples imported meat and meat products to ensure that they meet APHIS regulations (designed to protect the country from exotic plant and animal diseases).
- The U.S. Public Health Service (USPHS), housed in HHS, works with inspectors located at the ports of entry to regulate: dogs, cats, and monkeys (nonhuman primates); leather brushes made from hair and bristles; and human tissues, serum, blood, secretions, and excretions.
- USDA's APHIS officials evaluate imports of plants and animals. In cases where animals, plants, or their products fail to meet the requirements for importation, APHIS stipulates procedures to be followed by inspectors in handling the products. These may include the immediate exportation of the products, immediate destruction of the products under supervision of APHIS or CBP officials, or shipment to an approved establishment (e.g., one approved to receive and process restricted imported animal by-products).

Food and agriculture security officials have been focused on plant diseases for years. This photograph depicts plant inspection maintained by the USDA between Mexico and the United States in the 1930s; shoppers returning from Mexico are being required to open their packages for inspection. June 1937 photograph by Dorothea Lange. (Library of Congress)

APHIS plays an especially important role in facilitating safe international trade; besides monitoring the health of animals, animal products, and biologics offered for import and export, APHIS also regulates imports and exports of plant and plant products. APHIS, through its Plant Protection and Quarantine (PPQ) activities, regulates the importation of plants and plant products as provided for in the Plant Protection Act. The PPQ monitors the movement of high-risk plant materials to guard U.S. agriculture and natural resources against risks associated with importation of exotic plant pests, diseases, and noxious weeds. The PPQ protects the U.S. agriculture and natural resources through various means:

- By issuing import permits to entities who seek to import certain plants, plants products, or soil into the United States, those who seek to use the United States or its ports as transit points for certain plants and plant products, those who seek to import plant pests or biological-control organisms into the United States and those who seek to move plant pests or biological-control organisms between states in the United States;
- By conducting identification of plant pests and weeds of regulatory concern;
- By conducting pest-detection programs, which target harmful or economically significant plant pests and weeds;

- By cooperating with state departments of agriculture and local agencies to respond to introductions of exotic plant pests, plant diseases, and noxious weeds in order to eradicate, suppress, or contain them.

In addition to protecting the country from introduction of exotic plant pests, plant diseases, and noxious weeds through importation of plants, APHIS also protects the country from importation of plants pests and diseases by regulating the use of wood packaging material. Standards for wood packaging materials that are used in international trade were approved on March 15, 2002, by the International Plant Protection Convention (IPPC). The IPPC calls for wood packaging materials used in international trade to be either heat treated or fumigated with methyl bromide.[29]

The European Union's Approach to Managing Imports of Animal and Plant Species

The European Union's (EU's) import regulations on animals govern the introduction of animals into the EU from third countries. The EU has specific minimum animal-health requirements. These requirements are laid down under Council Directive 91/496/EEC, which seeks to harmonize import regulations for the various EU member countries by establishing minimum health conditions for importing animals into the EU. Harmonization ensures that the same principles for importation of animals are applied in all EU member states. This ensures that animals that carry infectious diseases that are dangerous to humans and animals are not allowed into EU territories.[30] EU Directive 2004/68/EC explains the basis of animal-health principles and the requirements that third countries must fulfill in order to be allowed to export animals to the EU. The EU takes into consideration the following parameters:

- Relevant legislation in the third country;
- The health status of the third country;
- Membership of the third country in the World Organization for Animal Health (OIE);
- The regularity and rapidity of information on infectious animal diseases provided by the third country to the European Commission and the OIE;
- The country's animal-health requirements for the production, manufacture, handling, storage, and dispatch of products of animal origin;
- The country's rules regarding the prevention and control of animal diseases; and
- The organization, structure, competence, and power of the country's veterinary services.

EU Directive 2004/68/EC elaborates additional, specific conditions regarding certain infectious diseases; the conditions listed must be met by third countries if they are to be permitted to trade with EU member states.[31] EU Directive 90/675/EEC prohibits entry into its territories, of animals which, upon examination, are found to have originated from third countries, territories, or part of a territory of a third country, which is not part of the list of countries from which the species of animals are to be imported, or countries that are prohibited from exporting certain animal species to the EU. Other prohibitions apply to animals which do not conform to the requirements under the EU import regulations, animals suffering or suspected of suffering from or infected by a contagious disease or a disease that presents significant risk to the health of human or other animals, animals from third countries that have not complied with EU requirements, animals that are not in a fit state to continue their journey, and animals accompanied by insufficient or unsatisfactory veterinary documents (e.g., certificates).

EU Directive 2004/68/EC lays down specific requirements that are to be met by EU border inspection posts that are situated at major ports of entry to facilitate the inspection of animal imports into the EU. The EU has laid down several import regulations dealing with importation of animal and animal products. The regulations—in the form of "Council Directives," address importation of animals and animal products into the EU.

With respect to the importation of plants and plant species, the EU requires certain plants, plant products, and items (which are listed under Part B of Annex V of Directive 2000/29/EC) be accompanied by a phytosanitary certificate issued by the national plant protection organization of the country of origin. Once the imports enter the EU, the phytosanitary certificates for the imported plants, plant products, or objects listed under Directive 2000/29/EC Part A Annex V are, in some cases, replaced by a plant passport. Phytosanitary certificates issued in countries where the imported plants, plant products, and other items originate should indicate that the plant or plant products have undergone appropriate inspections, are free from harmful organisms and pests, and conform to the phytosanitary regulations of the importing country. Other plant objects covered under Directive 2000/29/EC Part A Annex V include rough wood products, poles and stakes, wood meant for fuel, wood chips and particles, wood wastes and scraps, packing cases and crates, and wood pallets and other load boards.

The EU has also laid down the types of inspections that plants, plant products, and other imported items are subjected to upon entry into the EU from third countries.[32] Inspections conducted include documentary review, identity checks, and physical health examination of the imported plants or plant materials in order to ensure compliance with EU import regulations. Documentary review involves verification of documents accompanying imports (including the phytosanitary certificate); the certificates must be issued by an appropriate IPPC-recognized authority in the exporting country or country of reexportation. Identity checks involve verification that the consignment offered for import corresponds to the plants or plant products detailed in the certificate. Plant health checks consist of verification that the imported plants or plant products are free from harmful plant organisms.

The phytosanitary certificate accompanying plants, plant products, or items imported into the EU include, but are not limited to, the following:

- The name and address of the exporter as well as the consignee;
- The plant protection organization of the country of origin;
- The declared point of entry into the EU;
- The botanical names of plants;
- A certification that the consignment has not been subjected to risks of infestation or infection on the country of origin or country of reexport;
- A declaration of the treatment condition, disinfestations, or disinfection treatment which the imported material underwent (e.g., the kind of treatment administered, the chemical or active ingredient used, the duration of treatment, the temperature of treatment, the concentration of the chemicals used, etc.); and
- A stamp placed on the material, signed and dated by an authorized officer, indicating that the imported material has undergone satisfactory treatment for pests and parasites.

Role of IPPC Standards Regarding Import Security

Phytosanitary measures adopted by the United States, EU, and other countries ought to be in accordance with applicable IPPC standards. Article VII of the IPPC allows importing countries to prescribe and adopt phytosanitary measures concerning the importation of plants, plant products and other regulated articles (including, for example, inspection, prohibition on importation, and treatment); refuse entry (or detain or require treatment, destruction, or removal) of plants, plant products, and other regulated articles that do not comply with the phytosanitary measures prescribed and adopted by the importing country; prohibit or restrict the movement of regulated pests into their territories; and prohibit or restrict the movement of biological control agents and other organisms of biological concern claimed to be beneficial into their territories.

Article VII of the IPPC discourages countries from taking measures that would restrict international trade unless such measures are made by phytosanitary considerations and are technically justified or based on science. For the purpose of transparency, the IPPC requires WTO members to be proactive in publishing and transmitting phytosanitary requirements, restrictions, and prohibitions to other trading members if the measures adopted may directly affect trade.

Article VIII of the IPPC encourages WTO members to cooperate with one another through the exchange of information on plant pests, particularly reporting of the occurrence, outbreak, or spread of pests that may be of immediate or potential danger to the importing country. Countries are also encouraged to participate in particular campaigns for combating pests and diseases that may seriously threaten agriculture. Cooperation and sharing of technical and biological information is also encouraged when necessary for conducting import pest risk analyses.[33] Articles IX, X, and XI encourage WTO member countries to participate in regional as well as international plant protection organizations, and to participate in the developing of standards. WTO members are encouraged to settle, through bilateral consultations, trade disputes that arise as a result of prohibitions or restrictions on the imports of plants, plant products, or other regulated articles. If disputes cannot be resolved through consultation, Article XIII encourages countries concerned to request the Director-General of the Food and Agriculture Organization (FAO) of the United Nations to appoint a committee of experts to consider the question in dispute, in accordance with relevant rules and procedures. The established committee, to include representatives from the parties involved in the dispute, hears the case and prepares a report on the technical aspects of the dispute with the aim of resolving the dispute. The Director-General then transmits the report to the parties in dispute and may, upon request, transmit the report to a competent body of international organizations responsible for resolving disputes. While the recommendations of the committee are not binding in character, the concerned parties shall accept the recommendations as the basis for renewed consideration by the parties concerned.[34]

CONCLUSION

In the United States and elsewhere, import security plays a key role in food and agriculture security policy. Laws such as the 2002 Bioterrorism Act in the United States, multilateral standard-setting bodies such as the IPPC, and innovative collaborations (e.g., officials from multiple governments working together) greatly influence import security today. Food and agriculture security professionals evaluate what ought to be done to ensure that imported food, animals, and plants do not threaten food safety, agricultural biosecurity, and the capacity of a country to be agriculturally productive. In today's globalized society, where international trade is valued, thoughtful solutions are needed to maintain trade while protecting the safety and security of the food and agriculture sector.

NOTES

1. The estimates are from the year 1999 and earlier; it should be noted that these figures might be higher at present. The data is obtained from surveillance of food-borne illness.CDC, "Food-Related Illness and Deaths in the United States," National Center for Infectious Diseases; the Centers for Disease Control and Prevention, http://www.cdc.gov/ncidod/EID/vol5no5/mead.htm.

2. Committee on Energy and Commerce, Subcommittee on Health, *Testimony of Rep. Pallone,* in Hearing on Weaknesses Placing Americans at Risk, September 26, 2007.

3. In addition to the pet-food incident, and as chapter 4 alluded, melamine was also responsible for the deaths of 6 infants, 30,000 illnesses, and hospitalization of 50,000 infants in China after the chemical was used in infant formula. Food and Drug Administration, "Transcripts: FDA Press Conference on Pet Food Recall," United States Department of Health and Human Services, http://www.fda.gov/oc/opacom/hottopics/petfood/transcript040507.pdf.

4. Gardiner Harris, "U.S. Identifies Tainted Heparin in 11 Countries," *New York Times,* http://www.nytimes.com/2008/04/22/health/policy/22fda.html.

5. G. S. Becker, "U.S. Food and Agricultural Imports: Safeguards and Selected Issues" (Congressional Research Service, 2009).

6. U.S. Food and Drug Administration, "Federal Food, Drug, and Cosmetic Act," ed. Department of Health And Human Services (Department of Health And Human Services).

7. Section 801 21 U.S.C 381: Protection Against Adulteration of Food, "Title III—Protecting Safety and Security of Food and Drug Supply; the Public Health Security and Bioterrorism Preparedness and Response Act Section 801 21 U.S.C 381: Protection against Adulteration of Food," ed. Department of Health and Human Services; Food and Drug Administration (Code of Federal Regulations 2002).

8. FDA, "Part 110 Current Good Manufacturing Practice in Manufacturing, Packing, or Holding Human Food," Department of Health and Human Services, http://www.accessdata.fda.gov/scripts/cdrh/cfdocs/cfcfr/CFRSearch.cfm.

9. *Public Health Security and Bioterrorism Preparedness and Response Act,* 107–188.

10. G. S. Becker, "U.S. Food and Agricultural Imports: Safeguards and Selected Issues."

11. F D &C Act, "Imports and Exports," in *21 USC Chapter VIII,* ed. Department of Health and Human Services (U.S. Code: Food and Drug Administration).

12. G. S. Becker, "U.S. Food and Agricultural Imports: Safeguards and Selected Issues."

13. House Energy and Commerce Committee's Oversight and Investigations Subcommittee, *Testimony of Cross,* House Energy and Commerce Committee's Oversight and Investigations Subcommittee on the FDA Foreign Drug Inspection Program: Weaknesses Place Americans at Risk, April 22, 2008.

14. G. S. Becker, "U.S. Food and Agricultural Imports: Safeguards and Selected Issues."

15. C. MacLeod, "FDA Opens Office in China," *USA Today,* 2008.

16. Food and Drug Administration, "HHS Preparing to Open FDA Offices in China, India, Europe, and Latin America This Year," in *HHS News Release* (U.S. Department of Health and Human Services, 2008).

17. Dezan Shira & Associates, "FDA Opens Offices in Delhi, Mumbai," in *India Briefing* (2009).

18. Section 801 21 U.S.C 381: Protection Against Adulteration of Food, "Title III—Protecting Safety and Security of Food and Drug Supply; the Public Health Security and Bioterrorism Preparedness and Response Act Section 801 21 U.S.C 381: Protection against Adulteration of Food."

19. Article 2 of the WTO SPS Agreement, "Article 2 of the SPS Agreement," in *The Key Provisions of the Agreement,* ed. World Trade Organization (The World Trade Organization).

20. GAO, "Agencies Need to Address Gaps in Enforcement and Collaboration to Enhance Safety of Imported Food," in *Food Safety* (Report to Congressional Committees, 2009).

21. Interagency Working Group on Import Safety, "The Interagency Working Group on Import Safety Action Plan for Import Safety: A Roadmap for Continual Improvement" (Department of Health and Human Services, Department of State, Department of Treasury, Department of Justice, Department of Agriculture, Department of Commerce, Department of Transportation, Department of Homeland Security, Office of Management and Budget, United States Trade Representative, Environmental Protection Agency and Consumer Product Safety Commission., 2007).

22. Ibid.

23. Section 306 21 U.S.C 350c: Prior Notice of Imported Food Shipments, "Title III—Protecting Safety and Security of Food and Drug Supply; the Public Health Security and Bioterrorism Preparedness and Response Act of 2002: Section 306 21 Usc 350c: Prior Notice of Imported Food Shipments," in *Protecting the United States From Bioterrorism,* ed. Department of Health and Human Services; Food and Drug Administration (Code of Federal Regulations 2002).

24. Ibid.

25. Section 415 21 U.S.C 350d: Registration of Food Facilities, "Title III—Protecting Safety and Security of Food and Drug Supply; the Public Health Security and Bioterrorism Preparedness and Response Act of 2002: Section 415 21 Usc 350d: Registration of Food Facilities," ed. Department of Health and Human Services; Food and Drug Administration (Code of Federal Regulations 2002).

26. FDA Prior Notice Regulation, "Final Rule—Prior Notice of Imported Food under the Public Health Security and Bioterrorism Preparedness and Response Act of 2002 (68 Fr 58975)," in *21 CFR 110.310,* ed. Department of Health and Human Services; Food and Drug Administration (Federal Register 2002).

27. Section 306 21 U.S.C 350c: Prior Notice of Imported Food Shipments, "Title III—Protecting Safety and Security of Food and Drug Supply; the Public Health Security and Bioterrorism Preparedness and Response Act of 2002: Section 306 21 Usc 350c: Prior Notice of Imported Food Shipments."

28. CDC, "Importing Animals (Including Pets) and Animal Products," Centers for Disease Control and Prevention, http://www.cdc.gov/animal importation/.

29. USDA PPQ, "Animal and Plant Health Inspection Service: Plant Health," United States Department of Agriculture; Animal and Plant Health Inspection Service, http://www.aphis.usda.gov/plant_health/.

30. European Commission, "31991l0496 Council Directive 91/496/Eec," http://eur-lex.europa.eu/LexUriServ/LexUriServ.do?uri=CELEX:31991L0496:EN:HTML.

31. Ibid.

32. Directive 2009/29/EC Part B Annex V, "Harmful Organisms: Third Country Imports-Documents," http://ec.europa.eu/food/plant/organisms/imports/index_en.htm.

33. International Plant Protection Convention, "Article VII," ed. FAO (1997).

34. International Plant Protection Convention, "The Convention Text," ed. the 29th Session of FAO Conference (1997).

BIBLIOGRAPHY

Article 2 of the WTO SPS Agreement. "Article 2 of the SPS Agreement." In *The Key Provisions of the Agreement*, ed. World Trade Organization: The World Trade Organization.

Becker, G. S. "U.S. Food and Agricultural Imports: Safeguards and Selected Issues." Congressional Research Service, 2009.

CDC. "Food-Related Illness and Deaths in the United States." National Center for Infectious Diseases; the Centers for Disease Control and Prevention. http://www.cdc.gov/ncidod/EID/vol5no5/mead.htm.

CDC. "Importing Animals (Including Pets) and Animal Products." Centers for Disease Control and Prevention. http://www.cdc.gov/animalimportation/.

Committee on Energy and Commerce, Subcommittee on Health. *Testimony of Rep. Pallone*. Hearing on Weaknesses Placing Americans at Risk, September 26, 2007.

Dezan Shira & Associates. "FDA Opens Offices in Delhi, Mumbai." In *India Briefing*, 2009.

Directive 2009/29/EC Part B Annex V. "Harmful Organisms: Third Country Imports-Documents." http://ec.europa.eu/food/plant/organisms/imports/index_en.htm.

European Commission. "31991l0496 Council Directive 91/496/Eec." http://eur-lex.europa.eu/LexUriServ/LexUriServ.do?uri=CELEX:31991L0496:EN:HTML.

FDA. "HHS Preparing to Open FDA Offices in China, India, Europe, and Latin America This Year," In *HHS News Release:* U.S. Department of Health and Human Services, 2008.

FDA. "Part 110 Current Good Manufacturing Practice in Manufacturing, Packing, or Holding Human Food." Department of Health and Human Services. http://www.accessdata.fda.gov/scripts/cdrh/cfdocs/cfcfr/CFRSearch.cfm.

FDA. "Transcripts: FDA Press Conference on Pet Food Recall." United States Department of Health and Human Services. http://www.fda.gov/oc/opacom/hottopics/petfood/transcript040507.pdf.

FDA Prior Notice Regulation. "Final Rule—Prior Notice of Imported Food under the Public Health Security and Bioterrorism Preparedness and Response Act of 2002 (68 Fr 58975)." In *21 CFR 110.310*, ed. Department of Health and Human Services; Food and Drug Administration. Federal Register, 2002.

F D & C Act. "Imports and Exports." In *21 USC Chapter VIII*, ed. Department of Health and Human Services. U.S. Code: Food and Drug Administration.

GAO. "Agencies Need to Address Gaps in Enforcement and Collaboration to Enhance Safety of Imported Food." In *Food Safety:* Report to Congressional Committees, 2009.

Harris, Gardiner. "U.S. Identifies Tainted Heparin in 11 Countries." *New York Times*. http://www.nytimes.com/2008/04/22/health/policy/22fda.html.

House Energy and Commerce Committee's Oversight and Investigations Subcommittee. *Testimony of Cross*. House Energy and Commerce Committee's Oversight and Investigations Subcommittee on the FDA Foreign Drug Inspection Program: Weaknesses Place Americans at Risk, April 22, 2008.

Interagency Working Group on Import Safety. "The Interagency Working Group on Import Safety Action Plan for Import Safety: A Roadmap for Continual

Improvement." Department of Health and Human Services, Department of State, Department of Treasury, Department of Justice, Department of Agriculture, Department of Commerce, Department of Transportation, Department of Homeland Security, Office of Management and Budget, United States Trade Representative, Environmental Protection Agency and Consumer Product Safety Commission, 2007.

International Plant Protection Convention. "Article VII," ed. FAO, 1997.

International Plant Protection Convention. "The Convention Text," ed. the 29th Session of FAO Conference 1997.

MacLeod. C. "FDA Opens Office in China." *USA Today,* 2008.

Public Health Security and Bioterrorism Preparedness and Response Act. 107–188.

Section 306 21 U.S.C 350c: Prior Notice of Imported Food Shipments. "Title III—Protecting Safety and Security of Food and Drug Supply; the Public Health Security and Bioterrorism Preparedness and Response Act of 2002: Section 306 21 Usc 350c: Prior Notice of Imported Food Shipments." In *Protecting the United States From Bioterrorism,* ed. Department of Health and Human Services; Food and Drug Administration. Code of Federal Regulations, 2002.

Section 415 21 U.S.C 350d: Registration of Food Facilities. "Title III—Protecting Safety and Security of Food and Drug Supply; the Public Health Security and Bioterrorism Preparedness and Response Act of 2002: Section 415 21 Usc 350d: Registration of Food Facilities," ed. Department of Health and Human Services; Food and Drug Administration. Code of Federal Regulations, 2002.

Section 801 21 U.S.C 381: Protection Against Adulteration of Food. "Title III—Protecting Safety and Security of Food and Drug Supply; the Public Health Security and Bioterrorism Preparedness and Response Act Section 801 21 U.S.C 381: Protection against Adulteration of Food," ed. Department of Health and Human Services; Food and Drug Administration. Code of Federal Regulations, 2002.

U.S. Food and Drug Administration. "Federal Food, Drug, and Cosmetic Act," ed. Department of Health And Human Services: Department of Health And Human Services.

USDA PPQ. "Animal and Plant Health Inspection Service: Plant Health." United States Department of Agriculture; Animal and Plant Health Inspection Service. http://www.aphis.usda.gov/plant_health/.

CHAPTER 6

Managing Human and Animal-Health Threats: Additional Lessons from the 19th-century Trading World

Justin Kastner

Chapter 2 provided a historical analysis of one of the dilemmas faced by food and agriculture security thought leaders in the 19th-century, transatlantic trading world. This dilemma was experienced, in particular, by Great Britain as its government contemplated what trade policies and regulatory arrangements ought to be implemented to both (a) ensure the ongoing operation of the transatlantic trade in food (including the importation of live cattle from the United States) and (b) guard against the importation of animal diseases (i.e., contagious bovine pleuro-pneumonia). Several lessons emerged from this instructive episode in history; these lessons pointed to the influence of economic considerations, the valuable advent of new technologies, the necessity for robust risk-management practices, the importance of bilateral cooperation, and the reminder that food and agriculture security officials are real human beings who often must make decisions with incomplete and still-unfolding scientific information.

The 19th-century trading world offers sundry other lessons for today's—and tomorrow's—food and agriculture security officials. In keeping with the historical theme embodied in this book, this chapter focuses on two additional 19th-century episodes involving international trade, security, and the agricultural and food system. The first relates to a human health (i.e., food safety) risk posed by a parasite in pork products, and the second relates to an animal health concern—namely, the disease rinderpest.

HUMAN HEALTH: TRICHINOSIS AND THE TRANSATLANTIC PORK TRADE

As chapter 2 detailed, the diagnosis of contagious bovine pleuro-pneumonia among U.S. cattle exported to Great Britain, the decision by the British government to extend its immediate-slaughter policy to American cattle imports, and the resultant flurry of British and American diplomatic and regulatory action served to make 1879 an eventful year for the transatlantic trading world. But just as food and agriculture security officials began to tackle the pleuro-pneumonia issue, 1879 served up more health-related problems in the agricultural and food trade. The discovery of classical swine fever, or hog cholera, in imported American pigs and of foot and mouth disease (FMD) in American sheep prompted Great Britain's Privy Council to require the immediate slaughter of these two species, too. By May 1879, U.S. cattle, sheep, and swine were all subject to the policy of immediate slaughter at British ports of entry.[1]

The slaughter of pigs at the ports of entry offered an opportunity for the Privy Council to search for and discover yet another problem—one regarding food safety and human health. A year earlier, the London *Times* had reported the presence of *Trichina spiralis*, the parasite responsible for the human ailment trichinosis, in American hams.[2] This report had prompted European consumers, including some Britons, to question the safety of eating U.S. pork.[3] However, for the time being, the importation into Britain of U.S. pigs, ham, and bacon continued; not until May 1879, after the Privy Council had ordered the immediate slaughter (at ports of entry) of American pigs, would British scrutiny of American pig flesh have the opportunity to intensify. As pigs were slaughtered at ports such as Liverpool, carcasses were microscopically examined to ascertain the extent to which the *Trichina* parasite was present. One study found three infected samples out of a total of 279, and feeding trials proved that so-called trichinized American pork was capable of transmitting the parasite to humans. However, after discussing the matter with Liverpool's medical health officers, the Privy Council decided against restrictions on American pork. In their decision, the Privy Council cited enforcement problems. Furthermore, most countries in 1879 had *Trichina*-infected pigs, and any import prohibition would have to be applied to all countries—a move that was deemed imprudent.[4] This view was largely rooted in Great Britain's economic reliance on American bacon and ham; not unlike the considerations in operation with the U.S. cattle and pleuro-pneumonia issue, economic dependence on food imports was a major objection to any contemplated trade restrictions on U.S. pork.

On May 29, 1879, Britain's government was asked about the trichinosis risk faced by Britons consuming American pork. The Duke of Richmond, Lord President of the Privy Council, acknowledged the human health risk, and he assured his colleagues in the House of Lords that he would continue to study the matter. In the meantime, Richmond urged consumers to thoroughly cook their pork.[5] While Britain continued to resist any restrictions on the importation of American pork, trichinosis would continue to embarrass U.S. pork exporters and benefit British swine producers. Subsequent outbreaks in Britain and reports by British diplomats also served to stigmatize American pork and prompted a number of continental European countries to adopt bans on U.S. pork imports.[6] Cultural differences between Britain and continental Europe would affect the way the risk of trichinosis was managed; British consumers, unlike German pig-eaters, preferred cooked pork to raw.

Background

By the beginning of 1880, both food safety and animal disease risks were on the minds of U.S. food and agriculture security officials. Indeed, just as the U.S. Treasury Cattle Commission began its regulatory work regarding the troublesome pleuro-pneumonia issue (discussed in chapter 2), the U.S. government was reminded of an equally troublesome trade issue related to food safety. Trichinosis had first embarrassed U.S. pork exporters in 1878 (when *Trichina spiralis* was discovered in American hams) and then 1879 witnessed the first ban—by southern European countries—on the importation of American pork products.[7] In February 1880, Spain became concerned and also excluded all American pork products. The prohibition, however, proved to be economically painful for consumers, and American pork was soon reinstated subject to microscopic inspection.[8] Initially, southern Europe's trade restrictions did little more than embarrass the American trade, for the three largest importers of American agricultural products—namely, Great Britain, France, and Germany—continued to accept U.S. pork.[9]

Nevertheless, the perceived threat of trichinosis had begun to inch its way into northern Europe and even Britain. During 1880, British food-safety concerns emerged on account of a parasitic disease outbreak aboard the English reformatory school-ship *Cornwall*.[10] Forty-three boys on board the *Cornwall* had become ill and American salted pork was initially blamed. Postmortem investigations later revealed a nematode other than the *Trichina* parasite, and a British expert argued in April 1880 that contaminated water, not American meat, was the likely culprit.[11] While American pork was, for the time being, spared further embarrassment, British food-safety concerns were revived two months later when a fatal food-borne disease outbreak was traced back to American hams.[12] In June 1880, America's food-safety reputation further eroded as Germany banned American ground pork and sausage.[13]

By 1881, the trichinosis issue had made its way to the forefront of American-British trade relations. The previous December, the British consul in Philadelphia, George Crump, had composed a report that served to complicate the entire U.S. pork controversy. His report, widely published in the February 19, 1881, issue of the London *Times* and regularly cited by diplomats, pointed to rampant swine mortalities occurring on account of hog cholera; Crump's report claimed that 700,000 pigs had died in the state of Illinois alone. Crump's report also noted the tremendous volumes of pork being shipped yearly from the United States to Britain, and then provided some alarming descriptions of the human illness, trichinosis, tied to the parasite *Trichina spiralis*.[14] Most notably, Crump described in gruesome detail an alleged case of trichinosis reported in Kansas.[15] The report was somewhat confusing as it intimated a link between two different disease issues (i.e., hog cholera and trichinosis). Publication of Crump's report in the *Times* had been prompted by a question raised in the House of Commons in February 1881. On February 17, Sir James Paget, Queen Victoria's sergeant-surgeon and the very person who 40 years earlier had discovered the *Trichina* parasite,[16] had asked the president of the Board of Trade about Crump's report. The London *Times* promptly published it.[17]

Crump's report became public shortly before U.S. President Rutherford B. Hayes left and President James Garfield entered the White House.[18] The outgoing and incoming secretaries of state, William M. Evarts and James G. Blaine, respectively, were irate. On March 7, Secretary Evarts told Sir Edward Thornton, the British minister in Washington, D.C., that Crump's description of a hog cholera epidemic did not square with state and federal surveillance information and was to be regarded as false.[19] Thornton replied to Secretary Evarts, writing that Crump's report was based on reliable information.[20] Two days later, Secretary Blaine took over for Evarts. Attaching explanatory telegrams from the Merchants' Exchange of St. Louis and the Cincinnati Chamber of Commerce, Secretary Blaine suggested to Thornton that the good faith of Crump had been taken advantage of by people seeking to disrupt international commerce. Secretary Blaine, like his predecessor, wanted the British government to publicly refute the Crump report.[21] On March 10, however, Thornton demonstrated to Secretary Blaine that Crump's report was actually based on information from the Illinois state government. While Crump's 700,000 figure might have been an exaggeration, hog cholera was clearly a problem—14 percent of the state's hogs had recently died from the disease.[22] The absence of a visibly effective regulatory system served to embarrass U.S. agriculturalists. Thornton told Secretary Blaine that the lack of robust animal-disease regulations in America meant that the British government had to gather through its various consuls (e.g., George Crump) disease information from a hodgepodge of state and federal sources.[23]

Secretary Blaine wrote to Mr. J. R. Lowell, the new U.S. minister in London, complaining that Mr. Crump had unnecessarily caused panic amongst British consumers.[24] Indeed, the Crump report was confounding in that it had implied a link between trichinosis and hog cholera, two entirely unrelated diseases.[25] As already explained in this chapter, hog cholera (also termed classical swine fever) was the disease that had prompted the Privy Council two years earlier to extend its immediate-slaughter order to American hogs imported into Britain. While worthy of the immediate-slaughter order, hog cholera was of only animal health significance, and had no bearing on trichinosis—an issue of food safety and human health. Secretary Blaine understood this difference, but he lamented that the general public would have a difficult time separating the two.[26] Blaine was right; Crump's report, including his account of trichinosis in Kansas (which, incidentally, was never confirmed), served to stigmatize U.S. pork and spawn more restrictions across Europe.[27] On the very day the Crump report appeared in the London *Times*, France banned American pig products (except lard and grease) and used Crump's report to justify the restriction.[28]

Economic Considerations and Regulatory Responses

Secretary Blaine authorized Lowell to do whatever he could to restore the reputation of American pork.[29] As it turned out, American pork exporters had something working in their favor that was more powerful than diplomatic lobbying—economic considerations. As noted in chapter 2, 19th-century Britain had become economically dependent upon American meat supplies; approximately one-half of these meat imports were comprised of pork products. Even at the apex of the Crump report's publicity, restrictions on the American pork trade were resisted in Britain for economic reasons. The vice president of the British Privy Council, Anthony John Mundella, was one of the most vocal members of parliament in this regard. A proponent of education and affordable food for the poor,[30] Mundella had already, in May 1879, given public voice to Professor William Williams's contentions that the British authorities had made a "gross mistake" in diagnosing American cattle with pleuro-pneumonia.[31] In March 1881, when Crump's report had stigmatized American pork as unsafe, Mundella actually took the time to defend U.S. pork.[32] Lowell, seeing Mundella as an ally in the fight against British import restrictions, noted Mr. Mundella's aversions to restrictions on the importation of cheap food supplies, including those from the United States.[33]

While economic considerations would generally work in the Americans' favor, Lowell realized that the United States needed to improve its regulations. Evarts's and Blaine's public statements of denial regarding the hog cholera problem proved to be a profound mistake and, in terms of credibility, an expensive one.[34] From Lowell's perspective, this gave dangerously ample room for British protectionists to disrupt the transatlantic trade in agricultural and food products.[35]

The British foreign minister, Lord Granville, was loath to restrict American food imports, but he also recognized the political necessity of restoring British confidence in American pork. Aware that trichinosis and hog cholera were now, due to the Crump report, linked in the British public's mind, Granville requested prevalence-related information regarding both diseases and their causes.[36] American officials would continue to lament the stigmatizing effect of the Crump report, in particular the scientifically unjustified association of hog cholera with *Trichina spiralis*.[37] Nevertheless, American officials knew that they could not put the Crump report, like a metaphorical genie, back in the bottle; while scientifically justified, appeals to separate animal disease risks (e.g., hog cholera and pleuro-pneumonia) from food-safety risks (e.g., trichinosis) were simply too cumbersome.

The restoration of the United States' food safety reputation lay not in complex arguments designed to disentangle animal health and food safety; instead, better regulations for both food safety and animal disease were needed. Writing from the American Legation in London,[38] Lowell added his voice to the crescendo of calls for federal regulation. For animal health, he described the need for inspection and oversight in the west, on the rails, and at the ports,[39] and for food safety, he urged microscopic inspection of pork exports for *Trichina spiralis*.[40] At the time of Lowell's appeals, both food-safety and animal-health regulations were showing signs of maturation in the United States and elsewhere.

In the domain of food safety, where trichinosis was the principal issue of focus, preliminary studies were underway. Southern Europe's moves to restrict American pork imports had prompted, in 1879, the U.S. Senate to commission a scientific study of trichinosis.[41] Conducted by Dr. W.C.W. Glazier at the U.S. Marine Hospital Service, the 200-page report reviewed both foreign and American scientific literature regarding *Trichina spiralis* and trichinosis.[42] A separate study was conducted by the U.S. State Department in 1881. Coupled with an investigation of France's decision to restrict U.S. pork imports, the State Department's report was replete with information from Chicago, Cincinnati, and U.S. Consular offices throughout Britain.[43] The Glazier Report, which was published in December 1881, and the State Department study, completed in May 1882, concluded that while the *Trichina* parasite was sometimes present in American pork, thorough cooking eliminated the risk.[44] These reports emphasized that European pigs had carried the parasite long before American pork was ever exported to Europe.[45] Microscopic inspection, for the moment, would not appear in the U.S. food-safety regulatory menu of practices (although later, in the early 1890s, it would be adopted by the U.S. government to satisfy continental European countries persisting in their restrictions on U.S. pork imports). The common practice—in the U.S. and Great Britain at least—of thoroughly cooking pork was deemed sufficient to manage the risk.

Conclusion

Great Britain's economic dependence on American meat supplies was evident in food and agriculture security leaders' management of the trichinosis risk posed by U.S. pork. To be sure, trichinosis was a genuinely important food-safety-related concern in the late 19th-century transatlantic trading world. While the risk of trichinosis from American pork (as well as other countries' pork products) was indeed real, some continental European governments used the issue for purposes of economic protectionism; as historian John Gignilliat has explained, banning competitive American meat imports on health grounds offered these countries a convenient way to help economically protect their domestic producers.[46]

While some European governments used the trichinosis issue to further protectionist ends, Britain did not do this. When American pork was stigmatized as unsafe in 1881, MPs like Anthony Mundella stood up to defend American pork. Even the Duke of Richmond, the Privy Council decision maker who had a reputation for being an ally of British livestock producers (who might, in theory, economically benefit from restrictions on U.S. pork), was reluctant to restrict U.S. pork imports. Rather than explore trade restrictions on U.S. pork, the Duke of Richmond simply told Britons to cook their pork thoroughly. In essence, Great Britain's ability to tolerate American pork imports was influenced by a relatively straightforward—and culturally acceptable—method of controlling the trichinosis risk: cooking. However, Britain's allegiance to maintaining a lively transatlantic trade in agricultural and food products, and its economic reliance on American meat imports in particular, were most influential.

ANIMAL HEALTH: RINDERPEST AND DECISION MAKING IN THE 19TH-CENTURY LIVESTOCK-TRADING WORLD

Contagious bovine pleuro-pneumonia (discussed in chapter 2) and trichinosis (discussed earlier in this chapter) were not the only health-related concerns that preoccupied 19th-century food and agriculture security decision makers. The cattle disease rinderpest—a high-mortality-causing disease that contributed to the professionalization of veterinary science in both North America and Europe—also presented challenges to the era's livestock-trading world. In Europe, rinderpest surfaced during an era characterized by still-immature microbiological science; this situation fuelled interesting and lesson-illustrating instances of scientific decision making as well as trade diplomacy. Rinderpest—also known as the cattle plague—caused particular economic, social, and scientific chaos in the 19th century, and today's food and agriculture security scholars can learn much from the decisions (both good and bad) that were made with reference to the disease, which was not fully understood at the time.

Background

In 1866, on a special Fast Day during Lent, parishioners across England sang a hymn prepared by musician John Mason Neale on occasion of his country's experience with the ravages of rinderpest, a disease whose dire effects many rural parishes were presently lamenting.[47] Indeed, the agricultural heart of Great Britain had been broken by rinderpest, a disease that was frequently and grimly referred to as "the cattle plague." Britain's encounter with rinderpest was, in the view of one Edinburgh-based veterinary professor, Dr. John Gamgee, an inevitable extension of continental Europe's experience with the animal disease. In November 1863, Dr. Gamgee had authored two letters to the London *Times* arguing it was only a matter of time before Britain's herds would be affected by rinderpest.[48] Gamgee, who had convened an International Veterinary Congress in the summer of 1863 in Hamburg, was captivated by continental Europe's experience with the disease, which had taken root there years—even centuries—before. Nineteenth-century veterinary scientists understood that rinderpest had epidemiological roots dating back to fourth-century Central Asia and Europe, and they were aware that the first certified descriptions of the disease in Europe had occurred in the early 18th century.[49] Today, historians of science—armed with perspectives and animal-disease reports across time and the globe—note that rinderpest has maintained a reputation for emerging as an epidemic, becoming endemic, and then subsiding only to reemerge with renewed virulence. Due to this characteristic periodicity and its awful "three-D" symptoms (discharge, diarrhea, and death), rinderpest has indeed surprised and plagued civilizations throughout history.[50] Today, historical analyses suggest that rinderpest originated in central Asia and then, over a period of centuries, spread to Europe courtesy of the movement of people, cross-border trading of livestock, and war-related invasions.[51] In his book *The Cattle Plague*, Dr. Gamgee referenced rinderpest outbreaks in Prussia and Germany in 1598; outbreaks had erupted and faded, resurfacing in Italy in 1626 and in Poland in 1709, he noted.[52] During the early 18th century, rinderpest-infected Russian cattle were sold to western Europe, thereby seeding additional epidemics. Outbreaks during the 1740s and 1750s eliminated half of France's herd, prompting in 1762 the founding in Lyons of the first veterinary school.[53] The European rinderpest epidemics of the 1700s resulted in widespread disaster.[54]

While continental Europe had been embattled for centuries, Great Britain had, prior to 1865, eluded rinderpest. Both Gamgee's warnings (in 1863) and Neale's hymn (in 1866) pointed to what has come to be known as a defining moment in the history of animal diseases in Great Britain: May 29, 1865. On that day, the *SS Tonning* from the Baltic port of Revel (in modern-day Estonia) arrived into harbor at Hull, England. A consignment of cattle was unloaded, some of which were sent to London. Shortly thereafter, an insidious disease broke out in a London cattle market, and the scourge began to spider-web its way throughout Britain's agricultural network. By the end of June, reports of cattle deaths were emerging from communities across Great Britain. In July 1865, Gamgee himself diagnosed the disease; it was agreed that the cattle shipment from the Baltic had, as he had feared, escorted to Britain the highly contagious and lethal rinderpest, or cattle plague. By October, rinderpest had a footing in 29 counties in England, 2 in Wales, and 16 in Scotland.[55]

Gamgee, drawing on his experience gained in Hamburg at the International Veterinary Congress of 1863, was aware of methods used by continental European authorities to deal with rinderpest. Taking cues from them, he urged Britain to adopt aggressive disease-control policies that featured mandatory slaughter of infected stock, isolation of animals in contact with infected stock, and compensation to owners of slaughtered animals. The British agricultural and veterinary communities had reservations about Gamgee, a scientist considered by some to be an alarmist,[56] and were slow to welcome his policy recommendations.[57] There was, however, little disagreement about the devastating effects of rinderpest. It was an acutely expensive disease; as the prevalence of rinderpest grew, animals died, and livestock farmers encountered the threat of financial ruin. Consumers, meanwhile, faced higher meat prices. A Royal Cattle Plague Commission was appointed to investigate the increasingly calamitous situation, and the Church of England issued a series of public proclamations, prayers, and Neale's hymn.[58] Farming groups, most notably the Royal Agricultural Society of England, pressed parliament to adopt aggressive slaughter and containment policies—not unlike those suggested by Gamgee. In February 1866, parliament adopted legislation mandating the purchase and slaughter of all infected stock and authorizing the same for animals exposed to the disease. By September 1867 Britain was free from rinderpest. The success of hard-line disease control policies had convinced Britain of the value of aggressive animal-disease regulations; when rinderpest again returned to British shores in 1872 and 1877, authorities summarily reapplied the strict policies.[59]

European and Transatlantic International Trade Policy

Great Britain's 1865–1867 rinderpest outbreaks captured the attention of trade diplomats and animal-health regulators in the United States as well as continental Europe. Each side of the North Atlantic trading region responded differently, with European countries in closest proximity to Britain adopting the most stringent risk-management policies. As Britain began to bring her cattle-plague epidemic under control, Belgium and France instituted their own precautionary policies: strict regulation of movements on cattle imports and, in some districts, suspension of market activity. Holland brought out its military and enforced disease-control slaughtering campaigns, to the extent of even fighting off upset peasants.[60] The Belgian response is illustrative of the seriousness with which parts of continental Europe treated rinderpest—a disease with which they, in contrast to Britain, had centuries of experience.

Between 1865 and 1867, while rinderpest prevailed in Britain, Belgium largely avoided the destructive potential of rinderpest. The Belgian interior minister, Mr. Van Denpeereboom, proudly noted that Belgium had lost only 2,300 head of cattle to the plague while England and Holland had lost more than 230,000.[61] While Van Denpeereboom had reason to be proud, he had more reason to remain vigilant. Economic history reveals the 1860s as a decade during which western European countries sought to repeal trade restrictions on food imports.[62] By the mid-1860s, free-trade commercial diplomacy had prompted increased cross-border trading in livestock—and livestock diseases. In 1865, when rinderpest invaded Britain, the threat of animal disease was perceived by countries—like Belgium—across the English Channel. In September of that year, a Brussels-based diplomat indicated how susceptible Belgium was to rinderpest, by virtue of its trading relationships.[63]

Aware of its susceptibility on account of its proximity to Britain, Belgium quickly prohibited the importation and transport of cattle, hides, fresh meat, hay, straw, and manure.[64] These measures, along with restrictions on cattle markets and fairs, contributed to Belgium's containment of rinderpest. Furthermore, the Belgian interior minister knew that the highly contagious rinderpest required additional attention. In June 1866, Van Denpeereboom encouraged his country to remain vigilant, alluding to lessons from the past.[65]

Mr. Van Denpeereboom, and other European veterinary leaders such as the controversial Dr. Gamgee of Britain, perceived the wisdom of disease prevention and containment policies that, to some, seemed excessive. Others, including the U.S. government, responded to rinderpest differently. Britain's rinderpest outbreak captured the attention of U.S. officials, and transatlantic and domestic correspondence indicates their interest in European precautionary policy suggestions.[66] In an April 1866 report to the U.S. Senate, the U.S. commissioner of agriculture even went as far as to assert the need for biosecurity legislation.[67] However, and unlike the example of vigilance set by the Belgian government, the U.S. Congress felt compelled to do little more during the mid-1860s than adopt laws prohibiting the importation of cattle and cattle hides. While seemingly admirable first-steps in animal-disease preparedness, the laws were not truly rigorous; the U.S. treasury secretary could lift the prohibition on a country-by-country basis, and the U.S. president retained the authority to suspend the entire prohibition—which was the usual practice.[68]

In both Europe and the United States, rinderpest remained an important trade-related concern, especially for food and agriculture security decision makers. As it spread from continent to continent, rinderpest joined other animal diseases as subjects of trade scrutiny. One 1883 customs regulation, promulgated by the U.S. government, illustrates trade-related concern about rinderpest, a disease that, mercifully, never would make its way to American shores.[69]

Decision Making about Rinderpest in the 19th-century Cultural and Scientific Contexts

Britain's 1865–1867 rinderpest epidemic, a high-profile event that stimulated governments' affection for scientific inquiries, served to advance the careers of medical-research pathologists and veterinarians alike.[70] For the collective veterinary profession, this was very much welcomed. Despite progress in the democratization of power in Britain, class politics remained a significant cultural force in 19th-century Britain, and there was a desire among men to raise their professional status. Some, including veterinarians, were eager to legitimize their profession and raise it to an honorable status closer to that enjoyed by medical doctors. 19th-century accounts on the social position of the veterinarian are available,[71] and elsewhere historians have discussed class forces at work in the British veterinary community and, more generally, 19th-century British professional society.[72]

Despite some in Britain persisting in their perception of him as an alarmist, Dr. Gamgee capitalized on his enhanced reputation by engaging in veterinary consulting abroad—notably, in the United States. During the 1860s, while Britons were preoccupied with rinderpest, U.S. Midwestern livestock farmers were increasingly concerned about the cattle disease Texas Fever. Also termed Spanish Fever, Texas Fever was an anemia-inducing disease to which southern cattle were immune and northern cattle were susceptible. An etiological mystery at the time, the disease was controversial in states like Kansas where Texas longhorns would trample crops and spread the disease to northern herds following behind.[73] In 1867, the Kansas state legislature lamented recurrent outbreaks of Texas Fever and urged the U.S. government to conduct a scientific study of the matter.[74] In 1868, after further outbreaks of Texas Fever in America, the U.S. commissioner of agriculture hired Britain's Dr. Gamgee to investigate.[75] Gamgee's new post was, for him, a career-related boon; while Gamgee had spent much of his early career in Edinburgh, where he founded in 1857 a veterinary school, he had moved to London in 1865, transplanting his school with him, only to see it later fail.[76] Indeed, Gamgee gladly assumed his new employment as a veterinary advisor to the U.S. government.[77] Although Gamgee's original mandate was to study Texas Fever, his report cited his experiences with rinderpest, and it expanded to include other diseases and, significantly, the epidemiological history of contagious bovine pleuro-pneumonia (a disease whose trade-related significance is discussed in detail in chapter 2). Gamgee's report, published in 1869 and again in 1871, was thereafter cited by America's preeminent veterinary thought leader: Dr. James Law, a former colleague of Gamgee's and veterinary professor at Cornell University.[78]

In his report for the U.S. government, Gamgee wasted no time lamenting what he had perceived, during the 1865–1867 rinderpest epidemic in

Britain, as unscientific quackery and an unfortunate delay in adopting ambitious control policies such as the mandatory slaughter of infected stock.[79] Gamgee's warnings were of relevance to both sides of the Atlantic. In the summer of 1866, U.S. congressional leaders had received, from Britain, treatment-related correspondence regarding rinderpest, including excerpts from a pamphlet illustrating the fact that the 19th century was chock-full of opportunities for quackery and bizarre "solutions" to animal-health problems.[80] Indeed, during the second half of the 19th century, as European and U.S. scientists grappled with how to best manage the real and looming threat of rinderpest, modern microbiological science was in its infancy. Spontaneous-generation explanations of disease were to be discarded on the basis of Louis Pasteur's famous experiments (1861) and Robert Koch's validation of the germ theory of disease (1876), but Pasteur's and Koch's ideas were nonetheless new. In fact, and despite the fame of Pasteur's experiments, the spontaneous-generation theory was not finally discredited until 1876 and 1877, when John Tyndall and Ferdinand Cohn described how bacteria and their spores could be heat-resistant—a question that had thwarted resolution of the spontaneous-generation debate. Robert Koch, the German founder of bacteriology, proved with anthrax bacteria that a specific disease is caused by a specific organism (i.e., the germ theory of disease); although he used the principles in his 1876 anthrax experiments, not until 1884 and his etiological study of tuberculosis would Koch formally elaborate his famous "Koch's Postulates."[81]

In the veterinary community, competing theories of disease transmission and control had fuelled controversies during Britain's 1860s rinderpest epidemic. Both Sir Frederick Smith (in his 1933 *The Early History of Veterinary Literature and Its British Development*) and, more recently, Michael Worboys (in his 1991 study of germ theories of disease in 19th-century British veterinary medicine) have noted how the spontaneous-generation debate was alive at the time of Gamgee's diagnosis of rinderpest.[82] By the early 1870s, spontaneous generation was less accepted,[83] but some scientists and animal-disease regulators had yet to graduate from their commitment to miasmatic theories of disease. Indeed, as late as 1872, some European medical officers of health still confessed a belief in miasms—disease-causing atmospheric products of organic decomposition that mysteriously caused epidemics when inhaled.[84] The newness of Koch's and Pasteur's discoveries was evident in the North American as well as British veterinary communities during the 1870s; late in the decade, contemporaries of Gamgee—Drs. James Law and Thomas Walley are two such examples—took the time to refute spontaneous-generation arguments.[85] In Canada, rivalries between the Ontario Veterinary College (OVC) and the Montreal Veterinary College involved personalities with differing views of the germ theory of disease. Dr. Duncan McEachran, founder of the Montreal Veterinary College, criticized OVC Principal Dr. Andrew Smith, who was unwilling to work with the University of Toronto medical faculty and hesitant to accept Koch's etiological explanation of anthrax.[86] Rinderpest was joined by other trade-troubling animal diseases, such as contagious bovine pleuro-pneumonia, the diagnosis of which was also fuelling scientific and international debate in the transatlantic trading world.[87]

The novelty of Pasteur's and Koch's microbiological science was an important feature of the scientific context in which rinderpest plagued the North Atlantic trading world and, indeed, elsewhere. When rinderpest spread to Africa, where a tragic epidemic ensued during 1888–1898, leading European scientists such as Koch would keep their finger on the pulse of rinderpest-related events there.[88] Not unlike how the U.S. hired Gamgee to provide counsel regarding its animal-disease woes, governments in Africa employed experts to develop vaccines. While Koch did succeed in producing a serum, it was in short supply and did not consistently confer immunity. Other serums (e.g., one by Dr. Edington) were developed but were, quite simply, in short supply.[89] In Africa, where rinderpest had not been a continuously present disease requiring treatment, there were few if any successful traditional medicinal solutions to rinderpest (that is, traditional medicines were developed to treat common illnesses, not rare or novel ailments like rinderpest).[90] Complete identification of the rinderpest virus would elude scientists until 1902,[91] and it is, therefore, understandable that many 19th-century food and agriculture security officials would genuinely struggle in how best to prepare for and manage the animal disease rinderpest. However, the implementation of successful control measures did not necessarily hinge on the availability of complete scientific information. As Dr. Gamgee had learned from continental European countries, the best approach to controlling rinderpest was to adopt aggressive and ambitious regulatory measures—most significantly, the slaughter of diseased and exposed livestock.

CONCLUSION

The animal-health-related case of rinderpest in the 19th-century livestock-trading world well illustrates the importance of several characteristics among food and agriculture security decision makers, including today's and tomorrow's. While Gamgee was seen by many of his contemporaries to be an irritating alarmist, others could reasonably argue that he provided a good example of one of the forms courage can take in food and agriculture security decision making. Students of food and agriculture security ought to pay particular attention to Dr. Gamgee's willingness to speak out—not only in speech but also in writings in the popular press (i.e., the London *Times*)—about the looming threat of rinderpest, which he had observed in continental Europe. While "courage" does not necessarily have to take the form of proposing new disease-control measures,[92] there may be future seasons where this form may, in fact, be needed to preserve food and agriculture security. Another noteworthy characteristic illustrated in this case is that of being willing—and, perhaps, content—to make decisions on the basis of incomplete information. As this chapter attests, scientific knowledge about rinderpest was, in fact, incomplete and, moreover, there was a unique scientific culture in which this knowledge was being uncovered and communicated. The lesson for today's food and agriculture security students is a genuinely challenging one: be prepared to courageously make regulatory and trade decisions, even when information is incomplete or, quite simply, unavailable.

NOTES

1. Sheep-scab was also found in American sheep landed at Liverpool. Richard Perren, The Meat Trade in Britain *1840–1914*, ed. F.M.L. Thompson, Studies in Economic History (London: Routledge & Kegan Paul Ltd., 1978), pp. 113–14. 46th Congress (3rd Session), "Senate Ex. Doc. 5: Documents...Relative to Contagious Diseases of Cattle," *U.S. Serial Set*, no. 1941v.1 (1880), pp. 16, 18–19.

2. "Miscellaneous Foreign News," *Times*, June 11, 1878. The nomenclature for the parasite would later, in 1896, be changed to *Trichinella spiralis*. S. E. Gould, "The Story of Trichinosis," *American Journal of Clinical Pathology* 55 (1971), p. 5.

3. Later, several European governments actually banned U.S. pork. John L. Gignilliat, "Pigs, Politics, and Protection: The European Boycott of American Pork, 1879–1891," *Agricultural History* 35 (1961).

4. 46th Congress (3rd Session), "Senate Ex. Doc. 5," p. 19.

5. *Hansard's Parliamentary Debates* 246, no. May 9–June 16 (1879), column 1406.

6. Gignilliat, "Pigs, Politics, and Protection."

7. Italy, Portugal, and Greece were the first three countries to ban American pork on account of trichinosis. Ibid., p. 4.

8. Increased pork prices and protesting merchants persuaded the Spanish government in July 1880 to readmit pork subject to the inspection. Ibid.

9. It will be recalled from earlier in this chapter that when the trichinosis question first came up in parliament during the spring of 1879, the Duke of Richmond simply told Britons to thoroughly cook their pork.

10. The incident occurred in the early autumn of 1879, but it became the subject of a lengthy debate. See 48th Congress (1st Session), "House Ex. Doc. 106: Swine Products of the United States," *U.S. Serial Set*, no. 2206v.26 (1884), p. 120.

11. The postmortems were done on bodies exhumed two months after death, and worms of the genus *Pelodera* were identified. Some thought the worms entered the bodies after death, and others blamed American pork. Dr. T. Spencer Cobbold, MD, of the Scientific Club, believed that investigators should have looked at the water supply as opposed to any meat-related issues. Ibid., p. 120. T. S. Cobbold, "Trichinosis: Letter to the Editor (Dated 30 April)," *Times*, May 3, 1880.

12. The June 1880 incident occurred in Nottingham at an estate sale of the Duke of Rutland. Poor handling practices appear to have played a role and descriptions suggest a food safety nightmare in which food was placed near sewage, contaminated leftovers were given to the poor, and diarrhea and vomiting were experienced by many. Some suspected trichinosis, but a bacilli (i.e., bacteria) was probably responsible. See Francis Vacher, *The Transmission of Disease by Food*

(*Reprint of British Medical Journal of 16 September*) (1882; reprint, British Medical Journal, September 16, 1882), pp. 5–6. "Poisoned," *Times,* June 28, 1880. 47th Congress (1st Session), "House Ex. Doc. 209: Restrictions Upon the Exportation of Pork from the United States by the French Government," *U.S. Serial Set,* no. 2031 (1882), pp. 130–35.

13. Suellen Hoy and Walter Nugent, "Public Health or Protectionism? The German-American Pork War, 1880–1891," *Bulletin of the History of Medicine* 63, no. 2 (1989): 198. The June 1880 ban excluded ham and bacon, which were later subsumed in another German ban of 1883. Fred Wilbur Powell, *The Bureau of Animal Industry: Its History, Activities and Organization,* ed. Institute for Government Research, Service Monographs of the United States Government (Baltimore, MD: The Johns Hopkins Press, 1927), p. 8.

14. Extract of Crump's report, provided on page 580 of "Diplomatic Correspondence Paper No. 354: Sir Edward Thornton to Mr. Evarts, March 7, 1881," *Papers Relating to the Foreign Relations of the United States* (1881). See also "Hog Cholera in the United States," *Times,* February 19, 1881.

15. "[T]richinae were found; worms were in his flesh by the millions, being scraped and squeezed from the pores of the skin. They are felt creeping through his flesh, and are literally eating up his substance. The disease is thought to have been contracted by eating sausages." "Diplomatic Correspondence Paper No. 354: Sir Edward Thornton to Mr. Evarts, March 7, 1881," p. 580.

16. Paget had discovered the blade-dulling cysts and worms of *Trichina* in the muscles of an Italian man who had died, incidentally, from tuberculosis. The discovery was made in 1835 when Paget was a first-year student at London's St. Bartholomew's Hospital. Paget's colleague, Richard Owen, named the organism *Trichina spiralis*. Paget is recognized as one of the world's pioneers in microbiology. Gould, "The Story of Trichinosis," pp. 2–3. Albert S. Lyons and R. Joseph Petrucelli, *Medicine: An Illustrated History* (New York: Harry N. Abrams Inc., 1987), p. 518. D'Arcy Power, "Sir James Paget," in *The Dictionary of National Biography: Supplement, vol. 22,* ed. Sir Leslie Stephen and Sir Sidney Lee (Oxford: Oxford University Press, 1917).

17. "Parliamentary Notices," *Times,* February 17, 1881. "Hog Cholera in the United States."

18. President Garfield was sworn in on March 4, 1881. Gignilliat, "Pigs, Politics, and Protection," p. 5.

19. "Diplomatic Correspondence Paper No. 353: Mr. Evarts to Sir Edward Thornton, March 7, 1881," *Papers Relating to the Foreign Relations of the United States* (1881).

20. "Diplomatic Correspondence Paper No. 354: Sir Edward Thornton to Mr. Evarts, March 7, 1881."

21. The St. Louis and Cincinnati telegrams were refutations of Crump's claims of a hog cholera epidemic. "Diplomatic Correspondence Paper No. 355: Mr. Blaine to Sir Edward Thornton, March 9, 1881," *Papers Relating to the Foreign Relations of the United States* (1881). Evarts wanted an immediate public rejection of Crump's report. "Diplomatic Correspondence Paper No. 353: Mr. Evarts to Sir Edward Thornton, March 7, 1881."

22. The figures were from the State of Illinois agricultural department for the year 1878. "Diplomatic Correspondence Paper No. 356: Sir Edward Thornton to Mr. Blaine, March 10, 1881," *Papers Relating to the Foreign Relations of the United*

States (1881). Thornton would later be convinced that the 700,000 figure was perhaps an *under*estimation. "Diplomatic Correspondence Paper No. 357: Sir Edward Thornton to Mr. Blaine, March 21, 1881," *Papers Relating to the Foreign Relations of the United States* (1881).

23. "...Her Majesty's consular officers are in possession of peremptory instructions from Her Majesty's Government to make periodical reports of the sanitary condition of the domestic animals in this country, so many of which are now contributing towards the supply of food to the inhabitants of Her Majesty's dominions. In performing this duty they naturally endeavor to obtain the most correct data, and I know not where they are so much justified in looking for them as in the statistics collected by the authorities, whether of individual State or of the United States." "Diplomatic Correspondence Paper No. 357: Sir Edward Thornton to Mr. Blaine, March 21, 1881," p. 583.

24. Secretary Blaine wrote, "Had it been Mr. Crump's specific purpose to cause a panic among the British consumers, by misrepresenting and associating isolated statements, he could hardly have framed his report more appropriately." "Diplomatic Correspondence Paper No. 315: Mr. Blaine to Mr. Lowell, March 17, 1881," *Papers Relating to the Foreign Relations of the United States* (1881), p. 516.

25. Gignilliat, "Pigs, Politics, and Protection," p. 5.

26. Blaine wrote to the American minister in London, "No scientist need be informed that 'hog cholera' or 'hog fever,' as the disease is indifferently styled, is a contagious catarrhal pneumonia, analogous to pleuro-pneumonia among neat-cattle, and entirely distinct from trichinosis, which is due to the development in the muscular tissue of minute parasites, but to the popular mind the distinction is far from evident." "Diplomatic Correspondence Paper No. 315: Mr. Blaine to Mr. Lowell, March 17, 1881," p. 516.

27. See Hoy and Nugent, "Public Health or Protectionism?" Gignilliat, "Pigs, Politics, and Protection."

28. Gignilliat, "Pigs, Politics, and Protection," pp. 6–7.

29. "The injury having been done, no step should be omitted to undo it," Blaine instructed Lowell. "Diplomatic Correspondence Paper No. 315: Mr. Blaine to Mr. Lowell, March 17, 1881," p. 517.

30. Mundella was an employer in the hosiery trade in Nottingham and spent most of his public life as MP for Sheffield. He is revered for his fight for the Education Act, but he always had his eye on trade related matters. He would serve as president of the Board of Trade in 1886 and 1892–1894. "Anthony John Mundella," in *The Concise Dictionary of National Biography (Part I: From the Beginnings to 1900)*, ed. Sir Sidney Lee (Great Britain: Smith, Elder, & Co., 1903; reprint, 1961, by Oxford University Press).

31. On May 12, 1879, Mundella read aloud in parliament a letter of Professor Williams. Hansard's Parliamentary Debates 246, no. May 9–June 16 (1879), columns 128–29. For more on William Williams's involvement in the trade dispute regarding contagious bovine pleuro-pneumonia, see chapter 2 as well as Justin Kastner et al., "Scientific Conviction Amidst Scientific Controversy in the Transatlantic Livestock and Meat Trade," *Endeavour* 29, no. 2 (2005).

32. There were also suspicions that recent outbreaks of trichinosis in Dublin and Nottingham were tied to American pork, but Mundella explained on behalf of the Privy Council that the deaths were not traceable to U.S. pork. "Diplomatic Correspondence Paper No. 310: Mr. Lowell to Mr. Blaine, March 9, 1881," *Papers Relating to the Foreign Relations of the United States* (1881).

33. Lowell wrote to Secretary Blaine, "Mr. Mundella is fully aware of the great importance of the trade in cheapening food to the poorer classes in England, and entirely disposed to prevent any unnecessary restrictions upon it....I have kept Mr. Mundella supplied with whatever information I had on the subject..." Ibid., p. 511.

34. Gignilliat, "Pigs, Politics, and Protection," pp. 5–6.

35. Lowell wrote, "The present ministry is altogether well disposed in the matter and satisfied that this [livestock and meat] trade is as important to England as to the United States; but there is always the danger that the question may become political rather than economic, and that the theory of protection (which still has advocates here) may be disguised as a legitimate carefulness of the public health and of the interests of British agriculture." "Diplomatic Correspondence Paper No. 320: Mr. Lowell to Mr. Blaine, April 9, 1881," *Papers Relating to the Foreign Relations of the United States* (1881), p. 526.

36. Lord Granville requested of Lowell "evidence of the non-existence of hog cholera or trichinosis in the pork exported from the United States." April 8, 1881 Letter from Lord Granville to Lowell, in "Diplomatic Correspondence Paper No. 321: Mr. Lowell to Mr. Blaine, April 13, 1881," *Papers Relating to the Foreign Relations of the United States* (1881), p. 528.

37. A good example of this appears in "Diplomatic Correspondence Paper No. 326: Mr. Blaine to Mr. Lowell, June 10, 1881," *Papers Relating to the Foreign Relations of the United States* (1881).

38. Prior to 1894, the U.S. diplomatic office in London was termed a "legation"; sometime between 1893 and 1894, it was awarded embassy status. At the time of this upgrade, the U.S. legation/embassy was situated on Victoria Street. Anna Girvan, electronic mail message from the Information Resource Center, U.S. embassy, London, July 29, 2002.

39. It appears that Lowell learned this from Dr. Charles Lyman, with whom he had met during Dr. Lyman's 1880 mission to Britain, which was mentioned in chapter 2. "Diplomatic Correspondence Paper No. 320: Mr. Lowell to Mr. Blaine, April 9, 1881," p. 526.

40. On this point, Lowell was joined by the American ministers in Vienna and Paris. Gignilliat, "Pigs, Politics, and Protection," pp. 8–10.

41. According to F. W. Powell, the trichinosis study was commissioned in 1880, but the Glazier report indicates that the study was commissioned in June 1879. See 46th Congress (3rd Session), "Senate Ex. Doc. 9: Report on Trichinae and Trichinosis," *U.S. Serial Set*, no. 1941v.1 (1881). [46th Congress, 1881 #581@7] and Powell, *The Bureau of Animal Industry*, p. 8.

42. 46th Congress (3rd Session), "Senate Ex. Doc. 9."

43. The U.S. consular offices contributing to the report were in cities including Londonderry, Nottingham, and Newcastle-upon-Tyne. The State Department's Bureau of Statistics chief visited both Chicago and Cincinnati. 47th Congress (1st Session), "House Ex. Doc. 209," pp. 125–26, 130–31, 139, and 179–198.

44. See, for example, Ibid., p. 191, and 46th Congress (3rd Session), "Senate Ex. Doc. 9," p. 145.

45. Powell, *The Bureau of Animal Industry*, p. 8.

46. See Gignilliat, "Pigs, Politics, and Protection."

47. The song was "All Creation Groans and Travails," by John Mason Neale, available in *Collected Hymns, Sequences and Carols* (UK: Hodder & Stoughton, 1914). The author is also grateful to this Web site, accessed in September 2002: The Royal

School of Church Music, "The Cattle Plague Hymn," The Royal School of Church Music, http://www.rscm.com.

48. S. A. Hall, "The Cattle Plague of 1865," *Medical History* 6 (1962): 49.

49. "Cattle Plague or Rinderpest," in *Report of the Commissioner of Agriculture for the Year 1879*, ed. William G. Le Duc (Washington: Government Printing Office, 1880), p. 472.

50. M. Blystone, "Rinderpest: One Virus's Impact on Veterinary History," *Veterinary Heritage* 24, no. 1 (2001).

51. C. A. Spinage, *Cattle Plague: A History* (New York: Kluwer Academic/Plenum Publishers, 2003). I. A. Merchant and R. A. Packer, *Veterinary Bacteriology and Virology*, 6th ed. (Ames: Iowa State University Press, 1961).

52. J. Gamgee, *The Cattle Plague* (London: William Clowes and Sons, 1866).

53. Blystone, "Rinderpest: One Virus's Impact on Veterinary History." Iain Pattison, *The British Veterinary Profession, 1791–1948* (London: J. A. Allen, 1984).

54. One report noted that "not less than two hundred million head of cattle were carried off by the cattle plague." "Cattle Plague or Rinderpest" (1880), p. 472.

55. Hall, "The Cattle Plague of 1865." Perren, *The Meat Trade in Britain*. For a contemporary summary, see also 39th Congress (1st Session), "Senate Misc. Doc. 98: Letter of the Commissioner of Agriculture, Communicating...Information in Relation to the Rinderpest or Cattle Plague," *U.S. Serial Set*, no. 1239 v.1 (1866).

56. T. Duckham and G. T. Brown, "The Progress of Legislation against Contagious Diseases of Live Stock," *Journal of the Royal Agricultural Society of England*, 3rd ser., 4 (1893): 268.

57. S. A. Hall, "The Stimulus for the Statutory Control of Animal Diseases in Great Britain in the 19th Century," *Veterinary History* 6 (1976); Hall, "The Cattle Plague of 1865."

58. Thanks to the cue provided by S. A. Hall, the author and his wife have had the pleasure of viewing several colored plates published by the Royal Cattle Plague Commission. The plates are bound in an exceptionally large book in the library of London's Royal College of Physicians; the impressive plates depict in great detail the lesions of rinderpest. For our original lead, see Hall, "The Cattle Plague of 1865."

59. Ibid.

60. 39th Congress (1st Session), "Senate Misc. Doc. 98," (1866).

61. "Diplomatic Correspondence Paper No. 416: Mr. Sanford to Mr. Seward, March 22, 1867," *Papers Relating to the Foreign Relations of the United States* (1867).

62. Herbert Heaton, *Economic History of Europe*, ed. Guy Stanton Ford, Rev. ed., Harper's Historical Series (New York: Harper & Row, 1948).

63. "The cattle plague, which is causing such great ravages in England, has appeared in this country [Belgium], having spread from Holland, where it was brought by some Dutch cattle sent to London for sale, and reimported." "Diplomatic Correspondence Paper No. 309: Mr. Sanford to Mr. Seward, September 13, 1865," *Papers Relating to the Foreign Relations of the United States* (1865), p 92.

64. "Diplomatic Correspondence Paper No. 344: Mr. Sanford to Mr. Seward, February 12, 1866," *Papers Relating to the Foreign Relations of the United States* (1866), p 63.

65. "It is not impossible that some isolated cases [of rinderpest] may still appear in [our country]. Those fears are only too much justified by the experience of the past; they must make us [persist] in the measures of precaution and vigilance which have enabled us to escape until now, at the cost of not very onerous sacrifices

the ravages of a pestilence whose victims are counted elsewhere by thousands." "Diplomatic Correspondence Paper No. 365: Mr. Sanford to Mr. Seward, June—, 1866," *Papers Relating to the Foreign Relations of the United States* (1866), pp. 66–67.

66. See, for example, "Diplomatic Correspondence Paper No. 16: Mr. Harrington to Mr. Seward, November 3, 1866," *Papers Relating to the Foreign Relations of the United States* (1866).

67. "[I] urge the present necessity of additional legislation to provide prompt measures for isolating and exterminating the disease [rinderpest] in its inception, should any active germs of it, whether brought to our shores in hides or other animal refuse, or in the straw packing of crockery-ware, or any of the mysterious modes by which the contagion is communicated, engender the disease in this country." 39th Congress (1st Session), "Senate Misc. Doc. 98." (1866), p. 1.

68. Powell, *The Bureau of Animal Industry*.

69. See customs order, in pages 455–56 of "Diplomatic Correspondence Paper No. 246: Mr. Frelinghuysen to Mr. Lowell, October 1, 1883," *Papers Relating to the Foreign Relations of the United States* (1883).

70. Terrie M. Romano, *Making Medicine Scientific: John Burdon Sanderson and the Culture of Victorian Science* (Baltimore, MD: The Johns Hopkins Press, 2002).

71. For example, see R. H. Dyer, "The Social Position of the Veterinary Surgeon," *Veterinarian* 38(1865).

72. Harold Perkin, *The Origins of Modern English Society 1780–1880* (London: Routledge & Kegan Paul, 1969), pp. 260–70. Abigail Woods, "From Occupational Hazard to Animal Plague: Foot-and-Mouth Disease in Britain, 1839–1884" (Master's Thesis, University of Manchester, 1999); J. R. Fisher, "Not Quite a Profession: The Aspirations of Veterinary Surgeons in England in the Mid Nineteenth Century," *Historical Research* 66, no. 161 (1993); Pattison, *The British Veterinary Profession*.

73. Paul F. Clark, *Pioneer Microbiologists of America* (Madison: The University of Wisconsin Press, 1961), pp. 123–26. Jimmy M. Skaggs, *Prime Cut: Livestock Raising and Meatpacking in the United States, 1607–1983* (College Station: Texas A&M University Press, 1986), pp. 53, 65.

74. 39th Congress (2nd Session) and Kansas Legislature, "Senate Misc. Doc. 15: Resolution in Favor of an Appropriation to Enable the Department of Agriculture to Make a Scientific Investigation of...Spanish Fever," *U.S. Serial Set*, no. 1278v.1 (1867).

75. Hall, "The Cattle Plague of 1865," p. 57. For a description of Gamgee's commissioning orders, see page 1 of 41st Congress (2nd Session), "Diseases of Cattle in the United States: Report of the Commissioner of Agriculture, Including Reports from Professor Gamgee," *U.S. Serial Set*, no. 1430v.16 (1871).

76. Pattison, *The British Veterinary Profession*, p. 71.

77. Hall, "The Cattle Plague of 1865," p. 57.

78. Powell, *The Bureau of Animal Industry*, p. 3. As a later-published book alludes, Dr. James Law was a former professor of Gamgee's educational institution—the New Veterinary College, Edinburgh, which was moved to London in 1865 and renamed the Albert Veterinary College. See the title page of James Law, *The Farmer's Veterinary Adviser*, 11th ed. (Ithaca, NY: published by the author, 1897).

79. Gamgee wrote, "...as late as 1865 the outbreak of a virulent cattle plague in England developed in its train the compounders of drugs and filth, and the believers in the treatment of isolated cases of a plague; of a plague, indeed, which

advanced in direct ratio to the delay in extinguishing its virulent poison, and the rapidity of whose spread may be likened to that of the confluent mountain waters the form the inland seas and navigable streams. Let the people learn from the ancient history of veterinary medicine, as they can learn from recent events, that to dam the Mississippi and annihilate its waters is quite as easy a process as attempting to save a country form incalculable loss by the medical treatment of isolated cases of a specific and contagious cattle plague." 41st Congress (2nd Session), "Diseases of Cattle in the United States," (1871), p. 6.

80. The pamphlet extolled the "remarkable results attending the use of sulphurous acid gas for the prevention and cure of rinderpest and other diseases." 39th Congress (1st Session), "House Misc. Doc. 128: Report on Rinderpest from Mr. Bidwell, Chairman of the Committee on Agriculture," *U.S. Serial Set*, no. 1271v.3 (1866), p. 1.

81. Raymond W. Beck, *A Chronology of Microbiology in Historical Context* (Washington, D.C.: ASM Press, 2000), pp. 81, 93–95. Thomas D. Brock, *Robert Koch: A Lifetime in Medicine and Bacteriology* (Madison, WI: Science Tech Publishers, 1988), pp. vii, 2, 139.

82. Sir Frederick Smith, *The Early History of Veterinary Literature and Its British Development,* vol. 4: *The Nineteenth Century, 1823–1860* (London: Baillière, Tindall and Cox, 1933), pp. 90–91. Michael Worboys, "Germ Theories of Disease and British Veterinary Medicine, 1860–1890," *Medical History* 35 (1991), p. 310.

83. See 41st Congress (2nd Session), "Diseases of Cattle in the United States," (1871), p. 5.

84. Hall, "The Stimulus for the Statutory Control of Animal Diseases," p. 4.

85. Thomas Walley, *The Four Bovine Scourges: Pleuro-Pneumonia, Foot-and-Mouth Disease, Cattle Plague, Tubercle (Scrofula) with an Appendix on the Inspection of Live Animals and Meat* (Edinburgh: MacLachlan and Stewart, 1879), pp. 8–9. For insights on Professor James Law's thinking on animal disease, trade policy, and causation of disease, see James Law, *The Lung Plague of Cattle, Contagious Pleuro-Pneumonia* (Ithaca, NY: published by the author, 1879).

86. C.A.V. Barker and T. A. Crowley, *One Voice: A History of the Canadian Veterinary Medical Association* (Ottawa: Canadian Veterinary Medical Association, 1989); F. Eugene Gattinger, *A Century of Challenge: A History of the Ontario Veterinary College* (Toronto: University of Toronto Press, 1962).

87. For more on this matter, see chapter 2.

88. See letter dated December 9, 1896, in Robert Koch, *Reise-Berichte Über Rinderpest, Bubonenpest in Indien und Afrika, Tsetse-Oder Surrakrankheit, Texasfieber, Tropische Malaria, Schwarzwasserfieber* (Berlin: Verlag von Julius Springer, 1898).

89. C. van Onselen, "Reactions to Rinderpest in Southern Africa 1896–97," *Journal of African History* 13, no. 3 (1972): 483.

90. Deon van der Merwe, Personal communication to Julianne Jensby, research assistant to Dr. Kastner, October 16, 2007.

91. Merchant and Packer, *Veterinary Bacteriology and Virology*.

92. Other good examples of courage, occurring in different forms, include that of Professor William Williams, who in the pleuro-pneumonia trade dispute maintained—until his death—that British veterinary inspectors were wrong in their diagnoses of the disease in American cattle. Kastner et al., "Scientific Conviction Amidst Scientific Controversy in the Transatlantic Livestock and Meat Trade."

BIBLIOGRAPHY

39th Congress (1st Session). "House Misc. Doc. 128: Report on Rinderpest from Mr. Bidwell, Chairman of the Committee on Agriculture." *U.S. Serial Set*, no. 1271v.3 (1866).

39th Congress (1st Session). "Senate Misc. Doc. 98: Letter of the Commissioner of Agriculture, Communicating...Information in Relation to the Rinderpest or Cattle Plague." *U.S. Serial Set*, no. 1239v.1 (1866).

39th Congress (2nd Session), and Kansas Legislature. "Senate Misc. Doc. 15: Resolution in Favor of an Appropriation to Enable the Department of Agriculture to Make a Scientific Investigation of...Spanish Fever." *U.S. Serial Set*, no. 1278v.1 (1867).

41st Congress (2nd Session). "Diseases of Cattle in the United States: Report of the Commissioner of Agriculture, Including Reports from Professor Gamgee." *U.S. Serial Set*, no. 1430v.16 (1871).

46th Congress (3rd Session). "Senate Ex. Doc. 5: Documents...Relative to Contagious Diseases of Cattle." *U.S. Serial Set*, no. 1941v.1 (1880).

46th Congress (3rd Session). "Senate Ex. Doc. 9: Report on Trichinae and Trichinosis." *U.S. Serial Set*, no. 1941v.1 (1881).

47th Congress (1st Session). "House Ex. Doc. 209: Restrictions Upon the Exportation of Pork from the United States by the French Government." *U.S. Serial Set*, no. 2031 (1882).

48th Congress (1st Session). "House Ex. Doc. 106: Swine Products of the United States." *U.S. Serial Set*, no. 2206v.26 (1884).

"Anthony John Mundella." In *The Concise Dictionary of National Biography (Part I: From the Beginnings to 1900)*, ed. Sir Sidney Lee, p. 917. Great Britain: Smith, Elder, & Co., 1903. Reprint, 1961, by Oxford University Press.

Barker, C.A.V., and T. A. Crowley. *One Voice: A History of the Canadian Veterinary Medical Association*. Ottawa: Canadian Veterinary Medical Association, 1989.

Beck, Raymond W. *A Chronology of Microbiology in Historical Context*. Washington, D.C.: ASM Press, 2000.

Blystone, M. "Rinderpest: One Virus's Impact on Veterinary History." *Veterinary Heritage* 24, no. 1 (2001): 8–12.

Brock, Thomas D. *Robert Koch: A Lifetime in Medicine and Bacteriology*. Madison, WI: Science Tech Publishers, 1988.

"Cattle Plague or Rinderpest." In *Report of the Commissioner of Agriculture for the Year 1879*, ed. William G. Le Duc, pp. 472–84. Washington, D.C.: Government Printing Office, 1880.

Clark, Paul F. *Pioneer Microbiologists of America*. Madison: The University of Wisconsin Press, 1961.

Cobbold, T. S. "Trichinosis: Letter to the Editor (Dated 30 April)." *Times*, May 3, 1880, 12, column f.

"Diplomatic Correspondence Paper No. 16: Mr. Harrington to Mr. Seward, November 3, 1866." *Papers Relating to the Foreign Relations of the United States* (1866): 2:185–88.

"Diplomatic Correspondence Paper No. 246: Mr. Frelinghuysen to Mr. Lowell, October 1, 1883." *Papers Relating to the Foreign Relations of the United States* (1883): 454–59.

"Diplomatic Correspondence Paper No. 309: Mr. Sanford to Mr. Seward, September 13, 1865." *Papers Relating to the Foreign Relations of the United States* (1865): 3: 92.
"Diplomatic Correspondence Paper No. 310: Mr. Lowell to Mr. Blaine, March 9, 1881." *Papers Relating to the Foreign Relations of the United States* (1881): 510–11.
"Diplomatic Correspondence Paper No. 315: Mr. Blaine to Mr. Lowell, March 17, 1881." *Papers Relating to the Foreign Relations of the United States* (1881): 515–17.
"Diplomatic Correspondence Paper No. 320: Mr. Lowell to Mr. Blaine, April 9, 1881." *Papers Relating to the Foreign Relations of the United States* (1881): 525–27.
"Diplomatic Correspondence Paper No. 321: Mr. Lowell to Mr. Blaine, April 13, 1881." *Papers Relating to the Foreign Relations of the United States* (1881): 527–29.
"Diplomatic Correspondence Paper No. 326: Mr. Blaine to Mr. Lowell, June 10, 1881." *Papers Relating to the Foreign Relations of the United States* (1881): 534–35.
"Diplomatic Correspondence Paper No. 344: Mr. Sanford to Mr. Seward, February 12, 1866." *Papers Relating to the Foreign Relations of the United States* (1866): 2:63.
"Diplomatic Correspondence Paper No. 353: Mr. Evarts to Sir Edward Thornton, March 7, 1881." *Papers Relating to the Foreign Relations of the United States* (1881): 579.
"Diplomatic Correspondence Paper No. 354: Sir Edward Thornton to Mr. Evarts, March 7, 1881." *Papers Relating to the Foreign Relations of the United States* (1881): 579–80.
"Diplomatic Correspondence Paper No. 355: Mr. Blaine to Sir Edward Thornton, March 9, 1881." *Papers Relating to the Foreign Relations of the United States* (1881): 580–81.
"Diplomatic Correspondence Paper No. 356: Sir Edward Thornton to Mr. Blaine, March 10, 1881." *Papers Relating to the Foreign Relations of the United States* (1881): 581–83.
"Diplomatic Correspondence Paper No. 357: Sir Edward Thornton to Mr. Blaine, March 21, 1881." *Papers Relating to the Foreign Relations of the United States* (1881): 583–85.
"Diplomatic Correspondence Paper No. 365: Mr. Sanford to Mr. Seward, June—, 1866." *Papers Relating to the Foreign Relations of the United States* (1866): 2:66–67.
"Diplomatic Correspondence Paper No. 416: Mr. Sanford to Mr. Seward, March 22, 1867." *Papers Relating to the Foreign Relations of the United States* (1867): 1:623–27.
Duckham, T., and G. T. Brown. "The Progress of Legislation against Contagious Diseases of Live Stock." *Journal of the Royal Agricultural Society of England*, 3rd ser., 4 (1893): 262–86.
Dyer, R. H. "The Social Position of the Veterinary Surgeon." *Veterinarian* 38 (1865): 360–65.
Fisher, J. R. "Not Quite a Profession: The Aspirations of Veterinary Surgeons in England in the Mid Nineteenth Century." *Historical Research* 66, no. 161 (1993): 284–302.

Gamgee, J. *The Cattle Plague*. London: William Clowes and Sons, 1866.
Gattinger, F. Eugene. *A Century of Challenge: A History of the Ontario Veterinary College*. Toronto: University of Toronto Press, 1962.
Gignilliat, John L. "Pigs, Politics, and Protection: The European Boycott of American Pork, 1879–1891." *Agricultural History* 35 (1961): 3–12.
Girvan, Anna. Electronic mail message from the Information Resource Center, U.S. Embassy, London, July 29, 2002.
Gould, S. E. "The Story of Trichinosis." *American Journal of Clinical Pathology* 55 (1971): 2–11.
Hall, S. A. "The Cattle Plague of 1865." *Medical History* 6 (1962): 45–58.
Hall, S. A. "The Stimulus for the Statutory Control of Animal Diseases in Great Britain in the 19th Century." *Veterinary History* 6 (1976): 3–12.
Hansard's Parliamentary Debates. *Hansard's Parliamentary Debates* 246, no. May 9–June 16 (1879): columns 128–29.
Hansard's Parliamentary Debates 246, no. May 9–June 16 (1879): column 1406.
Heaton, Herbert. *Economic History of Europe*, ed. Guy Stanton Ford. Rev. ed. Harper's Historical Series. New York: Harper & Row, 1948.
"Hog Cholera in the United States." *Times*, February 19, 1881, 5.
Hoy, Suellen, and Walter Nugent. "Public Health or Protectionism? The German-American Pork War, 1880–1891." *Bulletin of the History of Medicine* 63, no. 2 (1989): 198–224.
Kastner, Justin, Douglas Powell, Terry Crowley, and Karen Huff. "Scientific Conviction Amidst Scientific Controversy in the Transatlantic Livestock and Meat Trade." *Endeavour* 29, no. 2 (2005): 78–83.
Koch, Robert. *Reise-Berichte Über Rinderpest, Bubonenpest in Indien und Afrika, Tsetse-Oder Surrakrankheit, Texasfieber, Tropische Malaria, Schwarzwasserfieber*. Berlin: Verlag von Julius Springer, 1898.
Law, James. *The Farmer's Veterinary Adviser*. 11th ed. Ithaca, NY: published by the author, 1897.
Law, James. *The Lung Plague of Cattle, Contagious Pleuro-Pneumonia*. Ithaca, NY: published by the author, 1879.
Lyons, Albert S., and R. Joseph Petrucelli. *Medicine: An Illustrated History*. New York: Harry N. Abrams Inc., 1987.
Merchant, I. A., and R. A. Packer. *Veterinary Bacteriology and Virology*. 6th ed. Ames: Iowa State University Press, 1961.
"Miscellaneous Foreign News." *Times*, June 11, 1878, 5, column d.
"Parliamentary Notices." *Times*, February 17, 1881, 8, column b.
Pattison, Iain. *The British Veterinary Profession, 1791–1948*. London: J. A. Allen, 1984.
Perkin, Harold. *The Origins of Modern English Society 1780–1880*. London: Routledge & Kegan Paul, 1969.
Perren, Richard. *The Meat Trade in Britain 1840–1914*, ed. F.M.L. Thompson, Studies in Economic History. London: Routledge & Kegan Paul Ltd., 1978.
"Poisoned." *Times*, June 28. 1880, 11, column f.
Powell, Fred Wilbur. *The Bureau of Animal Industry: Its History, Activities and Organization*, ed. Institute for Government Research, Service Monographs of the United States Government. Baltimore, MD: The Johns Hopkins Press, 1927.
Power, D'Arcy. "Sir James Paget." In *The Dictionary of National Biography:* Supplement. Vol. 22, ed. Sir Leslie Stephen and Sir Sidney Lee, pp. 1112–14. Oxford: Oxford University Press, 1917.

Romano, Terrie M. *Making Medicine Scientific: John Burdon Sanderson and the Culture of Victorian Science*. Baltimore, MD: The Johns Hopkins Press, 2002.

Skaggs, Jimmy M. *Prime Cut: Livestock Raising and Meatpacking in the United States, 1607–1983*. College Station: Texas A&M University Press, 1986.

Smith, Sir Frederick. *The Early History of Veterinary Literature and Its British Development*. Vol. 4, *The Nineteenth Century, 1823–1860*. London: Baillière, Tindall and Cox, 1933.

Spinage, C. A. *Cattle Plague: A History*. New York: Kluwer Academic/Plenum Publishers, 2003.

The Royal School of Church Music. "The Cattle Plague Hymn." The Royal School of Church Music. http://www.rscm.com.

Vacher, Francis. *The Transmission of Disease by Food (Reprint of British Medical Journal of 16 September)*1882. Reprint, British Medical Journal, September 16, 1882.

van der Merwe, Deon. Personal communication to Julianne Jensby, research assistant to Dr. Kastner, October 16, 2007.

van Onselen, C. "Reactions to Rinderpest in Southern Africa 1896–97." *Journal of African History* 13, no. 3 (1972): 473–88.

Walley, Thomas. *The Four Bovine Scourges: Pleuro-Pneumonia, Foot-and-Mouth Disease, Cattle Plague, Tubercle (Scrofula) with an Appendix on the Inspection of Live Animals and Meat*. Edinburgh: MacLachlan and Stewart, 1879.

Woods, Abigail. "From Occupational Hazard to Animal Plague: Foot-and-Mouth Disease in Britain, 1839–1884." Master's Thesis, University of Manchester, 1999.

Worboys, Michael. "Germ Theories of Disease and British Veterinary Medicine, 1860–1890." *Medical History* 35 (1991): 308–27.

CHAPTER 7

Looking Forward

Cobus Block, Jason Ackleson, and Justin Kastner

The authors of this book have devoted their pages to retrospective and contemporary analyses of food and agriculture security. Chapters 2, 4, and 6 each examined past instances where food and agriculture security thought leaders, officials, and other decision makers grappled with complex and interrelated problems confronting the global agricultural and food system. Lest it ignore present-day approaches, this book (in chapters 3 and 5) has also paid due attention to today's food and agriculture security policy frameworks, risk-management approaches, and import-security arrangements. In this chapter, the book continues to examine both history and the present while also contemplating the future; it encourages students to gaze forward in time and consider solutions to some of the 21st century's most pressing food and agriculture security challenges. The chapter begins with an analysis of an increasingly important player and stakeholder in world trade—China—and several of the food-safety-related challenges facing its agricultural and food system and, by extension, the world. The chapter expands to consider food and agriculture security issues confronting all countries engaged in the multilateral trading system, identifying two innovative approaches to international cooperation in the global agricultural and food trade: regionalization and compartmentalization. The chapter then concludes with a call for governmental and business leaders to pursue cross-border cooperation to ensure food and agriculture security.

CHINA

China boasts demographic and economic diversity that stems from its massive size and population. Moreover, as a transitional economy, China deals with a unique set of challenges. Indeed, properly understanding food and agriculture security issues in China requires the consideration of a wide range of topics. While all cannot be fully addressed here, this section considers some of the most salient issues facing China's agricultural and food industry, and then examines the reasons behind increased food-safety precautions, legislation and regulatory systems currently in place, and some particular areas where China could improve its efforts.

Background

The domain of food and agriculture security represents but one of many pressing issues with which China must grapple. For several years now, the most important topics in Chinese agricultural policy have revolved around basic food-security considerations, rural poverty, and environmental degradation. In the past, China's leadership was much more concerned with providing enough food to feed the country's population (i.e., food-security and food-supply issues) than it was with ensuring, for example, food safety.[1] Policy in China from the time of reform[2] until the present has essentially required that the country produce 95 percent of its own grain requirements.[3] A quantity-over-quality mind-set emerged and is still evident today in the actions of local governments that often favor economic growth over food-safety regulation.[4] While health regulation—at least in the domain of animal health and the food supply—has been recognized as directly relevant to the general food-security situation in China,[5] basic food-security matters have been the primary preoccupation of China policymakers. After food security, increasing farm-household income has been an important objective for the Chinese government. The massive rural-urban income gap is of concern to Chinese citizens and politicians alike. This is especially true since the rural poor have, in recent years, contributed to social unrest.[6] China's government views increasing rural per-capita income as one of the best ways to preserve stability. China must also deal with a number of problematic environmental issues, which have great bearing on the sustainability of its agriculture sector. China's northern and western areas are experiencing the increasingly harsh effects of desertification. One scholar has estimated that desertification takes up one-third of China's land base, while up to 90 percent of grasslands in China have been degraded.[7] Furthermore, increased agricultural production and population pressure has exacerbated the strain on China's water resources.[8]

Problems with food security, rural poverty, and the environment all affect food and agriculture security generally, and food safety particularly. Improving China's food-safety situation is not as simple as merely increasing inspection of food products; it requires addressing a number of other issues all of which have a bearing on the overall food and agriculture security situation in the country. While it is only one of many difficulties facing

China, calls for improved food safety have, in recent years, gained traction. This can be attributed to several recent developments including China's accession into the World Trade Organization (WTO), an increase in domestic income levels, and highly publicized food-safety scandals. China was initially compelled to pay more attention to food-safety concerns in the years leading up to 2001, as it pursued the process of becoming a member of the WTO (and a signatory to WTO agreements). Following accession to the WTO, the volume of agricultural items exported from China to the developed world markedly increased. Developed nations with high food-safety standards pushed Chinese exporters to address food-safety issues in order to market their goods overseas.[9] Another important development that helped bring food-safety issues closer to the forefront includes the increase in income levels amongst Chinese citizens, and, more specifically, the emergence of a new class of consumers able to afford higher quality food. According to one estimate, by 2010, the number of Chinese in the middle class is anticipated to reach 100 million.[10] As more Chinese citizens afford to pay higher prices for food, the demand for high quality food and food safety rises.[11] Finally, the most visible factor inducing real improvement in food safety has been a series of highly publicized incidents around the world that were subsequently linked back to China. Poisonous pet food, contaminants in exported seafood, and the melamine milk scandal of 2008 all drove home to the Chinese government the necessity of improved food safety.[12]

The New Food Safety Law

From 1994 to 2009, China's Hygiene Law served as the legislative basis for food safety administration and regulation in the country. During that time, the law was criticized for having too narrow a scope, lacking a risk-analysis basis, and failing to pinpoint producers as those primarily responsible for food safety. Although later regulations attempted to close loopholes in the Hygiene Law, it was not until 15 years later[13] that the National People's Congress (NPC) passed a new law addressing food safety—the Food Safety Law.[14]

The new law places responsibility for food safety on producers and processers. It also requires firms to have in place a system by which food products can be recalled. This is a welcome step toward traceability, though many firms have voiced concern over the expenses of new equipment and the time required to implement such a system.[15] The new law also recognizes the complications caused by multiple inspection procedures and varying standards for food safety. Article 5 of the Food Safety Law calls for the various levels and ministries of government to work in coordination (with reference to the national law) and manage inspection activities. It also emphasizes the need for standardization across all levels. Section 3 states that the implementation of standardized food safety is mandatory, and that this standardization should be made after obtaining results from risk assessment—one of the most important elements of the risk-analysis framework.[16] Standardization should also be made in consultation with international standards, consumer preferences, and industry advice.[17]

The central government has also taken steps to give added weight to the new law. In the past, one of the major problems in the Chinese food-safety inspection regime was a conspicuous lack of risk analysis. In July 2009, the Ministry of Health (MOH), in cooperation with several other ministries, established a committee of experts for the assessment of food-safety risks.[18] The committee consists of experts from a wide array of backgrounds and institutions, but among these experts there are no government officials. The most important attribute of the committee is that it does not represent any particular interest; it is explicitly and simply charged with the task of accurately assessing food-safety-related risks.[19] More recently, the NPC abolished some 220 outdated laws that it deemed incoherent and outside the scope of the Food Safety Law; this policy decision was made with the intent of streamlining the Chinese legal system as it relates to food safety.[20]

Administration

Article 4 of the Food Safety Law hands primary responsibility for food-safety administration over to the MOH, but calls for administration and inspection to be done in coordination with several relevant ministries.[21] The most important of these are the Ministry of Agriculture (MOA); the State Administration for Industry and Commerce (SAIC); the General Administration of Quality Supervision, Inspection, and Quarantine (AQSIQ); the Certification and Accreditation Administration (CNCA); and the Ministry of Environmental Protection (MEP).[22] Each ministry presides over a number of governmental branches at the provincial and subprovincial levels. Additionally, various ministries may also administer special bureaus (e.g., the Organic Food Development Center, which operates under the auspices of MEP).[23]

The agencies' most important food and agriculture security roles are as follows. The MOA oversees agricultural production, the marketing of farm chemicals and veterinary drugs, and the regulation of plant and animal diseases. The MOH is in charge of setting food sanitary standards and drafting laws addressing food-hygiene issues. The SAIC oversees food circulation and hygiene issues in the marketplace. The AQSIQ ensures food quality and safety in food processing. The CNCA inspects, approves, and registers certification institutions. Finally, the MEP is responsible for overseeing pollution issues that may apply to food safety.[24] Even with several ministries involved, robust and comprehensive regulation is difficult to attain. Part of this difficulty stems from China's geographic and demographic makeup. Millions of small farms provide products to the market through a complex chain of middlemen. Along the supply chain—from the farm gate to the table—almost all transactions are conducted in cash with little documentation. This makes traceability a major issue, which means that even if a food-safety-related problem is discovered, there is considerable difficulty in locating the source of trouble.[25]

Besides the hassle of dealing with a severely fragmented supply chain, Chinese governmental ministries must also work in less-than-ideal conditions. Inspection departments often do not have the proper equipment to perform their jobs; in many cases, the equipment in use is over 10 years old. Furthermore, inspection departments rarely have personnel with sufficient expertise.[26]

Another problem that persistently plagues China is that of inefficiency. Food-safety-related inspections often rely on end-product testing, which proves both difficult and expensive.[27] For example, in 2009, Haidian District, a district in Beijing, invested 900,000 RMB in 700 teams of food inspectors, who were employed to find harmful materials in market products.[28] In many cases, multiple "relevant" ministries are charged with the same task but lack the ability to effectively coordinate their efforts.[29] China would benefit greatly by directing more resources toward increasing the capability of its inspection systems. New equipment and new laboratory facilities should be provided to those entrusted with the job of detecting food-safety hazards. Additionally, communication should be fostered between those involved in inspection and experts from other fields. Exchanges between scholars—both foreign and domestic—could help improve personnel expertise.[30] With more expertise and better equipment, inspection activities could be applied earlier in the farm-to-table continuum, which would make for a more efficient use of resources.[31]

Standards

Technically, Chinese law requires food products to comply with a standard that takes into account Hazard Analysis and Critical Control Points (HACCP, which was discussed in chapter 3), but that standard is, in actuality, seldom strictly followed.[32] In order to deal with poor quality brands and help customers choose better products, various government ministries have established certification systems. In fact, nearly every ministry with the slightest connection to food production has established its own standard for quality and safety. These standards include China Top Brand, *Baojian Shipin* Health Food, Conversion to Organic, OFCC Organic, etc. This section will briefly address four of the most important certification labels: the Quality Safety (QS) standard, OFDC Organic Certification, Hazard-Free Food, and Green Food.

The AQSIQ's QS certification is the most visible food-safety standard in China precisely because it is actually mandated. Since it is compulsive, any processed-food items sold without the label are considered illegitimate and are liable to confiscation. The AQSIQ holds certified companies to standards on the quality of ingredients, sanitation in the workplace, and method of operation. It also subjects companies to periodic inspection in order to ensure an acceptable level of quality is being maintained.[33] The MEP established the Organic Food Development Center (OFDC) in 1994 to head up its push for organic food certification. The OFDC standard is strictly organic, and one of the most rigorous standards in China. It is International Federation of Organic Agricultural Movements (IFOAM) and European Union (ISO 65) accredited.[34] The OFDC's organic label should not be confused with the label offered by the China Organic Food Certification Center (OFCC), which was established by the MOA. Though the OFCC is certified by the CNCA, it is not accredited by IFOAM.[35] The two standards are unconnected but not necessarily incompatible. Thus, food items may carry both labels if they meet both OFDC and OFCC standards.

The MOA has pushed its own food-safety certification system, which includes Hazard-Free Food and Green Food. The Hazard-Free Food standard applies to food that is produced by conventional methods (i.e., with inorganic fertilizers, pesticides, etc.) but seeks to ensure that the food contains a limited amount of certain chemical residues.[36] The MOA's most significant project has been Green Food (*lüse shipin*), which comes in two grades. Grade A Green Food maintains standards for levels of pollution, health, and safety; inorganic chemicals are still used, but in smaller quantities. Grade AA Green Food, on the other hand, meets organic standards.[37] Initially, Green Food was marketed internationally as "organic food"; however, after the OFDC challenged this claim at the 1995 IFOAM conference, Green Food was redefined, and the Grade AA standard—already in development at the time—was introduced.[38] Overall, Green Food has been a genuine and remarkable success. It provides a level of food-safety assurance to consumers at an affordable price, and it also offers a niche market to farmers not engaged in organic agriculture. Chinese consumers' familiarity with the Green Food standard is generally high, and consumers have demonstrated a willingness to pay premium prices for food with the Green Food label.[39] China has begun to apply the Green Food label overseas. For example, in order to gain access to China's breweries, the Canadian Wheat Board secured Green Food accreditation for barley exports in 2007.[40]

Access to Information

One major problem that persistently appears in China relates to a general lack of information. This problematic phenomenon occurs at all levels and among all groups—from inspectors to producers to consumers—and it severely diminishes China's ability to ensure food safety. Increasing public awareness is a key step toward combating the production of unsafe and dangerous food. Most fake products slip through inspection because they are sold on small scales to consumers who have never actually encountered the real item.[41] Unscrupulous entrepreneurs have even taken to copying the government's successful accreditation and certification systems. One of the authors of this chapter has personally witnessed a misspelled label that claimed certification from a nonexistent "American" ministry.

Lack of information is a critical problem for not only consumers but also producers. Often times, producers are ill-informed about the essence of the national laws and what their implementation actually means. Lu Yongxiang, vice chairman of the NPC Standing Committee, notes that many in the fields of production and processing are not aware that they have primary responsibility for food safety. Moreover, in the process of examining various facilities and businesses, Chinese authorities discovered many manufacturing operations failed to implement safety measures because they were unaware of the requirements or were under the false impression that the requirements did not apply to them.[42]

One study has noted that food contamination is often the result of poor training and lack of education on the part of farmers and food manufacturers. Farmers may not realize that the chemicals they use are dangerous, or they may simply believe they have no other option when dealing with pests and poor soil. Any proposed food-safety solution must take into account producers' understanding (or misunderstanding) of the issue at hand.[43] (Chapter 4's case study on milk and its vulnerability in China alluded to the importance of this.) In Article 61, China's Food Safety Law leaves room for standards to be developed by private companies, producer associations, and even consumers, provided that their standards are based on the parameters established by the national law.[44] The Chinese government could do more to cooperate with nongovernmental organizations in order to create a more efficient and cost-effective regulatory system. Hiring, commissioning, or encouraging business associations, nonprofit organizations, and other groups to inform the public of how to avoid fake products would go a long way toward a solution.[45]

Additional Challenges, and Looking to the Future

One area of food and agriculture security not addressed in the Food Safety Law[46] is the threat of agricultural terrorism or biological attacks on the food system. Though the issue has been discussed in academic circles,[47] it has failed to garner much notice. This, however, may soon change. Ethnic tensions in the Xinjiang Autonomous Region in western China erupted in the late spring of 2009, causing brutal rioting in the city of Ürümqi. In response to the subsequent crackdown on Xinjiang's Muslim community, al Qaeda threatened to harm China wherever it could.[48] While terrorism-related concerns form part of the menu of food and agriculture security concerns in China, and while the issue of "food defense" (defined in chapter 3) is important, the prevailing and most pressing issue for China is that of food safety. New or revised legislation and regulatory approaches are ongoing and will help; however, a number of issues demand further attention. Ensuring food safety in China will require much more than merely shoring up regulations and increasing inspections; it will require new efforts by industry stakeholders as well as governmental officials from the lowest levels to the top. China should work speedily to implement the ideas already inscribed in law and standardize its regulations and administration. Most important, China needs to better inform consumers and producers of the importance of food safety.

These food-safety issues have begun to affect China's trade relationships. For example, U.S.-China trade relations have been disturbed in recent years by general food-safety problems, pet-food recalls, and disturbing revelations about seafood safety. This occurs against the backdrop of a heightened trade relationship in today's global economy. Some safety issues appear to be rooted primarily in corruption; responses that China has adopted include the arresting of liable regulators and the filing of criminal cases (in recent years, over 600 such cases have been filed within China in reference to the food and drug approval systems).[49]

Meanwhile, and as discussed above, Chinese officials have instituted new approaches to food-safety regulation, advocated new systems for export safety, and publicly acknowledged the importance of food safety for several (e.g., public health, national image, political, and international) reasons.[50] In addition, it may be helpful for China to consider some of the novel approaches to ensuring food and agriculture security for trade purposes; these are discussed in the next section of this chapter, and they include the concepts of regionalization and compartmentalization. The application of these concepts may make particular sense for China, which like other geographically large countries has problems in administering countrywide federal programs of regulation. Regional (similar to that outlined in regionalization) and supply-chain based (similar to that outlined in compartmentalization) approaches to improving food safety and quality are already occurring, albeit informally, in China. For example, food produced in mainland China's Guangdong province is held to higher quality controls when exported to Hong Kong.[51] Elsewhere, pressure to improve food safety has been communicated through market forces, mediated by the elevation of private-company standards.[52]

INNOVATIVE APPROACHES TO FOOD AND AGRICULTURE SECURITY FOR TOMORROW'S TRADING WORLD

In the agricultural and food trade, innovative approaches are needed to ensure food and agriculture security in an ongoing era of globalization and international trade. Two such innovative models include the trade-policy concepts of regionalization and compartmentalization. Both concepts enjoy general endorsement by the modern, rules-based multilateral trading system as it relates to the agricultural and food trade. This system includes, most notably, the WTO Agreement on the Application of Sanitary and Phytosanitary Measures (SPS Agreement), which encourages WTO members to heed the standards and guidelines developed by three international scientific standard-setting bodies: the World Organization for Animal Health or OIE, the Codex Alimentarius Commission, and the International Plant Protection Convention or IPPC.[53] Regionalization (also known as zoning) and compartmentalization refer to concepts sanctioned by the WTO and these organizations in the arena of food and agriculture security and international trade.[54] The SPS Agreement's Article 6, "Adaptation to Regional Conditions, Including Pest- or Disease-Free Areas and Areas of Low Pest or Disease Prevalence," alludes to these concepts,[55] and the OIE's Terrestrial Animal Health Code and Aquatic Animal Health Code provide additional context; for example, chapter 1.3.5. of the Terrestrial Animal Health Code recognizes both zoning (regionalization) and compartmentalization.[56] The following terms, briefly defined here in animal-health terms, and further explored below, offer unique opportunities for today's and tomorrow's food and agriculture security officials tasked with managing health and security concerns in the global agricultural and food trade:

- *Zone/region*: a clearly defined part of a country containing an animal subpopulation with a distinct health status with respect to a specific disease for which required surveillance, control, and biosecurity measures have been applied for the purpose of international trade.
- *Compartment*: one or more establishments under a common biosecurity management system containing an animal subpopulation with a distinct health status with respect to a specific disease or specific diseases for which required surveillance, control, and biosecurity measures have been applied for the purpose of international trade.[57]

Regionalization

WTO member countries have heeded the guidelines provided by the OIE and successfully adopted the concept of regionalization for the purposes of export; these countries have gained, from their trading partners who import their livestock and products, recognition for the maintenance of geographically isolated animal subpopulations with distinct animal-health situations. That is, these countries have successfully demonstrated the geographic separation of disease-free and infected areas. The food and agriculture security and international-trade consequences are indeed rewarding for these countries; regionalization offers the opportunity for the continued exporting of animals and animal products (i.e., those that are certified as coming from disease-free regions) even when other parts of the same country are not disease-free. Throughout history, governments have used regionalization and regionalization-like methods to differentiate, in the animal health realm, between infected and disease-free regions.[58]

South American food and agriculture security officials have used regionalization for years; that is, they have worked to maintain disease-free regions for the purposes of international trade. A 2007 regionalization effort involving Uruguay, in the context of its trade relationship with the United States, provides a good example. In that year, the United States issued a regionalization decision about Uruguay, specific animal diseases, and international trade; the decision, announced in the U.S. *Federal Register* demonstrated how regionalization enables government regulators to make distinctions between different diseases (in this particular case, regarding rinderpest and foot and mouth disease) and different subnational regions in a country.[59]

In the United States, regionalization decisions are based on 11 different factors, outlined in the U.S. Code of Federal Regulations. These include such issues and considerations as the authority, organization, and infrastructure of the veterinary-service organizations in the region in question; the status of the disease in the region as well as in adjacent regions; the nature and extent of disease-control programs; the operation of vaccination programs; the degree of separation between the region in question and adjacent regions with higher-risk status; control of animal and animal product movement among the regions (and the types of biosecurity controls present); the livestock demographics and marketing practices in the region; the nature and extent of disease surveillance efforts in the region; the availability and capacity of diagnostic laboratory resources; and emergency-response capabilities.[60] As exporting countries successfully implement regionalization for trade purposes, they assist in the ongoing operation of the global agricultural and food trade while also maintaining safety and security in their own agricultural and food systems.

Compartmentalization

While regionalization has enjoyed broad acceptance in the multilateral trading system, the concept of compartmentalization is relatively novel. The OIE definition, cited above, states that instead of geographically delineated risk boundaries, risks and their boundaries may be understood to be limited by a number of epidemiological factors. Compartmentalization may be applied to specific herds, feed-supply chains, establishments, premises, and so forth. Examples of compartmentalization applications might include (a) a confined animal-feeding operation with biosecurity and risk-management practices that confer virtually no risk from a particular disease and (b) a cattle operation certified as bovine spongiform encephalopathy (BSE) free through demonstrable feed-source management, animal-movement documentation, and livestock identification.[61] These are but two possible examples.

Among food and agriculture security officials, interest in compartmentalization is growing. Recent years have witnessed the development of guidelines for implementing the concept of compartmentalization, and the OIE has facilitated discussions regarding how poultry operations, for example, might implement compartmentalization to control for highly pathogenic avian influenza in biosecurity-certified supply chains. Compartmentalization has potential application in many agricultural and food sectors (not just that of poultry), and future applications ought to be explored. The ultimate purpose of compartmentalization, like regionalization, is to limit the disruption of trade by demonstrably limiting the spread of diseases through public as well as private biosecurity efforts.

CROSS-BORDER COOPERATION

This book has featured historical and contemporary illustrations of some of the challenges, dilemmas, and opportunities facing food and agriculture security officials. Both public (e.g., governmental) and private (e.g., business) decision makers must remember that in a globalized world, public-private partnerships as well as transnational collaboration are imperative to the successful maintenance of safety, security, and international trade. For example, the implementation of such innovative concepts like regionalization and compartmentalization (including in a cross-border fashion) require significant technical and administrative capacity—capacity that government agencies alone cannot deliver. Indeed, it seems that robust public-administration efforts (among governmental officials), reliable and transparent information sharing (between the governments of countries engaged in international trade), and sophisticated business management (among the private stakeholders involved) are all needed. In addition, strengthened international legal frameworks can help provide the structure and assurance necessary to efficiently implement such cross-border arrangements.

The objectives of ensuring efficient international trade practices, safe and secure food supplies, and national and international security are, quite simply, daunting. In an age of globalization—where both trade and security are increasingly valued—partnerships across national borders will become ever-more important. For such cross-border cooperation to occur, food and agriculture security thought leaders must publicly embrace the concept of reaching across borders in the areas of public administration and regulation, information sharing, and business management. By publicly and enthusiastically embracing cross-border cooperation in these areas, food and agriculture security decision makers can help promote an international culture conducive to genuine bilateral and multilateral cooperation. Such a culture will, it is hoped, make more common the kinds of international partnerships that, in the future, will be even more essential for global food and agriculture security.

NOTES

1. Ministry of Agriculture, *Report on the State of China's Food Security* (Beijing 2004).
2. That is, the reforms that opened China to the world in 1979.
3. Andrzej Kwiecinski et al., *OECD Review of Agricultural Policies* (China 2005).
4. Aleda V. Roth et al., "Unraveling the Food Supply Chain: Strategic Insight from China and the 2007 Recalls," *Journal of Supply Chain Management* 44, no. 1 (2008).
5. China, which is home to 1.5 billion consumers, has in recent years faced food-supply worries due to animal diseases; for example, a pig disease outbreak in 2007 caused (food-security) concerns about China's pork supplies. See Richard McGregor and Jamil Anderlini, "Pig Disease Adds 30% to China's Pork Price and Fuels Inflation Fear," *Financial Times*, May 29, 2007.
6. T. Lum, *Social Unrest in China* (Washington, D.C.: Congressional Research Service, 2006).
7. K. Morton, *China and the Global Environment: Learning from the Past, Anticipating the Future* (Double Bay, New South Wales: Lowy Institute for International Policy 2009).
8. B. Lohmar and J. Wang, "Will Water Scarcity Affect Agricultural Production in China?" in *China's Food and Agriculture: Issues for the 21st Century*, ed. F. Gale (Washington, D.C.: Economic Research Service, 2002).
9. Linda Calvin et al., "Food Safety Improvements Underway in China," *Amber Waves* 4, no. 5 (2006).
10. Z. Xin, "Dissecting China's 'Middle Class'," *China Daily*, October 27, 2004.
11. C. van der Meer, A. Fock, and Z. Zhu, *China's Compliance with Food Safety Requirements for Fruits and Vegetables: Promoting Food Safety Requirements for Fruit and Vegetables* (World Bank, 2006); X. Zhang, *Tianjin Consumer Study: With Special Attention to Food Safety* (The Hague: Agricultural Economics Research Institute, 2003).
12. National Development and Reform Commission et al., *Naiye Zhengdun He Zhenxing Guihua Gangyao [Plan for the Rectification and Revitalization of the Dairy Industry]* (China 2008).
13. It should be noted that while no new, comprehensive food-safety law was passed for 15 years, efforts to create one began as early as 2004. J.-M. Chaumet and F. Desevedavy, "Food Consumption and Food Safety in China," *Asie Visions* 21(2009). J. Chen and N. Xu, "Chaoyue Bumen Liyi Mai Chu Jianku Yi Bu [Taking a Step over the Difficulty of Ministry Interests]," in *Nanfang Zhoumo* (Guangzhou: Nanfang Baoye Zhuanmei Jituan Zhuguan, 2010).
14. K. Malik, ed., *Advancing Food Safety in China* (United Nations in China, 2008).
15. Chaumet and Desevedavy, "Food Consumption and Food Safety in China."
16. The risk-analysis framework consists of risk assessment, risk management, and risk communication.
17. *Zhonghua Renmin Gonghe Guo Shipin Anquan Fa [People's Republic of China Food Safety Law]* (China: Xinhua, 2009).
18. Ministry of Health, "Weishengbu Bangongting Guanyu Chengli Diyi Miao Guojia Shipin Anquan Fengxian Pinggu Zhuanjia Weiyuanhui De Tongzhi

[General Office of the Ministry of Health Notice Concerning the Establishment of the First Meeting of the National Food Safety Assessment Expert Committee]," http://www.moh.gov.cn/sofpro/cms/previewjspfile/zwgkzt/cms_0000000000000000131_tpl.jsp?requestCode=44735&CategoryID=2746.

19. Chen and Xu, "Chaoyue Bumen Liyi Mai Chu Jianku Yi Bu [Taking a Step over the Difficulty of Ministry Interests]."

20. T. Li, *Quanguo Renda Tuidong Shipin Anquan Peitao Falü Tixi Jianshe [National People's Congress Promotes Food Safety and Constructs Supporting Legal System]* (Jiankang Baowang, 2010).

21. Deploying multiple ministries for food-safety administration is not unique to China. In the United States, at least 12 federal agencies (not to mention state and local governments) administer 35 different laws related to food safety. Roth et al., "Unraveling the Food Supply Chain: Strategic Insight from China and the 2007 Recalls." *Zhonghua Renmin Gonghe Guo Shipin Anquan Fa [People's Republic of China Food Safety Law]*.

22. The MEP was formerly known as the State Environmental Protection Agency (SEPA).

23. Malik, ed. *Advancing Food Safety in China*; van der Meer, Fock, and Zhu, *China's Compliance with Food Safety Requirements for Fruits and Vegetables: Promoting Food Safety Requirements for Fruit and Vegetables;* Organic Food Development Center, "OFDC Introduction," http://www.ofdc.org.cn/english/about/about.asp.

24. van der Meer, Fock, and Zhu, *China's Compliance with Food Safety Requirements for Fruits and Vegetables: Promoting Food Safety Requirements for Fruit and Vegetables.*

25. Roth et al., "Unraveling the Food Supply Chain: Strategic Insight from China and the 2007 Recalls."

26. X. Chen and N. Deng, *Zhongguo Shipin Anquan Zhanlüe Yanjiu [Researching China's Food Safety Strategy]* (Beijing: Chemical Industrial Press, 2004).

27. Malik, ed. *Advancing Food Safety in China.*

28. H. Chen, "Shequ Pei Shipin Anquan Jiance Xiang [Community to Have Food Safety Inspection]," *Beijing Daily,* March 25, 2009.

29. Malik, ed. *Advancing Food Safety in China*; van der Meer, Fock, and Zhu, *China's Compliance with Food Safety Requirements for Fruits and Vegetables: Promoting Food Safety Requirements for Fruit and Vegetables.*

30. Chen and Deng, *Zhongguo Shipin Anquan Zhanlüe Yanjiu [Researching China's Food Safety Strategy].*

31. Malik, ed. *Advancing Food Safety in China.*

32. M. Zhu et al., "Shipin Anquan Yu Kongzhi [Food Safety and Control]," in *Shipin Anquan Congshu [Food Safety Series],* ed. M. Zhu, L. Wang, and L. Deng (Beijing: Chemical Industry Press, 2008).

33. Li Bai et al., "Food Safety Assurance Systems in China," *Food Control* 18, no. 5 (2007); Chen and Deng, *Zhongguo Shipin Anquan Zhanlüe Yanjiu [Researching China's Food Safety Strategy];* General Administration of Quality Supervision Inspection and Quarantine, *Shipin Shengchan Jiagong Qiye Zhiliang Anquan Jiandu Guanli Banfa [Quality and Safety Supervision of Food Production and Processing Enterprises]* (2003).

34. Organic Food Development Center, "OFDC Introduction."

35. N. Baer, "The Spread of Organic Food in China," in *China Environment Forum*, ed. J. Turner (Woodrow Wilson International Center for Scholars, 2007).

36. L. Liu, "Enhancing Sustainable Development through Developing Green Food: China's Option," in *Sub-Regional Workshop, Dfid Ii Project,* ed. United Nations in Bangkok (2003).

37. Grade AA Green Food always meets the standards of the OFCC for organic but not always those of the OFDC. Zhu et al., "Shipin Anquan Yu Kongzhi [Food Safety and Control]."

38. P. Thiers, "China's "Green Food" Label and the International Certification Regime for Organic Food: Harmonized Standards and Persistent Structural Contradictions," *Sinosphere* 3, no. 3 (2000).

39. X. Zhang, *Tianjin Consumer Study: With Special Attention to Food Safety.*

40. A number of other countries have taken similar actions. J. Paull, "Green Food in China," *Elementals Journal of Bio-Dynamics Tasmania* 91(2008); Canadian Wheat Board, "CWB Gains Edge in World's Largest Beer Market," http://www.cwb.ca/public/en/newsroom/releases/2007/110107.jsp.

41. F. Zhang, "Lun Zhongguo Shipin Anquan Jianguan Tizhi De Xiuzheng [Discussing the Revision of China's Food Safety Inspection System]," *Dongfang Faxue* 2(2009).

42. Chen and Deng, *Zhongguo Shipin Anquan Zhanlüe Yanjiu [Researching China's Food Safety Strategy].* Shipin Shangwu Wang, "Shipin Anquan Fa" Zhifa Jiancha Jieguo Gongbu [Announcement on the Results of The "Food Safety Law" Inspection] (Shipin Shangwu Wang, 2010).

43. Roth et al., "Unraveling the Food Supply Chain: Strategic Insight from China and the 2007 Recalls."

44. *Zhonghua Renmin Gonghe Guo Shipin Anquan Fa [People's Republic of China Food Safety Law].*

45. F. Zhang, "Lun Zhongguo Shipin Anquan Jianguan Tizhi De Xiuzheng [Discussing the Revision of China's Food Safety Inspection System]."

46. The law does not feature a single mention of the words "terror," "attack," or "war."

47. A. Li, Y. Yu, and B. Shi, "Kongbu Xiji Xin Shouduan: Nongye Kongbu [New Means of Terror Attacks: Agricultural Terror]," *National Defense* 4(2007); J. Guo and Y. Guo, "Cong Shengwu Kongbuzhuyi Kan Zhongguo Nongye Jiaoyu De Fazhan [Looking at China's Agricultural Education Development through Biological Terrorism]," *Higher Agricultural Education* 8(2005).

48. "Al-Qaeda Claims Revenge of Uygur Deaths in Xinjiang Riot," *Global Times,* July 15, 2009.

49. Geoff Dyer, "China Arrests 774 in Product Crackdown," *Financial Times,* October 30, 2007.

50. Mure Dickie, "China Publishes First Food Safety Five-Year Plan," *Financial Times,* June 7, 2007. National Development and Reform Commission et al., *Naiye Zhengdun He Zhenxing Guihua Gangyao [Plan for the Rectification and Revitalization of the Dairy Industry].*

51. These types of improvements are occurring in part because of the income gap between coastal and inland regions. The coastal regions of China generally feature higher per capita GDP, and consumers in those regions can afford to pay more for quality food (as already discussed in this chapter, in its reference to the growing middle class in China). This phenomenon may also be observed near Shanghai, in Zhejiang, Jiangsu, Fujian, Shandong, and around Beijing—that is, around the more developed cities.

52. Robin Kwong, "Chinese Food Gets Grilling in Hong Kong," *Financial Times,* August 8, 2007.

53. WTO, "Agreement on the Application of Sanitary and Phytosanitary Measures," in *The WTO Agreement Series: Sanitary and Phytosanitary Measures,* ed. WTO (Geneva: World Trade Organization, 1998). The three standard-setting organizations recognized by the WTO and the SPS Agreement are sometimes referred to as the "three sisters."

54. A. Scott et al., "The Concept of Compartmentalisation," *Rev. sci. tech. Off. int. Epiz.* 25, no. 3 (2006).

55. WTO, "Agreement on the Application of Sanitary and Phytosanitary Measures."

56. World Organization for Animal Health, "Chapter 1.3.5. Zoning and Comparmentalisation," in *Terrestrial Animal Health Code* (Paris: World Organization for Animal Health, 2006). With respect to phytosanitary issues, the IPPC also provides guidelines for regionalization.

57. Ibid.

58. For additional historical perspective, see Jason Ackleson and Justin Kastner, "Territoriality and Functionality in Health Regulation and the Agri-Food Trade," forthcoming in 2010 in the journal *Geopolitics*.

59. U.S. Department of Agriculture Animal and Plant Health Inspection Service, "Foot-and-Mouth Disease Status of Uruguay," *Federal Register* 72, no. 218 (2007).

60. The factors are codified in 9 CFR 92.2 (Title 9, Animals and Animal Products, and Part 92, Importation/procedures for requesting recognition of regions—recognition of regions for imports). The authors thank Donald Link, import risk analyst with the U.S. Animal and Plant Health Inspection Service's National Center for Import and Export, for his invaluable help in identifying and explaining the 11 factors to *Frontier* students during a December 2008 *Frontier* field trip to Washington, D.C.

61. Scott et al., "The Concept of Compartmentalisation."

BIBLIOGRAPHY

"Al-Qaeda Claims Revenge of Uygur Deaths in Xinjiang Riot." *Global Times,* July 15, 2009.

Baer, N. "The Spread of Organic Food in China." In *China Environment Forum,* ed. J. Turner: Woodrow Wilson International Center for Scholars, 2007.

Bai, Li, Chenglin Ma, Shunlong Gong, and Yinsheng Yang. "Food Safety Assurance Systems in China." *Food Control* 18, no. 5 (2007): 480–84.

Calvin, Linda, Fred Gale, Dinghuan Hu, and Bryan Lohmar. "Food Safety Improvements Underway in China." *Amber Waves* 4, no. 5 (2006): 16–21.

Canadian Wheat Board. "CWB Gains Edge in World's Largest Beer Market." http://www.cwb.ca/public/en/newsroom/releases/2007/110107.jsp.

Chaumet, J.-M., and F. Desevedavy. "Food Consumption and Food Safety in China." *Asie Visions* 21 (2009).

Chen, H. "Shequ Pei Shipin Anquan Jiance Xiang [Community to Have Food Safety Inspection]." *Beijing Daily,* March 25 2009, 8.

Chen, J., and N. Xu. "Chaoyue Bumen Liyi Mai Chu Jianku Yi Bu [Taking a Step over the Difficulty of Ministry Interests]." In *Nanfang Zhoumo*, C13. Guangzhou: Nanfang Baoye Zhuanmei Jituan Zhuguan, 2010.

Chen, X., and N. Deng. *Zhongguo Shipin Anquan Zhanlüe Yanjiu [Researching China's Food Safety Strategy]*. Beijing: Chemical Industrial Press, 2004.

Dickie, Mure. "China Publishes First Food Safety Five-Year Plan." *Financial Times,* June 7, 2007, 8.

Dyer, Geoff. "China Arrests 774 in Product Crackdown." *Financial Times,* October 30, 2007, 2.

General Administration of Quality Supervision Inspection and Quarantine. *Shipin Shengchan Jiagong Qiye Zhiliang Anquan Jiandu Guanli Banfa [Quality and Safety Supervision of Food Production and Processing Enterprises]* 2003.

Guo, J., and Y. Guo. "Cong Shengwu Kongbuzhuyi Kan Zhongguo Nongye Jiaoyu De Fazhan [Looking at China's Agricultural Education Development through Biological Terrorism]." *Higher Agricultural Education* 8 (2005): 13–15.

Kwiecinski, Andrzej, Stephen Apted, Dirk Bezemer, Fabrizio Bresciani, Brian Morrissey, John Nash, Joe Dewbre, Hsin Huang, Wayne Jones, Wilfrid Legg, Pete Liapis, Claude Nenert, Stefan Tangermann, and Martin von Lampe. *OECD Review of Agricultural Policies*. China 2005.

Kwong, Robin. "Chinese Food Gets Grilling in Hong Kong." *Financial Times,* August 8, 2007, 3.

Li, A., Y. Yu, and B. Shi. "Kongbu Xiji Xin Shouduan: Nongye Kongbu [New Means of Terror Attacks: Agricultural Terror]." *National Defense* 4 (2007): 79–81.

Li, T. *Quanguo Renda Tuidong Shipin Anquan Peitao Falü Tixi Jianshe [National People's Congress Promotes Food Safety and Constructs Supporting Legal System]*: Jiankang Baowang, 2010.

Liu, L. "Enhancing Sustainable Development through Developing Green Food: China's Option." In *Sub-Regional Workshop, Dfid Ii Project,* ed. United Nations in Bangkok, 2003.

Lohmar, B., and J. Wang. "Will Water Scarcity Affect Agricultural Production in China?" In *China's Food and Agriculture: Issues for the 21st Century,* ed. F. Gale, 41–43. Washington, D.C.: Economic Research Service, 2002.

Lum, T. *Social Unrest in China*. Washington, D.C.: Congressional Research Service, 2006.

Malik, K., ed. *Advancing Food Safety in China*: United Nations in China, 2008.

McGregor, Richard, and Jamil Anderlini. "Pig Disease Adds 30% to China's Pork Price and Fuels Inflation Fear." *Financial Times,* May 29, 2007, 1.

Ministry of Agriculture. *Report on the State of China's Food Security*. Beijing 2004.

Ministry of Health. "Weishengbu Bangongting Guanyu Chengli Diyi Miao Guojia Shipin Anquan Fengxian Pinggu Zhuanjia Weiyuanhui De Tongzhi [General Office of the Ministry of Health Notice Concerning the Establishment of the First Meeting of the National Food Safety Assessment Expert Committee]." http://www.moh.gov.cn/sofpro/cms/previewjspfile/zwgkzt/cms_0000000000000000131_tpl.jsp?requestCode=44735&CategoryID=2746.

Morton, K. *China and the Global Environment: Learning from the Past, Anticipating the Future*. Double Bay, New South Wales: Lowy Institute for International Policy 2009.

National Development and Reform Commission, Ministry of Agriculture, Ministry of Industry and Information Technology, Ministry of Commerce, Ministry of Health, General Administration of Quality Supervision Inspection and Quarantine, Ministry of Finance, People's Bank of China, China Banking

Regulatory Commission, China Insurance Regulatory Commission, and Propaganda Department and Ministry of Supervision. *Naiye Zhengdun He Zhenxing Guihua Gangyao [Plan for the Rectification and Revitalization of the Dairy Industry]*. China 2008.

Organic Food Development Center. "OFDC Introduction." http://www.ofdc.org.cn/english/about/about.asp.

Paull, J. "Green Food in China." *Elementals Journal of Bio-Dynamics Tasmania* 91 (2008): 48–53.

Roth, Aleda V., Andy A. Tsay, Madeleine E. Pullman, and John V. Gray. "Unraveling the Food Supply Chain: Strategic Insight from China and the 2007 Recalls." *Journal of Supply Chain Management* 44, no. 1 (2008): 22–39.

Scott, A., C. Zepeda, L. Garber, J. Smith, D. Swayne, A. Rhorer, J. Kellar, A. Shimshony, H. Batho, V. Caporale, and A. Giovannini. "The Concept of Compartmentalisation." *Rev. sci. tech. Off. int. Epiz.* 25, no. 3 (2006): 873–79.

Shipin Shangwu Wang. *"Shipin Anquan Fa" Zhifa Jiancha Jieguo Gongbu [Announcement on the Results of The "Food Safety Law" Inspection]*: Shipin Shangwu Wang, 2010.

Thiers, P. "China's "Green Food" Label and the International Certification Regime for Organic Food: Harmonized Standards and Persistent Structural Contradictions." *Sinosphere* 3, no. 3 (2000): 8–18.

U.S. Department of Agriculture Animal and Plant Health Inspection Service. "Foot-and-Mouth Disease Status of Uruguay." *Federal Register* 72, no. 218 (2007): 63796–97.

van der Meer, C., A. Fock, and Z. Zhu. *China's Compliance with Food Safety Requirements for Fruits and Vegetables: Promoting Food Safety Requirements for Fruit and Vegetables*: World Bank, 2006.

World Organization for Animal Health. "Chapter 1.3.5. Zoning and Compartmentalisation." In *Terrestrial Animal Health Code*. Paris: World Organization for Animal Health, 2006.

WTO. "Agreement on the Application of Sanitary and Phytosanitary Measures." In *The WTO Agreement Series: Sanitary and Phytosanitary Measures*, ed. WTO, pp. 29–49. Geneva: World Trade Organization, 1998.

Xin, Z. "Dissecting China's 'Middle Class'." *China Daily*, October 27, 2004.

Zhang, F. "Lun Zhongguo Shipin Anquan Jianguan Tizhi De Xiuzheng [Discussing the Revision of China's Food Safety Inspection System]." *Dongfang Faxue* 2 (2009).

Zhang, X. *Tianjin Consumer Study: With Special Attention to Food Safety*. The Hague: Agricultural Economics Research Institute, 2003.

Zhonghua Renmin Gonghe Guo Shipin Anquan Fa [People's Republic of China Food Safety Law]. China: Xinhua, 2009.

Zhu, M., L. Deng, J. Sun, L. Wang, and W. Zhou. "Shipin Anquan Yu Kongzhi [Food Safety and Control]." In *Shipin Anquan Congshu [Food Safety Series]*, ed. by M. Zhu, L. Wang and L. Deng. Beijing: Chemical Industry Press, 2008.

APPENDIX

Available Resources Related to Food and Agriculture Security

Kathryn Krusemark and Justin Kastner

CARVER PLUS SHOCK

Chapter 3 mentioned the CARVER plus Shock tool, which may prove useful by those conducting vulnerability assessments in the food industry. Three noteworthy FDA Web sites provide information:

- URL: http://www.fda.gov/Food/FoodDefense/CARVER/default.htm
- URL for food manufacturing: http://www.accessdata.fda.gov/scripts/email/CFSAN/reg_feedback/carverdl.cfm
- URL for agriculture: http://www.accessdata.fda.gov/scripts/email/CFSAN/reg_feedback/carverag.cfm

COMMODITY- AND SECTOR-SPECIFIC HACCP INFORMATION

The USDA National Agricultural Library and its Food Safety Information Center provide information on HACCP, mentioned in chapter 3. The following resources are available:

- URL for meat and poultry: http://foodsafety.nal.usda.gov/nal_display/index.php?info_center=16&tax_level=2&tax_subject=177&level3_id=0&level4_id=0&level5_id=0&topic_id=1147&&placement_default=0
- URL for seafood: http://foodsafety.nal.usda.gov/nal_display/index.php?info_center=16&tax_level=2&tax_subject=177&level3_id=0&level4_id=0&level5_id=0&topic_id=1148&&placement_default=0

- URL for juice and produce: http://foodsafety.nal.usda.gov/nal_display/index.php?info_center=16&tax_level=2&tax_subject=177&level3_id=0&level4_id=0&level5_id=0&topic_id=1149&&placement_default=0
- URL for food service: http://foodsafety.nal.usda.gov/nal_display/index.php?info_center=16&tax_level=2&tax_subject=177&level3_id=0&level4_id=0&level5_id=0&topic_id=1150&&placement_default=0

CONGRESSIONAL RESEARCH SERVICE REPORTS

The Congressional Research Service (CRS) provides reports to members of the U.S. Congress on a variety of topics relevant to food and agriculture security. While there is no systematic way to obtain all CRS reports, the Center for Democracy and Technology has developed *Open CRS*, which provides access and links to CRS Reports that are in the public domain.

- URL: http://opencrs.com/

FDA'S FOOD DEFENSE AND EMERGENCY RESPONSE INFORMATION

This resource describes the FDA's collaborations with other U.S. agencies as well as private sector organizations; these resources are intended to help reduce the risk of tampering as well as malicious, criminal, or terrorist actions on the food supply.

- URL: http://www.fda.gov/Food/FoodDefense/default.htm

FDA'S ALERT INITIATIVE

This FDA program, described in chapter 3, is designed to raise awareness of food defense and preparedness.
URL: http://www.fda.gov/food/fooddefense/training/alert/default.htm

FOOD AG SECTOR CRITICALITY ASSESSMENT TOOL FROM NCFPD

The National Center for Food Protection and Defense (NCFPD), a Department of Homeland Security Center of Excellence, has made available the Food Ag Sector Criticality Assessment Tool (FASCAT) tool.

- URL: http://www.ncfpd.umn.edu/docs/FAS-CAT%20Version%201.2.xls

FOOD POLICY ISSUE ANALYSIS FROM THE INTERNATIONAL FOOD INFORMATION COUNCIL

The International Food Information Council (IFIC) provides information on health, food safety, and nutrition issues.

- URL: http://www.foodinsight.org/

FOODSAFETY.GOV

This online resource, provided by multiple U.S. government agencies, provides a gateway to a variety of food-safety-related information.

- URL: http://www.foodsafety.gov/

FRONTIER PROGRAM RESOURCES

The Kansas State University–New Mexico State University *Frontier* program for the historical studies of border security, food security, and trade policy maintains a Web site featuring a number of resources (e.g., podcasted commentaries) as well as announcements about unique homeland security related educational opportunities (e.g., the *Frontier* Interdisciplinary eXperiences, or FIX, program). The *Frontier* program also routinely provides resources and opportunities to help food and agriculture security scholars both (a) acquire interdisciplinary learning experiences and (b) develop invaluable lifelong skills.

- URL: http://frontier.k-state.edu

FSIS's FOOD DEFENSE AND EMERGENCY RESPONSE INFORMATION

The USDA Food Safety and Inspection Service (FSIS) provides information on food defense.

- URL: http://www.fsis.usda.gov/Food_Defense_&_Emergency_Response/index.asp

GLOBAL AGRICULTURAL TRADE SYSTEM

The USDA Foreign Agricultural Service maintains the Global Agricultural Trade System (GATS), which provides trade-related statistics concerning agricultural products.

- URL: http://www.fas.usda.gov/gats/default.aspx

HOMELAND SECURITY DIGITAL LIBRARY

The Homeland Security Digital Library (HSDL) compiles open-source resources related to homeland-security policy, strategy, and organizational management. The HSDL is sponsored by the U.S. Department of Homeland Security and the Naval Postgraduate School Center for Homeland Defense and Security.

- URL: https://www.hsdl.org/

IFT'S RESEARCH REPORTS

The Institute of Food Technologists provides publicly available scientific reports that address topics related to food science and food and agriculture security.

- URL: http://members.ift.org/IFT/Research/

PRIOR NOTICE OF IMPORTED FOODS

As chapter 5 mentioned, the 2002 Bioterrorism Act created new requirements, including that of prior notice, for food imports into the United States. For more on this requirement, visit the following FDA Web site:

- URL: http://www.fda.gov/food/guidancecomplianceregulatoryinformation/priornoticeofimportedfoods/default.htm

PROMED-MAIL

The International Society for Infectious Diseases maintains a global, open-source, electronic reporting system for outbreaks of emerging infectious diseases and toxins.

- URL: http://www.promedmail.org/

SANITARY AND PHYTOSANITARY INFORMATION MANAGEMENT SYSTEM

The World Trade Organization (WTO) provides information on WTO member countries' trade-related sanitary (food safety and animal health) and phytosanitary (plant health) measures; these are researchable through the WTO's Sanitary and Phytosanitary Information Management System (SPS IMS).

- URL: http://spsims.wto.org/web/pages/search/other/Search.aspx

U.S. SERIAL SET

The U.S. Library of Congress has made available online selected portions of the *U.S. Serial Set*, which contains historical Congressional reports and executive-branch materials related to food and agriculture security.

- URL: http://lcweb2.loc.gov/ammem/amlaw/lwss.html

Appendix

WORLD FOOD REGULATION REVIEW

World Food Regulation Review is a subscription-based news source regarding international trade and food and agriculture security issues.

- URL (introduction): http://www.researchinformation.co.uk/wfrr.php
- URL (subscription page): https://www.secure-website.com/researchinformation/wfrrsubf.shtml

Index

Accessibility score, 50
Accidental contamination, 44
Aggressors, 47–48
Agreement on the Application of Sanitary and Phytosanitary Measures (SPS Agreement), 87, 137
Agricultural Marketing Service (AMS), 35, 95
Agricultural Research Service (ARS), 35
Albertson's grocery store, 69–70
ALERT (Assure, Look, Employees, Reports, and Threats), 52
Animal and Plant Health Inspection Service (APHIS), 34–35, 95–97
Animal and plant species, importation of, 94–100; EU's management of, 97–99; IPPC standards regarding security of, 99–100; U.S. management of, 94–97
Animal health threats: in Britain, 9–10; European international trade policies and, 113–14; history of, 111–13; international trade policies, 113–14; livestock-trading world and, 111–17; rinderpest epidemic, 115–17; in United States, 9–10

Armour & Co., 6, 19
Assure, Look, Employees, Reports, and Threats (ALERT), 52
Attackers, 49
Automated Import Information System (AIIS), 87
Avalos, Ava Kay, 69–70

Biological agents, 47
Bioterrorism, 7, 34
Blaine, James G., 108–9
Blood thinner contamination, 84
Blue cheese salad dressing, 67, 70
Bovine pleuro-pneumonia, 9, 106, 107, 115
Bovine spongiform encephalopathy (BSE), 4, 138
Britain: agricultural investments by, 7; animal health threats in, 9–10; cattle trade in, 6; economic circumstances in, 8; economic dependence of U.S. in, 11; exportation to, United States, 18–19; food importation in, increased, 8; Foreign Animals Order Number 452 in, 13–14, 15; Foreign Animals Order Number 467 in, 18; international trade with

United States, 5–6; livestock diseases in, 12–13; livestock importation in, 6, 8, 14; pleuropneumonia in, 12–17; railroads investments by, 6–7; slaughter regulations in, 10–11; steamship transportation investments by, 7
Britain's Society of the Arts, 6
British Privy Council, 12, 106–7, 109; Veterinary Department of, 13, 16, 21
Brown, George T., 15–16, 21–22
Bureau of Animal Industry, 22
Bush, George W., 89

C. botulinum (Clostridium botulinum), 39
C. jejuni, 36
Caliciviridae, 37
Caliciviruses, 37
Campylobacter, 36
Canada, 12–13
Canadian Wheat Board, 134
CARVER plus Shock, 2, 48–53; conducting, 48–52; food supply chain, detailing, 49–50; instituting, 51–52; parameters for, 49; purpose of, 48; scoring, assignment of, 50–51; software, development of user-friendly, 52–53; subject matter experts, assembling, 49
Cattle plague. *See* Rinderpest
Cattle Plague, The (Gamgee), 112
Cattle trade, 6
Cattle Trade Association of Liverpool, 18
Centers for Disease Control and Prevention (CDC), 35, 83–84
Central Chamber of Agriculture in Britain, 11
Certification and Accreditation Administration (CNCA), 132
Chamberlain, Carla, 67, 68
Chaplin, Henry, 22
Chemical agents, 47
China, 70–73, 84
China, food and agriculture security in: accessibility to information on, 134–35; administration for, 132–33; challenges of, additional future, 135–36; future issues concerning, 129–36; history of, 130–31; laws for, new, 131–32; standards for, 133–34
China Organic Food Certification Center (OFCC), 134
Cholera, 35
Church of England, 113
Cilantro, 63
Cincinnati Chamber of Commerce, 108
Codex Alimentarius Commission (Codex), 87, 137
Coffee creamers, 67, 70
Cohn, Ferdinand, 116
Commercialization, 7–8
Compartmentalization, 138–37
ConAgra Foods, 65–66
Contagious Diseases (Animals) Act of 1869, 12–13, 14
Contamination, 44, 62
Continental Europe, 9, 12
Cornell University, 115
Cornwall, 107
Corrective actions, 43
Council Directive 91/496/EEC, 97
Countermeasures, 51–52
Criminals, 48
Critical control points (CCPs), 42
Critical infrastructure and key resources (CIKRs), 45–46
Criticality score, 50
Crump, George, 107–10
Cryptosporidiosis, 38–39
Cryptosporidium, 38–39
Current Good Manufacturing Practices (cGMPs), 43
Customs and Border Protection (CBP), 95

Dairy industry in China, 70–72
Dairy pricing system, 71
Decision making: about rinderpest epidemic, 115–17; food and agriculture security and, 11–19; regulatory, 11–19
Denpeereboom, Van, 114
Department of Homeland Security (DHS), 34, 95

Index

Detention of food, 93–94
Diarrheal disease, 36
Directive 200/29/EC Part A Annex V, 98
"Disease-free west," 20–21
Disgruntled insiders, 48
Documentation procedures, 43
Duguid, W., 16

E. coli O157:H7 (*Escherichia coli*), 36–37
Eastman, Timothy, 6, 7, 19
Economic Research Service (ERS), 35
Effect score, 51
Egg Products Inspection Act, 92
Epidemic Intelligence Service (EIS), 67
European international trade policies, 113–14
European Union, 97–99
EU Directive 90/675/EEC, 98
EU Directive 2004/68/EC, 97–98
Evarts, William M., 10, 16, 108
Exotic animal disease, 94–95

Farm-to-fork continuum. *See* Farm-to-table continuum
Farm-to-table continuum, 2, 33–53; CARVER plus Shock and, 48–53; contamination and, accidental *vs.* intentional, 44; food-borne disease agents and, common, 35–39; food safety *vs.* food defense and, 47–48; HACCP and, 40–43; infrastructure protection and (*See* specific types of); regulatory complexity of, 34–35
Federal Bureau of Investigation (FBI), 69
Federal Food, Drugs, and Cosmetic Act (FD&C), 84, 85
Federal Meat Inspection Act, 92
Federal Trade Commission, 35
Fish and Wildlife Service (FWS), 95
Fleming, George, 9, 14–15
Fonterra Cooperative Group, 72
Food, defined, 92
Food additives, 84–85
Food and Agriculture Organization (FAO), 100
Food and agriculture security. *See* China, food and agriculture security in: commodities and sectors of (*See* specific types of); cross-border cooperation concerning; defined; food safety laws concerning; infrastructure protection and (*See* specific types of); innovative approaches to
Food and agriculture security, contemporary challenges of, 5–25; decision making and, regulatory, 11–19; economic backdrop to, 5–11; regulatory cooperation and, bilateral, 19–23
Food and Drug Administration (FDA), 34; detention of food by, authorized, 93–94; *Food Protection Plan* for, 89–90; global offices for, increase in, 86–87; notice of prior food shipments to, required, 92–93; PREDICT as tool for, 88; purpose of, 84–85; registering of food facilities with, required, 91–92; regulations made by (*See* specific types of); regulatory approaches by, 88; role in foreign inspections, 85–86
Food bioterrorism, 7
Food-borne disease agents. *See* specific types of
Food Code, 43, 67
Food defense, 2, 47–48, 135
Food establishments, 66–67
Food facilities, 91–92
Food importation, 8
Food processing, 64–66
Food protection, 2
Food Protection Plan, 89–90
Food safety, 2, 47–48
Food Safety and Inspection Service (FSIS), 34
Food Safety Enhancement Act (H.R. 2749), 88
Food Safety Law, 131–32, 135
Food Safety Modernization Act (S. 510), 88
Food sanitation, 35–36
Food security, 2
Food shipments, 92–93
Food supply chain, 49–50

Food supply safety, 90–94
Food terrorism, defined, 44
Foot and mouth disease (FMD), 4, 9, 12, 106
Foreign animal disease, 94–95
Foreign Animals Order Number 452, 13–14, 15
Foreign Animals Order Number 467, 18
Foreign Animals Wharf, 18
Foreign Cattle Market at Deptford, 12
Foreign Trade Zones, 92
France, 113
Francisella tularensis, 69
Frontier program, 1

Gamgee, John, 15, 112–17
Garfield, James, 108
Gastroenteritis, 37, 67
General Administration of Quality Supervision, Inspection, and Quarantine (AQSIQ), 132
Germ theories, 116
Giardia lamblia, 38
Giardiasis, 38
Glazier, W.C.W., 110
Glazier Report, 110
Good Manufacturing Practices (GMP), 85
Grade AA Green Food, 134
Grade A Green Food, 134
Grain Inspection, Packers and Stockyards Administration (GIPSA), 35
Granville, Lord, 109–10
Green Food, 133, 134

HACCP (Hazard Analysis Critical Control Point), 2, 40–43, 133
Hayes, Rutherford B., 21, 108
Hazard, defined, 41
Hazard-Free Food, 133, 134
Health and Human Services (HHS), Department of, 84
Hemolytic uremic syndrome (HUS), 37
Hepatitis A, 38
Hepatitis A virus (HAV), 38
Hog cholera, 106, 109–10
Holland, 113
Homeland Security Act of 2002, 45

Hong Kong, 136
Hot chili peppers, 63–64
Hot dog production, 49–50
HSPD-8: National Preparedness (Homeland Security Presidential Directive-8), 46
HSPD-5: Management of Domestic Incidents (Homeland Security Presidential Directive-5), 44–45
HSPD-9: Defense of the United States Agriculture and Food (Homeland Security Presidential Directive-9), 46, 61
HSPD-7: Critical Infrastructure Identification, Prioritization, and Protection (Homeland Security Presidential Directive-7), 45–46
Hulse, William, 68, 70
Human botulism, 39
Human health threats: history of, 107–9; pork trade and, transatlantic, 106–11; regulatory responses to, economic considerations and, 109–10; trichinosis and, 106–11
Hygiene Law of China, 131

Illinois, 108
Immediate-slaughter order, 11–19; bilateral regulatory cooperation concerning, 19–23; in Canada, 12–13; Contagious Diseases (Animals) Act of 1869 and, 12–13, 14; in Liverpool, 12, 13, 15–18; requirements of, 18–19; in United States, 12–13, 19
Immigration and Naturalization Service (INS), 69
Importation, 83–100; of animal and plant species, 94–100; background of, 83–85; FDA regulations concerning (*See* specific types of); inspections related to, 85–87; multilateral trading system for, 87
Importation inspections, 85–87
Importation security, 99–100
Imported food shipments, 92–93
Infrastructure protection. *See* specific types of
Intentional contamination, 44

Index 157

Interagency Working Group on Import Safety, 89–90
International Federation of Organic Agricultural Movements (IFOAM), 134
International Plant Protection Convention (IPPC), 87, 97, 137; animal and plant species and, importation of, 99–100; import security and role of, 99–100
International trade policies, 5–6, 113–14
International Veterinary Congress, 112, 113

Jalapeño peppers, 63–64

Kansas, 108, 109
Knapp, David Berry, 69–70
Koch, Robert, 116–17
"Koch's Postulates," 116

Law, George, 14–15
Law, James, 21–22, 115
Le Duc, William G., 10, 15–16, 20
Liverpool, 6, 8, 11; immediate-slaughter order in, 12, 13, 15–18
Liverpool Provision Trade Association, 6
Livestock diseases, 12–13
Livestock importation, 6, 8, 14
Livestock-trading world. *See* Animal health threats
London, 8
Lord President, 16
Lord Salisbury, 15–16
Lowell, J. R., 108, 109–10
Lutgens, Dave, 67
Lyman, Charles, 21

MacDonald, James, 7
Massachusetts, 9
Matador Land and Cattle Company, 7
McCall, Principal, 17–18
McEachran, Duncan, 16, 116
Melamine additive, 70
Melamine incident, 72–73
Merchants' Exchange of St. Louis, 108
Messrs. Flinn, Main & Montgomery, 13

Metropolitan Cattle Market, at Islington (London), 12
Mid-Columbia Medical Center, 67
Milk, 70–73. *See also* China; raw, 71–72; from Sanlu Group, 72
Ministry of Environmental Protection (MEP), 132
Ministry of Health (MOH), 132
Minnesota Department of Health, 63
Misbranded products, 85
Monitoring procedures, 42–43
Montreal Veterinary College, 116
Moore (Privy Council's inspector), 15–16
Multilateral trading system for importation, 87
Mundella, Anthony John, 10, 109

National Advisory Committee on Microbiological Criteria for Foods (NACMCF), 40
National Aeronautics and Space Administration (NASA), 40
National Agricultural Statistics Service (NASS), 35
National Guard, 69
National Incident Management System (NIMS), 44–45
National Infrastructure Protection Plan (NIPP), 45
National Marine Fisheries Service, 35
National People's Congress (NPC), 131, 132
National Preparedness Guidelines (NPG), 46
National Response Framework (NRF), 45
National Response Plan (NRP), 45
National School Milk Program, 71
Naturalistic decision making (NDM), 74
Neale, John Mason, 111–12
New Mexico Department of Health, 62
Norwalk-like viruses (NLVs), 37
Novel Influenza A, 4

OFDC Organic Certification, 133–34
Ontario, 16–18, 20
Ontario Veterinary College (OVC), 116

Operational and Administrative System for Import Support (OASIS), 85
Oregon State Public Health Laboratory, 67
Organic Food Development Center (OFDC), 134
OutbreakNet, 65

Paget, Sir James, 108
Pasteur, Louis, 116–17
Peanut butter, 65–66
Pet food contamination, 84
Phytosanitary certification, 98–99
Pillsbury Company, 2, 40
Pizza processing, 64–65
Plant Protection Act, 96
Plant Protection and Quarantine (PPQ), 96–97
Pleuro-pneumonia, 9, 10, 12–17
Pork trade: economic considerations concerning, 109–10; history of, 107–9; human health threats and, 106–11; regulatory responses to, 109–10; transatlantic, 106–11; in United States, 109–10
Poultry Products Inspection Act, 92
Predictive Risk-Based Evaluation for Dynamic Import Compliance Targeting (PREDICT), 88
PREDICT tool, 88
Produce, 62–64
Protesters, 48
Puja, Ma Anand, 69–70
Pulsed-field gel electrophoresis (PFGE) patterns, 62, 65
PulseNet, 65
Pythagoras Medical Clinic, 69

Quality Safety (QS) certification, 133–34
Queen Victoria, 6

Railroad, investments in, 6–7
Rajneesh, Bhagwan Shree, 68, 69–70
Rajneeshees, 68–70
Rajneesh Medical Corporation, 69
Rajneeshpuram, 68
Raw milk, 71–72

Recall authority, 88
Recognizability score, 51
Record-keeping, 43
Records, establishment and maintenance of, 90–91
Recuperability score, 50–51
Refrigerated beef, 6, 7–8, 19
Regionalization, 137–38, 139
Regulatory cooperation, 19–23
Regulatory decision making. *See* Immediate-slaughter order
Retail, 66–70
Richmond, 17, 18
Rinderpest, 9, 12; decision making about, 115–17; history concerning, 111–13; international trade policies and, European and transatlantic, 113–14; symptoms of, 112; treatment for, 117
Royal Agricultural Society of England, 113
Royal Cattle Plague Commission, 113

S. aureus (Staphylococcus aureus), 39
S. boydii, 37
S. dysenteriae, 37
S. flexceri, 37
S. sonnei, 37
Salad bars, 67–70
Salmon, Daniel, 22
Salmonella, 36; outbreak in peanut butter, 65–66; outbreak in salad bars, 67–70
Salmonella serotype Paratyphi, 69
Salmonella serotype Saintpaul outbreak, 62–64
Salmonella serotype Tennessee outbreak, 65–66
Salmonella serotype Typhi, 69
Salmonella typhimurium outbreak, 67–70
Salmonellosis, 67
Salt-preserved meats, 6
Sanlu Group, 72
Serrano peppers, 63–64
Seward, Frederick, 14, 15
Shakey's Pizza, 67
Sheela, Ma Anand, 69, 70
Sherman, John, 15, 20–21

Shigella, 37
Shigella dysenteriae, 69
Shigellosis, 37
Shock score, 51
Smith, Andrew, 116
Smith, Sir Frederick, 116
Smithfield Meat Market, 6
Snapshot safety inspections, 89
Spoilage, 90–91
Spontaneous-generation, 116
SPS Agreement (Agreement on the Application of Sanitary and Phytosanitary Measures), 87, 137
SS Tonning, 112
Staphylococcal "staph" food poisoning, 39
State Administration for Industry and Commerce (SAIC), 132
Steamship transportation, 7
Subversives, 48
Swine fever, 106, 109
Sylvester, Georgia, 65–66

Tamaulipas, Mexico, 62–63
Target Capabilities List (TCL), 46
Tauxe, Robert V., 69
Terrorists, 48
Texas Fever, 115
The Dalles, Oregon, 67–70
Thomas, Principal, 17–18
Thornton, Sir Edward, 15, 108
Thrombotic thrombocytopenic purpura (TTP), 37
Tomatoes, 62–64
Toothpaste contamination, 84
Transatlantic international trade policies, 114
Transatlantic pork trade, 106–11
Treasury Cattle Commission, 10, 21
Trichina spiralis, 106–8, 110
Trichinosis. See Pork trade: defined; Pork trade: human health threats and
Tuberculosis, 35
2002 Public Health Security and the Bioterrorism Preparedness Act (2002 Bioterrorism Act), 85, 90; U.S. food supply safety, provisions to, 90–94

Tyndall, John, 116
Typhoid fever, 35

United States: animal and plant species in, importation of, 94–97; animal health threats in, 9–10; British investment in, 7; commercialization in, expansion of, 7–8; exportation by, 18–19; food supply safety in, 90–94; immediate-slaughter order and, 12–13, 19; international trade with, 5–6; pleuro-pneumonia in, 12–17; pork trade in, 109–10; railroads investments in, 6–7; steamship transportation investments in, 7
U.S. Agriculture Department, 15
U.S. Air Force Space Laboratory Project Group, 40
U.S. Army Laboratories at Natick, 40
U.S. Code of Federal Regulations, 138
U.S. Department of Agriculture (USDA), 34, 84, 92
U.S. Department of Agriculture Bureau of Animal Industry, 10
U.S. Department of Commerce, 35
U.S. Department of Health and Human Services (HHS), 34
U.S. Department of the Treasury's Alcohol and Tobacco Tax and Trade Bureau, 35
U.S. Environmental Protection Agency (EPA), 35
U.S. Government Accountability Office (GAO), 34
U.S. Marine Hospital Service, 110
U.S. Public Health Service (USPHS), 95
U.S. State Department, 15, 110
U.S. Treasury Cattle Commission, 107
U.S. Treasury Department, 15
Universal Task List (UTL), 46
Urmqi, 135
USDA FSIS, 34–35, 95

Verification procedures, 43
Veterinary Department of British Privy Council, 13, 16, 21

Walley, Thomas, 9, 18, 116
Wasco-Sherman Public Health Department, 67
Wheat farmers, 8
Williams, William, 18, 20, 109
Windsor Castle, 6
Worboys, Michael, 116
World Health Organization (WHO), 44

World Organization for Animal Health (OIE), 87, 137
World Trade Organization (WTO), 2, 99–100, 137

Xinjiang, 135

Yongxiang, Lu, 135

Zoning, 137–38

About the Editor and Contributors

JUSTIN KASTNER, Assistant Professor of Food Safety and Security at Kansas State University, codirects the *Frontier* program for the historical studies of border security, food security, and trade policy. Through various projects (e.g., the Department of Homeland Security's Career Development Grants program), he conducts interdisciplinary research while coaching undergraduate and graduate students to do the same. A Fulbright and Truman Scholar, Dr. Kastner holds graduate degrees from Canada (PhD, University of Guelph) and the United Kingdom (London South Bank University and the University of Edinburgh). He teaches courses related to the multilateral trading system and multidisciplinary research and writing.

JASON ACKLESON is Associate Professor of Government at New Mexico State University and codirector of *Frontier*, an interdisciplinary program for the historical studies of border security, food security, and trade policy. As a Truman and British Marshall Scholar, he earned his PhD in International Relations at the London School of Economics. Working and publishing on questions of security, borders, and globalization, Dr. Ackleson actively pursues research and education projects supported by the U.S. Department of Homeland Security's Centers of Excellence Program. In 2009–2010, he was an American Political Science Association Congressional Fellow in Washington, D.C.

COBUS BLOCK is an undergraduate student majoring in International Studies at the University of Wyoming. In 2008 he was awarded the Chinese

Ambassador's Wyoming Scholarship and spent a year studying Chinese language at Zhejiang University. From 2009 to 2010 he continued his stay in China by taking courses in International Governance at Zhejiang University and Chinese Literature at Capital Normal University. While in China, he has worked in cooperation with the *Frontier* program to research developing agriculture in China. His field of study has included food supply chain management, food safety, public-private partnerships, and certification systems.

KATHRYN KRUSEMARK is a former Department of Homeland Security Career Development Fellow. She holds a BS degree in Food Science and a minor in Leadership Studies from Kansas State University. She recently finished her MS degree (2009, Food Science, Kansas State University), focusing on the DHS research area of food and agriculture security. Her research project considered task and setting factors relevant to decision making in food safety and food defense. While at K-State, she was actively involved with the *Frontier* program. Beyond food safety and defense, Kathryn is interested in the global food supply chain and food product development.

EDWARD NYAMBOK is a PhD student in Food Science at Kansas State University. He serves as a research assistant with the *Frontier* program; his focus areas include food safety, food import security, and trade policy. He holds a bachelor of science honors degree from Egerton University, Kenya (2005). He has conducted food safety and security, trade policy, and food safety risk analysis training events for the United States Department of Agriculture Foreign Agricultural Service Cochran Fellowship Program. He has also been involved in developing and administering online classes in trade policy at Kansas State University.